ANIMAL STORIES

posthumanities

Cary Wolfe SERIES EDITOR

ANIMAL STORIES

Narrating across Species Lines

Susan McHugh

posthumanities **15**

University of Minnesota Press

Minneapolis

London

Portions of the Introduction were previously published as "Literary Animal Agents," *PMLA: Publication of the Modern Language Association* 124, no. 2 (2009): 487–95. An earlier version of chapter 3 was published as "Marrying My Bitch: J. R. Ackerley's Pack Aesthetics," *Critical Inquiry* 27, no. 1 (2000): 21–41. A revised version of chapter 4 was previously published as "Bringing Up *Babe,*" *Camera Obscura* 49 (2002): 149–87.

Published by the University of Minnesota Press
111 Third Avenue South, Suite 290
Minneapolis, MN 55401-2520
http://www.upress.umn.edu

Library of Congress Cataloging-in-Publication Data

McHugh, Susan.
    Animal stories : narrating across species lines / Susan McHugh.
        p. cm. — (Posthumanities ; v. 15)
    Includes bibliographical references and index.
    ISBN 978-0-8166-7032-1 (alk. paper)
    ISBN 978-0-8166-7033-8 (pbk.: alk. paper)
    1. American fiction—20th century—History and criticism. 2. English fiction—20th century—History and criticism. 3. Animals in literature. 4. Human–animal relationships in literature. 5. Agent (Philosophy) in literature. I. Title.
    PS374.A54M39 2011
    813'.6080362—dc22

                                                    2010032186

Printed in the United States of America on acid-free paper

The University of Minnesota is an equal-opportunity educator and employer.

17 16 15 14 13 12 11   10 9 8 7 6 5 4 3 2 1

My mother-in-law's collie bitch Susan and my sister's paint gelding Sioux inspire this dedication to those for whom names can serve as powerful reminders of how kinship is only one among many powerful forms of relating.

Contents

Acknowledgments

WHEN I BEGAN THIS BOOK over a decade ago, I never anticipated how much it would depend on the work of others in cultivating the field of animal studies. Citations in the following pages often serve a double purpose, not only noting the work of but also paying homage to scholars and artists who make room for discussions of animals and animality despite prevailing (and, in the humanities, often ugly) prejudices against what too often remain thought of as bad intellectual object-choices. Citations can never say enough about the heroic contributions that these folks have made to this field of inquiry, let alone my deep appreciation for their work and friendship.

For their exceptional generosity with responses, references, translations, and other direct contributions to this manuscript, I am most grateful to Ali Ahmida, Karla Armbruster, Philip Armstrong, Rod Bennison, Lynda Birke, Sally Borrell, Dorothee Brantz, Ron Broglio, Jonathan Burt, Rebecca Cassidy, Una Chaudhuri, Jonathan Clark, Jay Clayton, Marion Copeland, Maryann Corsello, Istvan Csicsery-Ronay, Andrew Cuk, Marianne DeKoven, Margo DeMello, Jane Desmond, Amy Deveau, Elizabeth De Wolfe, Tom Dietz, Karin Dienst, Brian Duff, Jody Emel, Leesa Fawcett, Cathrine Frank, Erica Fudge, Carol Gigliotti, Noreen Giffney, Anita Guerrini, Natalie Hansen, Rikke Hansen, Donna Haraway, CoryAnne Harrigan, Jane Harris, Eva Hayward, Tora Holmberg, Linda Kalof, Ivan Kreilkamp, Andrew Kunka, Michelle Lindenblatt, Lisa Lynch, William Lynn, Anouar Majid, Kathleen Maloney, Teresa Mangum, Garry Marvin, Jennifer Mason, Robert McKay, Alyce Miller, Robert Mitchell, Deborah Mix, Brett Mizelle, Heather Lyons Narver, Richard Nash, Jovian Parry, Susan Pearson, Annie Potts, Alan Rauch, Harriet Ritvo, Carrie Rohman, Nigel Rothfels, Clinton Sanders, Heather Schell, Lavina Shankar, Kenneth Shapiro, Jo-Ann Shelton, Aaron Skabelund, Julie Ann Smith, Krithika Srinivasan, Karen Syse, Stephanie Turner, Tom Tyler, Lisa Uddin, Sherryl Vint, Priscilla Wald, Joseph Walker, Kari Weil, Bart Welling, Mary Weismantel, Jennifer Wolch, Michael Wolf, Cary Wolfe, and Wendy Woodward.

For sharing images and helping me to become more literate in visual narrative, I thank Giovanni Aloi, Steve Baker, Oron Catts, Wendy Coburn, Sue Coe, Jason Courtney, Deanna Deignan, Paul and Sandra Fierlinger, Catherine Fisher, Tim Flatch, Amy Freund, Carol Gigliotti, Kate James, Bruce Kellner, Rosemarie McGoldrick, Maura McHugh, Mik Morrisey, Alan Rosmarin, Bette and Sam Savitt, Gabrielle Schueler, Bryndís Snæbjörnsdóttir, Meri Stockford, Norman Twain, Jessica Ullrich, William Wegman, Mark Wilson, and Ionat Zurr. And for supporting this project (or something like it) right from the start, I am ever indebted to Vincent B. Leitch, Patrick O'Donnell, Arkady Plotnitsky, Siobhan Somerville, and above all Richard Dienst.

A delightful afternoon discussion of a draft of chapter 1 with William Lynn's graduate students at Tufts University provided the inspiration to draft key portions of the Introduction. Likewise, the enthusiasm of undergraduates in my "Animals, Literature, and Culture" course at the University of New England (UNE) and more specifically the thoughtful responses and contributions of Kristen Aloisio to chapter 1 and Ty Gowen to chapters 3 and 4 were indispensable to the drafting process. I thank Jeanne Blackwell for her patience and skill in sidesaddle instruction. And I am grateful to Don Weeks for teaching the fundamentals of obedience to me and the mutt, along with so many others in our community.

My involvement in collaborative projects has been especially helpful in thinking beyond disciplinary structures, and for that I thank my colleagues on the editorial boards of *Antennae: The Journal of Nature in Visual Culture* and *Society & Animals*, the *H-Animal Discussion Network* Editorial Group, the *Humanimalia* Editorial Collective, the New Zealand Centre for Human–Animal Studies, UNE's Seeds reading group, UNE's Department of English and Language Studies (especially administrative assistant Elaine Brouillette), the Georgia Institute of Technology's Brittain Fellowship Program, the *Modern Fiction Studies* editorial staff, and Purdue University's Unruly Women, the best graduate-student collective ever.

This project was made possible by grant funding and other research support. As a recipient of the John H. Daniels Fellowship Program of the National Sporting Library, I was able to conduct much of the historical research for chapter 2. Martha and Marty Daniels, Jacqueline Mars, and, most of all, Liz Tobey deserve special recognition for making my stay there exceptionally pleasant. Through support from the Animals & Society Institute, the British Animal Studies Network, and the University of New England—particularly the offices of the Dean of the College of Arts and Sciences, the Vice President for Research, and the Provost—I was able to travel to wonderfully organized meetings of animal studies scholars, which led to exceptionally productive exchanges around successive drafts of chapters 3 and 4.

Ongoing research support of a different sort was provided by many dedicated librarians, including Paul Camp, who located documents in the Baynard Kendrick Papers in the Special Collections of the University of South Florida Library; Lisa Campbell at the National Sporting Library; Barbara Kolk at the American Kennel Club Library; Randall Scott and Kris Baclawski at the Michigan State University Library's Comic Art Collection; and the UNE libraries staff, including Cadence Atchinson, Brenda Austin, Janice Beal, Sharon Eckert, Cally Gurley, Bethany Kenyon, Laurie Mathes, and, most especially, Barb Swartzlander (who is also my canine-agility adviser).

I greatly appreciate the careful editorial assistance of Doug Armato, Cherene Holland, Danielle Kasprzak, Daniel Ochsner, Alicia Sellheim, and the rest of the team at the University of Minnesota Press; Neil West at BN Typographics West; and Roberta Engleman for her indexing work. Drafts of portions of the Introduction and chapters 3 and 4 were previously published, and for their help with developing these pieces I also thank the editors—especially Jay Williams and Lauren Berlant—along with the anonymous readers at *Critical Inquiry;* Patsy Yeager and Eric Wirth at *PMLA;* and Jeff Scheible, Lynne Joyrich, Jeanne Scheper, Sharon Willis, and the anonymous readers at *Camera Obscura.*

In ways too numerous to mention, I have enjoyed the support of my extended family, particularly my aunt Alice Smith, who for as long as I can remember has encouraged me to write and continues to send me animal novels. My deepest gratitude goes to my parents, Ed and Eileen McHugh, and to my love, Mik, for indulging my pet passions.

Introduction   **Animal Narratives and Social Agency**

A CENTURY AGO, Irish novelist George Moore addressed the troubled history of the English novel—a "hackney," in pointed contrast to its thoroughbred Russian and French counterparts—in a series of imaginary conversations with Edmund Gosse in which literary animals prove much more than mere metaphors.[1] Arguing that the so-called great English novels of the eighteenth century "lack intimacy of thought and feeling," Moore points to a profound absence: "No one sits by the fire and thinks what his or her past has been and welcomes the approach of a familiar bird or animal. I do not remember any dog, cat, or parrot in *Vanity Fair*, and I am almost certain that *Tom Jones* is without one."[2]

Moore's position may be hard to take seriously, in part because for so long it has been tantamount to heresy in literary criticism. From the eighteenth century onward, the rise of the novel among English reading publics dovetails with that of identity politics. So it has seemed that novels gain in popularity because they give voice to the individual subject of representation, showing and telling the significance of being a human in full.[3] How, then, could animals matter in fiction, except as gauges of its inhuman limits?

The gaping hole in this argument, as Moore suggests, is that forms do not automatically follow the functions of literature. More sustained research into animal narrative suggests that literature mediates formal along with social developments in complex ways. Extending this line of inquiry in the pages that follow, I propose an alternate theory, namely, that the success of the novel form follows instead from its usefulness for experiments with multiple perspectives and processes that support models centered on agency rather than subjectivity, reflecting as well as influencing ongoing social changes.

Never simply capturing the voice of the past, fiction localizes mutable historically and physically contingent perspectives. Strict humanists diagnose fractured or fragmentary identities as the final frontiers of contemporary

1

fiction. But scholars of animals and animality today are mapping more permeable species boundaries, and, for reasons that are less clear, locating narrative as a zone of integration, one that does not end in literary studies so much as it begins to explain how story forms operate centrally within shifting perceptions of species life. Through their very indeterminacy, narrative processes thus appear to concern the very conditions of possibility for human (always along with other) ways of being.

It is important to note that animal narratives do not make self-evident the ongoing negotiations required of aesthetic representation. Rather, they only seem to do so amid crises of political and aesthetic representation. The preponderance of modernist and narrative examples in the growing literary discussions of representing animals (not to mention the timing of Moore's comments) begs greater scrutiny of why these questions arise with increasing urgency in the twentieth century.

Published in 1919, Moore's dialogues reject the terms of realism and naturalism (in which he and his interlocutor were cast as opposing figures) that dominated discussions of the novel form at that time, and more. By proposing that social life shared across species be the measure of literary representation, these discussions, deliberately presented in fictional form, attempt to shift the terms of representation away from human subjectivity. In other words, the content questions regarding animals and animality arise inextricably from this play with narrative form. Notably echoed in J. M. Coetzee's influential novel *The Lives of Animals* (1999), this approach models a much broader course for posthumanistic inquiry out of disciplinary forms in the century that has followed, even as it raises huge concerns for cultural theory.

How do animal agents appear in literature, and with what material effects on the worlds around them? Although my thesis is that animal narratives prove critical to aesthetic explorations of others' contributions to the fiction of the human subject, I hesitate to claim that distinguishing agency from subjectivity simply resolves concerns about deconstructive and other refutations of the foundational discourses of the humanist subject. Agency may never be completely or purely represented apart from this peculiar subject form. This complexity emerges through explorations of narrative that situate the individual as a molecule, as a hybrid formal structure integrating disparate materials, and it is far from exclusive to animal representation. Now that scientists are identifying the interdependence of life forms even below the cellular level, the pervasive companionship of human subjects with members of other species appears ever more elemental to narrative subjectivity, a dark matter of sorts awaiting literary analysis.

Fictional animals nonetheless provide a crucial entry point into discussions of the social effects of these shifting perceptions. Switching metaphors for a moment from particle physics to chemistry illuminates the pervasiveness of these concerns, for the case of chemical gradients suggests how interactions exceed any straightforward struggle over who is most important, even of who has agency even at the most elemental levels. Rather, the choice in engaging chemical reactions is either in terms of a continuous field (akin to the literary subject-form) or a language of intensities in which agency operates as a verb, not a subject. This extremely localized registering, or interaction of what happens between at least two properties, provides an altogether different problematic for companion-species relations, helping to explain how other creatures become important not as supplements to human subject forms but rather as actors joining us in continuously shaping this one alongside a range of other narrative forms.

The difficult emergence of this very contemporary social sensibility becomes visible through the halting developments of literary animal agency. Tracing the formation of some patterns specific to modern and contemporary fictions of cross-species companionship, this book focuses on trends in which, as fictions record the formation of new and uniquely mixed human–animal relations in this period, they also reconfigure social potentials for novels and eventually visual narrative forms. As narratives of distinctly modern human–animal ways of living move to media forms like film and television, they situate subjectivity more clearly as a collective production, a disciplinary form of power complementing rather than negating other biopolitical options.[4]

By locating these key creative developments in fiction, my point is not to claim that literature has some inherently privileged place. Rather, this story of animal narrative underscores how, in certain historical and cultural moments, some literary and visual narrative forms become inseparable from shifts in the politics and sciences of species, such that questions about animal narratives come to concern the formal and practical futures of all species life. To underscore this point, I will group along two major lines stories that reconfigure human–animal relationships across novels, films, television, and digital media.

Part I, "Intersubjective Fictions," focuses on a pair of distinctly modern interspecies and intersubjective relations, an anthropological term for a culturally valued sense of interdependence rooted in shared human–animal actions. This analysis grounds an analytical framework for understanding the social challenges of modern human–animal relations that immediately and obviously exceed the terms of the human subject.[5] Narratives of guide-dog users and female professional riders sharpen this focus on effects that cannot be reduced to the terms of human individuality. In the stories gathered here, companions of different species demonstrate no magical or otherwise supernatural powers of connection, but instead act ordinarily (except perhaps with unusually dogged determination) to live and work together successfully in unprecedented—and surprisingly hostile—conditions.

Part II, "Intercorporeal Narratives," addresses the broader social transformations that attend these sensibilities by zeroing in on intercorporeal intimacies, by which I mean the permutations of boundaries that have always shaped species and now are proliferating wildly through genetic and genomic science.[6] Although fictions of cross-species intersubjectivity ostensibly work to displace the centrality of individuals, they incur a serious risk of denying embodied differences. By framing sex and food as sites of entanglement, other fictions of this period elaborate how more generally human–animal relations mutate into the worldly structures of non-human-centered agency. Traditional notions that aesthetic forms follow from scientific thinking about animals, along with more reactionary views, for instance, that the novel gives form only ever to human subjectivity, become unsettled by this sense of embodiment as interconnecting species and social agency, effecting changes across literature, science, and indeed life itself.

Through chapters focused on stories of service-animal users, female professional riders, backyard pet breeders, and meat industry workers, the bulk of this book explores narrative histories of companion-species relations that not only exceed the abilities of individual subjects, troubling the terms of humanistic inquiry, but also are historically contingent. These stories are significant partly because they contradict conventional assumptions about the displacement of animals by machines in the everyday life of modernity. The fictions of Seeing Eye dog users and women "jump jockeys" (or riders in events such as steeplechase that are centered on horses jumping over obstacles), at the heart of chapters 1 and 2, respectively, seemingly imagine into being professional opportunities for people with animals as never before.

But their minor role in literary history is just one of many ambivalent social outcomes that give the lie to positive role modeling. My goal in recovering these rarified narrative histories is to demonstrate how integrations of forms and ideas about species in turn inform current and pervasive ideas about how people live with animals. Although the spectacular achievements of people who choose to share their lives with animals may be more readily recognizable, the effects of modern living on cross-species companionship may be more acutely felt through such long-established (if likewise changing) animal practices as urban pet breeding and industrial meat production. Again viewed through the lens of intercorporeality, narrative tropes of queer petkeepers in chapter 3 and clever pigs in chapter 4 flag the ways in which any given human–animal relationship triangulates outward in the social histories of literary and visual representation.

I will explore the broader implications of forms of species and social life in the book's conclusion, which argues for a narrative ethology, or ongoing and systematic analysis of how forms of species remain embedded in storytelling processes. Missing from so many attempted interventions into species extinctions and overpopulations alike is the recognition of the endangered knowledges that come and go with the possible stories of shared lives. Neither simply a new or better means for articulating an emergent sense of nonhuman social agency, narrative ethology suggests an irreducibly relational ethics, a way of valuing social and aesthetic forms together as sustaining conditions of and for mixed communities.[7] My overall aim is to show how certain engagements with narrative configure people and animals as working together to do things that do not add up to a sum of individual efforts, and so invite more precise considerations of agency and narrative form.

Toward this end, the remainder of this introduction offers a brief overview of the problems of animals for literary aesthetics, and then turns to the question of how fiction and other narrative forms offer a limited means of intervention into this disciplinary history, especially via visual media, in subsequent chapters. This is not to claim that these discussions are (or ever could be) settled. From the start, the mid-eighteenth- or nineteenth-century origins of this kind of animal story remain the subject of debates within literary studies.[8] As I argue below, their contested places in literary history instead indicate how interests in animals and representation fuel rather than resolve the problems of narrative and agency forms.

Literary Animal Agents

Literary animal studies started for me when the question of animal agency arose in a survey-course discussion of a short, forgettable William Wordsworth poem titled "Nutting." A shy undergraduate, I hesitantly volunteered an interpretation of the text as reflecting the squirrel's thoughts on the subject of seasonal change.

"That's insane," said the truly venerable professor, as the class fell silent. "Animals don't think, and they certainly don't write poetry."

Twenty years or so later, this moment of candor remains stunning, only for different reasons. My reading certainly failed to take into account the poem's original context, and attests instead to sensibilities peculiar to late twentieth-century America, where (unlike in Wordsworth's England) squirrels abounded. But this rebuke says so much more.

Animals locate a peculiar paradox of disciplinary concern, one that threatens to render literary studies irrelevant to the species discourses permeating other areas of thought, today most obviously through forms like genes, genomes, and proteins. Although animals abound in literature across all ages and cultures, only in rarified ways have they been the focal point of systematic literary study. Serving at once as a metaphor for the poetic imagination and voicing the limits of human experience, a figure like Wordsworth's squirrel gains literary value as dissembling the human, as at best metaphorically speaking of and for the human. What matter who's speaking, someone squirrelly said, what matter who's speaking (to corrupt the Samuel Beckett line made famous by Michel Foucault).[9] That is, viewed as one among many peculiar operations of agency, the metaphorical animal's ways of inhabiting literature without somehow being represented therein present tremendous opportunities for recovering and interrogating the material and representational problems specific to animality. But this work also necessarily involves coming to terms with a discipline that appears organized by the studied avoidance of just such questioning.

These textual politics of literary animals contain the potential for a thoroughgoing epistemic critique attuned to the traces of species, the markings of different orders of agency implicated in the making of human subjects that I once so naively imagined as figured by Wordsworth's squirrel.[10] To elaborate on this point, I sketch below a few of the ways in which literary animal studies begin to realize an empirical potential to develop these alternate terms, methods, and concepts of species relations, and so offer a means of productively intervening in a looming crisis of disciplinary ways of knowing. Although its beginnings (let alone name) may never be agreed upon, the formation of animal studies, an interdisciplinary field of inquiry that coalesces around questions of representation and agency, or the "unnatural" histories of species, clearly propels this movement.[11]

Far beyond the domain of science (within which "animal studies" initially signaled a limited, literal distinction from human medical case studies), the creative, activist, and scholarly endeavors coming together under this umbrella term are united not by commitments to common methods or politics so much as to the broader goal of bringing the intellectual histories and other stories of species under scrutiny. Such work sharpens ethical commitments not by following the mandates of philosophy (or for that matter any dominating discipline) for individuals' rights or groups' welfare. Rather, the work of interdisciplinary animal studies more effectively engages these objectives through examinations of aesthetic practices along with other intellectual traditions as deeply rooted in mixed-species life, and, more to the point of this book, by accounting for the ways in which creative as well as intellectual engagements have distinct values in mediating these relations.

Animal practices, in the broadest sense, become the stakes of moving from any given perspective (or project) to animal studies as a discursive formation.[12] Most effectively, this emergent discourse unsettles humanistic faith in knowledges of animal life as ends in themselves, insisting instead that concerns about their accumulation, endangerment, and other operations can never be exclusive to any creature. In this way, animal studies pushes the limits of exclusively human ways of being, and reveals among other things the ways in which species-being works in literary texts precisely as a function of what we think of as their literariness, even within and beyond humanist traditions.

Again this may seem counterintuitive because literary history supports my professor's formal lesson: animals appeared as significant figures in English literature only strictly in terms of metaphor.[13] "A Poet is a nightingale," proclaims poet Percy Bysshe Shelley in his famous 1821 defense of poetry, at once citing the most famous animal representation of the romantic artist's transcendence of human society (John Keats's 1819 poem "Ode to a Nightingale"), and limiting the literary animal's value to a figure for expressing the romantic artist's increasing sense of political alienation.[14] Recent studies of this kind of literary animal challenge its operations but not its underlying value, venturing that, among British romantics, metaphorical animals serve literary purposes even as they model ways of thinking outside literary forms, for instance, in medicine and law. Once serving as reference points for the poet-critic as gatekeeper of truth, animals gain further significance for scholars who are interrogating how this kind of cultural work proceeds directly from earlier Enlightenment views that such figures teach people (especially on the early modern British stage) how to become human.[15] Although this new consensus insists on the complex dynamics of reading literary animals as substitutes for human subjects-in-the-making, it also illustrates how the aesthetic structures of metaphor, though precariously supporting the human subject, seem unable to bear animal agency.[16]

By suggesting a different story, or rather, by shifting the focus of attention to the ways in which animality permeates literature, my reading of "Nutting" (however inadvertently) brought to class questions that have come to plague not just literary studies but the whole of disciplinary thought. The constitution of the subject, in the broadest sense, was at stake in this discussion, as my professor well knew. An American immigrant, Jewish veteran of World War II, and pioneering feminist scholar, my professor had fought on many lines for more rigorous and inclusive responses to the query coming to crisis in the twentieth century: What is the human? From this perspective, metaphor provides a strong defense for poetics in the service of anthropocentrism, for communicating (even becoming a means whereby people can learn how to read) messages about our own "essential" humanity.

"Like fish seen through a plate glass aquarium," says novelist and cultural critic John Berger in an infamous argument about animals in modernity, this approach to representational mechanisms makes animals appear to be eternally "disappearing" or distanced always in relation to the human.[17] That is, the point of metaphorical and other aesthetics beholden to animal-really-means-human and likewise substitutive logics may be to preserve human singularity, but their ongoing reliance on erasures invokes other potentials as perpetually deferred. Positing the "intimate caesura" of in/human division as a productive and never absolute intervention, philosophers like Giorgio Agamben have begun to call attention to the ways in which species divide only ever through fluctuating convergences of representational forms.[18] Today flagrant perforations of species boundaries—proliferating, for instance, through genetically modified organisms in agri-food flows—cast literary aesthetics in a pivotal moment, in which it has become both a critical peril to analyze anthropocentrist models as well as a creative imperative to elaborate new forms of agency.

Although insufficient as an end in itself, critiquing the wrongs (or rights) of anthropocentrism calls attention to profound disagreements about what literature and criticism uniquely contribute to emergent understandings of species life. The structuralist and poststructuralist problems of animals as written into the metaphysics of speech and subjectivity inform strikingly different conclusions about the roles that animal representations play. To some, it seems that animal studies gains legitimacy in literary circles with newfound attention to Jacques Derrida's movement toward questions about the subject's inscription in the erasure of animal traces. Derrida himself rejects "the distinction between animal and human language" itself as deliberately obfuscating: "The treatment of animality, as of everything that finds itself in submission by virtue of a hierarchical opposition, has always, in the history of (humanist and phallogocentric) metaphysics, revealed obscurantist resistance."[19] And in his final series of lectures on the subject, he locates the potential for countering this resistance in the interactions across species, more specifically, in his own pet cat's possession of a "point of view regarding me."[20]

In this formulation, nonhuman traces serve as deconstructive elements that betray human attempts at self-representation, and ultimately elaborate the logic of substitution through which the animal's sacrificiality (its real and representational consumption) supports the human. While this approach to animal traces can and does contribute to productive critiques of humanism, it also legitimates a much narrower focus on representing human animality, for instance, within the existing literary canon. In these and other ways, Derridean critiques of language create more problems for literary animal agents than they resolve.[21]

Intriguing in hindsight as a striking absence from the identity debates, for some literary critics animality thereby gains intellectual appeal as a repressed deconstructive element, a marker of difference internalized in human species-being.[22] Support for such arguments abounds in modernist fiction, where animal subjectivity gains significance as an essentially negative force against which the purportedly post-Darwinian human is asserted. The formal imbrications of human animality in Darwin's theory of the mutability of species trace an even more specific literary trajectory, first deconstructed in Margot Norris's account of why modernist writers and artists explicitly rejected metaphor in favor of the more plastic structures of narrative and visual media in their experiments with antirepresentational forms.

Norris's analysis emphasizes how these particular forms work to critique anthropocentrist aesthetics more coherently than they serve as vehicles for expressing human animality. Although the modernist "biocentric" tradition of representing human animality ended in failure, she points to the exceptional case of Franz Kafka's animal narratives, which cast this dynamic in terms of a narration or tentative narrative logic of animal being that "retracts itself."[23] More specifically, "a negative side of narration," that is, "a phantom narration, a trace," hangs in the balance of Kafka's "tale-spinning" approach to species life, a process of narrating narration itself that unravels in human animality.[24] While this Derridean deconstruction clarifies how internal breakdowns of the humanist subject render animal subjectivity all the more impossible, it also remains circumscribed by literature's disciplinary structures of the human subject, remaining illustrative of rather than accounting for the textual significance of animality.[25] The question remains: How might species life be configured in texts?

Narrating Animal Studies

Even by the time of my fateful class, scholars working in and across literature and other disciplines were making the case for animal studies around three interrelated imperatives. First, conceptualize agency itself as more than simply a property of the human subject form. Second, recover the spectrum of agency forms central to a variety of cultural traditions that (even as they are put under erasure) challenge the process of literary-canon formation. Complementing this historical work, the third charge concerns the interrelations of the representational forms and material conditions of species life, the processes whereby the agency of literary animals comes to consist precisely in the way that they cannot finally be enlisted in the tasks set for them. These mandates illustrate not just the magnitude of the problems that this book touches upon through twentieth-century narratives of interspecies life, but also their postdisciplinary or posthumanistic implications for twenty-first-century life.

Although no one to date seriously argues that squirrels write poetry, animals are being reconceptualized as key players in all sorts of cultural productions, and with material and methodological consequences for literary scholarship. Analysis of the varied involvements of animals in the production of disciplinary and other knowledges, often inspired by Donna Haraway's account of animals as "active participants in the constitution of what may count as scientific knowledge," sparks all sorts of claims about the textual evidence of animal imprints.[26] Authors' household pet-keeping histories, agricultural employments, blood-sport hobbies, and other participations in cultural traditions centered on animals subsequently gain new interest and bolster more widespread speculations about the relations of biographical details to creative responsibilities in representing animals.

Historically, specific engagements with animals tie the material contexts of textuality with knowledge production and dissemination. These conditions are perhaps most plainly evinced in the "rabbit" glue that was used to bind all books, whatever their politics, until commercial synthetic adhesives became widely used in the final decades of the twentieth century. Poorly documented textual production scenes render the material traces of any given relationship of life and text largely unrecoverable, hindering accounts of the influences of animals on literary representations. Particularly controversial animal practices, understood to be systematic integrations of animals in cultural productions of (and often against some) human subjects, arguably present an even greater challenge as sources of affect in textual along with social politics.[27]

Messy entanglements of human and animal agents become sedimented even in cultural practices without immediate ties to animals, and with time and distance become ripe for damaging distortion (for example, the French colonial usage of *animalicide* to mean killing a "native").[28] Indeed, the predominantly symbolic interpretation of literary animals into the twentieth century emerges as just such a practice from the perspective of new studies focused on authorial creativity, particularly "shamanism," in non-European literary traditions.[29] Moreover, they suggest that positing animals as mechanisms of transcendence, whether via foundational human knowledges or prediscursive fellow feelings for other species, only exacerbates this problem. Whatever the motive, such approaches to species risk a dangerous sort of end game for animal agency, one that imagines animals into political life only by bracketing off the significance of embodiment in space and time.

Such concerns lead animal studies scholars along a second track to interrogations of the convergences of agency forms and values. Now that genetic chimera-like pet clones are being produced on demand, the plasticity of certain species forms may be taken for granted, but in ways that further threaten to mystify their production. Domesticates, or members of species adapted to flourish alongside humans, appear instead as collaborative cross-species productions through cultural histories that intimately involve specific representational mutations. Published a few years before my "Nutting" lesson, Harriet Ritvo's history of animals in Victorian England provides an early example of how to analyze animals as both bearers of meaning and catalysts of social changes. As metaphors, she argues, animals like the show dog stand for their nonelite owners' aristocratic pretensions, yet this animal's potential for success also manifests human owners' desires for upward social mobility.[30] Likewise betraying a range of metonymic possibilities, the prizing of metaphorical relationships in literature begins to make sense as part of a representational continuum that becomes all the more compelling and confusing as it strikes closer to home.

In the past decade, poststructuralist aesthetic accounts of contemporary animal representations highlight the ways in which the mechanisms of representation more deliberately confront the singularity or closure of meaning with forms that build in gaps, fissures, or ruptures. Contrived metaphorical breakdowns and other ostentatiously mismanaged animal representations invite critique as unequivocal formal failures, only to prompt queries about (and arguably make efforts to respond to) the inadequacies or shortcomings built into representational processes concerning animals.[31] Viewed thus, early post-Darwinian experiments with voicing human animality might be said to continue through contemporary narrative engagements that appear all the more meaningfully to break signifying chains in ways that foreground—even possibly at times redress[32]—the historic paradox of the animal agent as subsumed by literary forms.

Enframed in film and new-media environments, animal acts signal profound ruptures to identity forms and less clearly extensions of struggles to represent animals as nonhuman social agents.[33] Informed by Haraway's and others' theories of human and nonhuman agency alike as co-constitutive, studies that take a longer historical view akin to Ritvo's further illuminate the unsettling ways in which animal representations themselves pry apart forms of agency and the human subject.[34] But it is arguably the focus on embodiment, surfaces, and exteriority in film and other representations of live animals that distinguishes animals in this sense as agents of a different order from human subjectivity, more precisely as film actors operating in accordance with a different narrative logic from that of human intentionality or psychological interiority.[35] That these concerns about animal agency appear to arise most comprehensively in response to modern urban conditions spurs my conclusions in the chapters that follow that animal agency can never simply oppose human identity, and in turn that animal agents are never entirely separable from human forms or presences.

Moreover, the linkage of aesthetics and social viability binds both ways, and follows from the reframing of community in terms of species as inherently mixed. This understanding proceeds from Mary Midgley's forerunning philosophical account of human sociality as premised not on domestication (conceived by others as absolute domination), but rather on people's interactions with members of other species who also happen to be social.[36] Against those who say, for example, that the rights of guide dogs and steeplechase horses are unequivocally violated by such use, narratives of their lives in working partnerships locate these peculiar agency forms as inextricable from deeply mixed social scenes, in turn informed by the shifting politics and aesthetics of representation.

And so they beg more comprehensive engagements with the discourses of animals and animality. Through her own training relationships with dogs and horses, Vicki Hearne's attempts to develop a narrative poetics of the responsiveness required of such relations at every turn emphasizes her experiences with "the sketchiness of the tokens of English," and in general the instructive inadequacies of linguistic representation in the lives of species.[37] The primacy of historically companionate relations to such arguments prefigures the relevance of what Haraway terms "companion species" relationships to the ongoing study of the social consequences of nonhuman agency. Self-styled as a hybrid poet-critic in the tradition of Shelley, Hearne also clearly implicates literature as a deeply ambivalent humanistic endeavor. Noting how everyone in industrial societies participates in the brutal management strategies of irreducibly human and animal cultures, literary and cultural critics are only just beginning to respond in coherent ways to her challenge to reckon with shared lives on their own terms.[38]

Success in conveying this sensibility hinges on the textual development of a sense of social power as irreducible to the human subject form. So it becomes all the more important to uncouple the concept of agency (the social movement or impact attributed to an agent of social power) from identity (the humanist form of subjectivity through which an agent is understood to have a history, in the broadest sense). And it is with some trepidation that, in order to clarify this point, I appeal throughout to a particular poststructuralist model that has been distorted, even explicitly disowned, within animal studies.

Elaborating their provocative (if poorly understood) theory of becoming-animal, Gilles Deleuze and Félix Guattari together develop a triangulated structure with these coordinates: animals in individuated forms, "the only kind of animal psychoanalysis understands" as stand-ins for human egos; icons built from the "characteristics or attributes" of certain animals; and collectivities, "pack or affect animals that form a multiplicity, a becoming, a population, a tale."[39] Read in context, this model responds to the ramifications of later twentieth-century identity politics, virulently reacting against the trends that institutionalize psychoanalysis as the regulator of capitalist subjects. Elaborated through their critique of Sigmund Freud's case studies, the animality triangle illuminates an interpretive pattern of documenting but otherwise explicitly avoiding dealing with the intensely affective, multifarious, and lateral connections people share with animals. Consequently, this animal model provides a strong plank in the platform from which Deleuze and Guattari launch their project of "schizo-analysis."

Animals are key elements in Freud's case studies, they argue, because they are not just icons, metaphors conveying meanings among humans, nor are they simply stand-ins for human animals. The nonhuman forms and meanings repressed even by the famous analyst most importantly serve as reminders of how animals can function as "demonic" or menacing figures of multiplicity.[40] While recent discussions in animal studies clarify that their example of the little old woman with "my cat, my dog" all too cleverly conflates the critique of ego and icon by pandering to social prejudices against especially postmenopausal women (not to mention all gay people) with pets, especially little dogs—prejudices that span cultures, continents, even millennia[41]—I counter that the value of this argument lies not in its choice of illustrations but rather in its modeling of alternative and no less contingent foundations to those of disciplinary subjects.

Deleuze and Guattari's approach rejects from the start the animal's exclusion from language and representation, for such positions ultimately submit to the problem of being a human animal as it is posited by language. Far from simply a defining property internalized by the human, animality pervades the forms of agency, permeating language, literature, and every living thing potentially engaged with processes of becoming. More than just recording or reflecting acts of (in their terms) "becoming-animal," stories might be seen as key points of ethical negotiation across artistic and scientific models of species and social life.[42] And it is in narratives of companion species that this book traces emergences of what they see as a distinct "logic of becoming."[43]

For the beauty of their triangulated structure is that it does not fix mutually exclusive or otherwise limiting alternatives, but rather sets all adrift in flows of interrelated potentials, which include the possibility that "any animal can be treated in all three ways."[44] My explorations of this model in what follows admittedly present only partial pictures, by way of attempting to address a more widespread problem of assuming that (rather than explaining how) narrative has become the preeminent form of working through the representational problems of species. Starting from intersubjective forms, this book appeals to the tripartite structure in order to localize eruptions of nonhuman-agency forms, and ultimately to make sense of the intercorporeal relations in which we cannot help but find ourselves alongside others.

Several of the narratives that I bring together in the following chapters engage in this critical problematic in ways that illuminate changes in literary history and recent theories of animality across the disciplines. Read together, they make a compelling case for animal narratives as pivotal to species formations in popular culture, public policy, and science by the twenty-first century. And as a whole they indicate that part of what makes it necessary to tell and retell these tales is that they contradict received notions of animals as anathema to technology.

Nostalgic tales of cowboys' horses and sentimental representations of faithful pet dogs work to retrench a sense of the human individual as ultimately unable to escape with (or like) the animal. Scholars who point to these examples as proof that the production of the modern human subject proceeds from a definitive displacement of organic/biological by machinic/technological beings argue this point.[45] However, these animals' kin and kind, who joined people in Neolithic conditions and persist in the puppy-mill purebreds and packaged pet foods that distinguish the aggressively individualistic cultures of contemporary consumerism, flesh out far more unsettling histories in which the conditions of modernity utterly transform the lives, and perhaps more important, the deaths of virtually all species.

The mind-boggling ways and numbers in which such animals are killed in our time are unprecedented, as are the mechanisms of rendering these processes invisible. Although these conditions may have been developed to serve expansions of capitalism and empire, they also create new opportunities for dismantling these structures. Often the impetus for accounts of the impossibility of animal subjectivity, twentieth-century stories of disappearing and dead animals contribute in surprising ways to more challenging models that represent the irreducible multiplicity of species and social life. Previewing the chapters that follow in greater detail, the next section also elaborates further how, practically and theoretically, literary narrative migrates across disciplines into biopolitical stories of companion species.

Companion-Species Stories

In a 1924 essay, Virginia Woolf made the famous claim that "on or about December 1910, human nature changed."[46] So common has it become to read this line as marking the historic arrival of modernist aesthetics that hardly anyone asks of its context: what (and who) else changed along with the human? A contemporary of Moore's and likewise appreciated as a hybrid novelist-critic confronting a literary system geared to serve others unlike them, Woolf's own animal writing offers some clues about this oversight.

Woolf's lone best seller during her lifetime, her 1933 novel *Flush: A Biography,* hangs warily on the fringes of the literary tradition, avoided like so many other stray animal books by authors whose significance thereby becomes reinvented for future generations in terms of their expression of the (exclusively) human conditions of modernity. But the story itself resists such reduction. It is a love story of the poet Elizabeth Barrett and her betrothed, Robert Browning, that pivots on her beginning the process of asserting her own agency in the name of saving her beloved companion from dog thieves. Formally, its narration wavers between the voice of an avowedly human biographer and the fictional animal's perspective. Like so many other modern narrative forms, this canine biography thus intimates why, when human nature changed more decisively, it could never do so alone.[47] That so few of Woolf's critics have wanted to follow her to this conclusion underscores one of the perils of my project here, namely, that literary institutions are set up to be inauspicious places for the investigation of shared human–animal stories. And these conditions also require attention to narrative beyond literary forms.

Setting out to trace some patterns of animal representation across the past century, this book does not arrive at a comprehensive analysis of modern and contemporary animal life. Instead it uses literary fiction as a lens for understanding how narrative forms become part of the processes whereby some kinds of people and animals move together between domestic and working (what used to be called private and public) spheres, both in new relations specific to urban industrial societies as well as in traditional configurations adapting within these emerging conditions. Visual art often makes these narrative processes most apparent, but I have included images also to open the discussion out from the fraught disciplinary history of companion species and into the properly postdisciplinary investigation commanded by engagements with species life.

Chapter 1, "Seeing Eyes/Private Eyes: Service Dogs and Detective Fictions," opens the discussion of cross-species intersubjective operations by examining how literary fictions and popular media increasingly make manifest what is at once a profound admiration for and misunderstanding of service-animal relationships. Starting in the 1930s with Baynard Kendrick's mystery novel series that features the first fictional Seeing Eye dog, and leading to popular visual narratives like the 2005 ABC television series *Blind Justice,* this chapter traces direct points of contact between narrative representations of human–animal "working units" and the simultaneously evolving terms of social rights movements. This history reveals how public accessibility for these human–animal partnerships grows along with this small but persistent narrative strain. But their ongoing social conflicts, embodied by the blinded, white male detectives exclusively cast with German shepherd guides in fiction, also reflect deep social contradictions that characterize this period, troubling the very terms of the question: How may a human enter into a rights relationship with an animal?

Chapter 2, "Velvet Revolutions: Girl–Horse Stories," develops an inverse representational history through growing ambivalence about another form of intersubjective relations taking shape in the twentieth century. Starting with Enid Bagnold's best-selling novel *National Velvet, or The Slaughterer's Daughter* (1935) and its rapid transformation into the blockbuster film classic *National Velvet* (1944), this chapter explores how, as quickly as girls and women come to compete on equal footing with their male counterparts as equine professionals, particularly in jumping sports, girl–horse relations become distinctly sexualized and infantilized, their participants even brutalized in the popular imaginary. Relating these narrative shifts to a broader cultural history of equestriennes as well as to the technological developments informing their entry into equine professions, I argue that these stories provide more than just a mirror for elements of human identity, asserted at the expense of cross-species intimacies. In this case, more explicitly film and other visual media can be said to inspire as well as endanger the emergence of modern forms of human–animal relationships. The insistence of these stories on visual media literacy as central to the formation of human–animal (which, as the titles suggest, are never far from national and globalizing) models of community in turn reveals how cross-species companionship may be embraced in resistance to threats of violence in ways that both complement the guide-dog fictions and inform rising concerns about professional (mis)managements and other interventions into traditional patterns of species life.

Chapter 3, "Breeding Narratives of Intimacy: Shaggy Dogs, Shagging Sheep," fleshes out one such trajectory by examining how modern authors arguably exceed the limits of queer life writing by crafting narratives that frankly depict the sex lives of their pets, intimacies that become increasingly troubled by changing biological and social structures of sexuality. In this context, J. R. Ackerley's *My Dog Tulip* (1956), the first and perhaps queerest example of what has become the intensely popular genre of the dog memoir, proves more startlingly innovative for its argument about the significance of canine sex to human society. Disrupting the identity conventions of human heteronormative coupling (such as the mainstreaming impulse surrounding the current politics of gay marriage) by showing how they are aligned with the conventional and often coercive methods of "marrying" animal breeders' stock, Ackerley's memoir joins his other narratives in modeling an alternate, triangulated structure of sexuality in which pets and people become involved not only in each other's love lives but also in social possibilities for sexuality. Thus, these narratives prove exceptionally helpful for unpacking contemporary scientific and popular attitudes toward animal sex, underpinning biological claims to have identified homosexual animals—erupting in the so-called gay sheep controversies of recent years—as well as the less controversial de-sexing of pets as suburban furniture. As the next chapter argues, this appreciation for the ways in which agency concerns lives that are intimately shared across species blazes still queerer trails to the final frontiers of livestock production.

Chapter 4, "The Fictions and Futures of Farm Animals: Semi-Living to 'Animalacra' Pig Tales," examines how industrial meat narratives frame more widespread anxieties about the failure of representation regarding animal agency, and less predictably the hopes as well as fears for genetically modified farm animals and other recent technological interventions into these histories. Narratives of meat animals from George Orwell's *Animal Farm* (1946) through Margaret Atwood's *Oryx and Crake* (2003) posit shared human–animal lives in these conditions as points of access into public life, anticipating how the future of such creatures in agri-food flows hinges on perceiving as much as transfiguring collective agency forms. Pigs in particular gain peculiar cultural resonances as avatars of animal agency in a startlingly coherent narrative history of barnyard revolutions, and more recently as representative meat animals baring visual media devices. In the process, they also become living links between locally sustained agriculture and globalizing biotech communities stretched to their limits amid systems increasingly concerned with vertical coordination, consumer perceptions, and industry regulation. Amid these changing fields of power, pig stories come to embody creative potentials for collective life, enframing images akin to the processes that biologist Lynn Margulis terms "symbiogenesis" and Deleuze terms "heterogenesis," even as their transgenic narratives figure the greatest threats to the futures of species life.

The book's conclusion, subtitled "Toward a Narrative Ethology," highlights some specific ways in which animal narrative forms prove useful not only for interrogating key elements of identity and society but also for confronting the limitations of disciplinary knowledges. If, by the mid-twentieth century, it seems increasingly to be the exclusive work of literature to serve and protect our humanity (if not *the* humanities), then it also makes it difficult to reconcile literary criticism's avoidance of animals with accounts of preeminent, popular ethologists as disparate as Konrad Lorenz and Jane Goodall, who cite their own uses of animal novels as models enabling significant epistemological shifts within animal science. Comparing larger trends in animal narratives through the period across studies of literature and scientific ethology, this final chapter argues for further explorations of the ways in which posthumanistic structures of species and social agency not only prove necessary but also necessarily become articulated through postdisciplinary discursive formations like animal studies.

So often dismissed as creative or imaginary alternatives to real life or, as Erica Fudge puts it, "always-already only representations," animal stories in many ways seem to set the limits of disciplinary perspectives, even to exemplify the bad object choices of academics (in stilted characterization, at least) as against real-life activist interests.[48] Challenging the assumption that literature is merely a reflection of ideology, the following chapters highlight some of the ways in which animal narratives also pointedly appeal to the power of affect to defy the regimes that benefit from separation, isolation, and fragmentation of our lives and theirs.[49] Reframing the significance of these textual processes, this book ultimately offers a partial theory of narrative ethology that underscores the ongoing relevance of the humanities to studies of species in the life sciences, and more specifically integrations of narrative practice and research to defy disciplinary divisions of knowledge. For narrative ethology foregrounds the ethical relations of agency and narrative form, locating species squarely within populations as continuous fields that distinguish biopolitical—or, in Isabelle Stengers's terms, "cosmopolitical"—processes.[50]

Put plainly, my main purpose in sketching these very specific animal narrative histories is to insist that story forms serve as spawning grounds for forms of species and social agency. Partly because the politics of literary canonicity obscure how central these operations have become to the novel form, the migrations of particular narrative forms to visual media prove more important than their origins for exposing the inadequacies of the singular form of human identity. Again this is why, in addition to literary examples, the chapters that follow also address visual texts, in order to show how creative thinkers constantly engage lived conditions that demand more responsive and responsible approaches to bodily imbrications. But I admit, too, that the literary texts examined here are often obscure, except to those immediately concerned with the issues they address. So examples from television, gaming, and other popular cultural forms creep in to reveal the ongoing relevance of a wide range of story forms to human and animal lives. Although easily overlooked or trivialized on their own, together such texts highlight contemporary frames of reference in which the stories of peculiarly modern human–animal relations remain influential long after their debuts, shaping our worlds in subtle but effective ways.

Against the fixed formal dynamic that some see as characterized by (literally and figuratively) disappearing animals, these narrative developments provide an important, if limited, record of how and why some cross-species relationships arise and even flourish amid urban industrial landscapes. Moreover, they speak directly to the conditions characterizing the twenty-first century, predicted to witness not only the slaughter of animals in the greatest numbers on record but also the relocation of a global majority of people to cities. These stories of people making (and unmaking) themselves together with animals as urban creatures illuminate how adapting to these conditions entails learning how to read and write about the companionship of species. Before moving on to examine exactly how they do so, I conclude here by speculating about how modern novelists began to address these concerns, and with what implications for scholarly and social developments today.

Tellingly, few of the authors and none of the texts I examine in this book have a secure place in the literary canon. And I am not arguing that they should. Often emerging as popular and critical successes, and continuing to inspire sequels, remakes, and imitations, these narratives resurface often within visual forms, in ways that reveal how narrative prompts transformations of knowledges and even feelings that resist disciplining. The most obvious case in point has been the shifting trends from interpreting Orwell's *Animal Farm* as a parable of Soviet history to reading it at face value as an animal story. As I argue in chapter 4, the novel sustains these pressures not simply as proof of its author's genius but, more important, as an extension of the complex forms of animal narrative agency, as an example of how the boundaries of species can be neither simply transcended by nor subsumed within the human.

Bringing these minor texts together contributes to a more comprehensive picture of the relations of biological, social, and aesthetic forms, more precisely of how poststructuralist inquiry into species and narrative offers new, contingent foundations for ethical relatings, which (as Haraway argues) at minimum involve "getting on together," and at best expand the biopolitical potentials for love.[51] The narratives central to my elaboration of narrative ethology so often deliberately cast human–animal relations amid contexts that are often violently hostile to these social ideals that it seems worth pondering the historical significance of such stories in the decades immediately following Woolf's remark. For at face value, their authors' direct wartime experiences would appear to inform more personal struggles with not writing about animals.

The disciplinary history of literature outlined above indicates why modern writers' interests in animals were not considered significant during their lifetimes, and perhaps too why they flag transformative moments in their careers and cultures. Reflecting on Ackerley's instantly acclaimed early play *The Prisoners of War* (1925), based on his own experiences as a POW detained for years in Switzerland after being captured on the front in France, early in my research I began to wonder why the suicidal gay officer at the center of the play articulates his fear of advancing insanity as a state of being rendered merely animal. When attended to at all, this play is seen as a working-out of the author's sense of guilt about his only brother having been killed in action, and this emotion is assumed to be psychologically sublimated in the author's growing affinity for telling dog stories instead. Yet such readings do not explain Ackerley's growing awareness (and wariness) of Freudian reductions, of the self-serving dangers of retreating to psychological interiority or social atomism, and his shift to narrative forms in which animals anchor a different vision of irreducibly social or molecular models.

Ranged alongside Ackerley's contemporaries' formal experiments, these stories seem all the more clearly to work through and beyond war as a social experience, rather than as the prompt for the traumatic retreat to modern individualism in the novel. Orwell's fateful service in the Spanish Civil War is so well documented that it hardly seems worth mentioning that it informs the subsequent evolution of filmic interpretations and literary critical readings of his fiction. While his famous animal story (or, again depending on how you read it, human-as-animal story) *Animal Farm* addresses implications for collective life, the influence of wartime actions and their aftermath also may be felt keenly in narratives of human-animal intersubjectivity.

In this sense, it is important to note up front that Kendrick's blind detective fictions were crafted didactically, to help his fellow servicemen to reenter the workforce. An American who joined World War I early by signing up to serve for Canada, Kendrick subsequently was denied veterans' benefits by both countries. Becoming a fiction writer at the same time that he was living with another similarly shafted vet, only one whose difficulties were compounded by having been blinded in the line of duty, he used fiction to promote service-dog organizations in ways that led to public advocacy work for disabled veterans. Thus animal narratives provide a way of working through shared solutions to the self-defeating suffering of isolated individuals, all the more surprisingly when they are least expected to do so.

Recovery efforts to document women's direct involvements in the Great War lately have renewed interest in Bagnold's first best seller, the anonymously published *A Diary without Dates* (1922), told from her own perspective as a volunteer nurse's aide working with wounded soldiers. Among the many social problems that it exposes with the war effort, one horrific standout case is that of the shell-shocked dairyman ridiculed in the rehab clinic, an anecdote that speaks to this memoir's overarching sense of outrage not at any particular individuals but at the ways in which war diminishes social sensibilities. Never having lived away from the farm beforehand, this nameless man becomes a rare soldier psychologically wounded by cavalry training before combat, and his condition worsens as his "treatment" includes being subjected to the daily sounds of new recruits being trained on horseback next door to the hospital. The problem unfolding here is not that the dairyman fails to modernize, that is, that his characteristic indirectness and reticence relegate the rube, stupidly "soft" about animals, to a passing or past era. It is that others fail to appreciate how social senses and sensibilities are cultivated through animal practices.

Lives are at stake in these scenes, as are whole ways of life. A century and a continent away, witnessing the family-run dairies of New England all but dying from industrial intensification and relocation to other regions of the United States, I recognize a version of the shy shuffle that Bagnold describes in the young soldier through my interactions with elderly neighbors who are fast losing farms to suburban sprawl and the confinement-operations driving down the price of milk. Visual media make it especially tempting to contemplate how a sense of nonhuman "neighborliness" might transcend touch.[52] What these novelists suggest, however, is that the tactile, olfactory, and other senses that are engaged through shared lives across species are central (if also unwieldly) to their representation as sustainable models of collectivity.

Although these are not the sorts of examples that literary and cultural critic Raymond Williams had in mind when formulating the concept "structures of feeling," by which he means the primary sensibilities of having lived in a particular place at the same time that tie people together, they do indicate how much confusion about animal ethics proceeds from what can only ever be partially recovered by others.[53] Practically speaking, the secondary way in which he says witnesses document and so share some of the threads of a social fabric that is by definition lost to all the rest of us (who must resort to access in a tertiary way, exclusively through documentation), might be the most important aspect of animal narrative. But I want to argue further that, particularly in an era characterized by genocides and extinctions on an ever-increasing scale, these textual processes also sustain a sense of what else is possible, of what has been and still can be achieved through cross-species relationships.

Returning to my primal scene of literary animal education, I want to suggest that the more important lesson for future research lies in a growing sense of responsibility to relate critical practice to the (inter)disciplinary consequences of taking literary animals seriously. As literature becomes one of many locations for negotiating the representational problems of animals, forcing new questions about the ways in which literary histories bind animals with linguistic forms (like metaphorical chains of substitution) to the terms of human individuals, writers and artists gain greater opportunities for intervening in the problems of species mutating through the technologies of xenotransplantation, genetic modification, and cloning, which appear to be changing the terms of life itself. Particularly by furthering the investigative work of animal studies into new and old means of representing animals, literary animal studies can contribute to broader understanding of narrative as modeling more porous forms of species and social agency. But this can happen only if scholars forgo the politics and privileges of knowledges conceived in exclusively disciplinary terms and train their attention to the biopolitical implications of affect.

It is well worth questioning what kinds of knowledge we as humans ever can have about other species. If the forgoing sketch history of literary animal agents shows how such self-questioning all too often comes at the expense of discovering what happens when we move from studying animals with any established methodology or preset value system to imagining ourselves working within (even against) a newly formulated discursive field that brings together complex and different constructions of and methods for studying (with) animals, then the need for narrative ethology becomes all the more apparent. More comprehensive productions along with analyses along these lines might undermine commitments to disciplinary ways of knowing even as they offer the best argument for the relevance of the feelings of animals, humans, and others enmeshed in companion-species relationships.

Part I

Intersubjective Fictions

Chapter 1   **Seeing Eyes/Private Eyes: Service Dogs and Detective Fictions**

SEVERAL URBAN AMERICAN dog people have shared with me a peculiar passing fantasy of disability. They imagine equipping themselves with dark glasses and their pet dogs with harnesses in order to enjoy universal access to public transportation, restaurants, and parks otherwise forbidden to their canine companions. One asked, "Who would stop me?"[1]

The problems with this kind of imagining are legion. Not the least is how it demonstrates just plain ignorance of the difficulties faced by guide-dog users, who are often barred entry to public places even though the Americans with Disabilities Act (ADA) supposedly now guarantees their right of access.[2] But two aspects of these fantasies intrigue me.

One aspect is that these able-bodied people are clearly wanting to pass as disabled—or, more precisely, as vision-impaired and canine-assisted. In other words, guide-dog relations change social perceptions (of sighted dog owners at least), such that a person with a disability has an attractive, even enviable identity. And another curious aspect is that, whether the dog folks are aware of it or not, their fantasies closely follow the history of guide-dog fictions, a representational pattern that, even as it promotes the political rights of the canine-assisted blind public, also comes to contribute to the ongoing problems of perceiving what exactly is so special about service-animal partnerships.

Long before public access was guaranteed for disabled people in the United States, this cause was effectively promoted through novels, films, and television shows featuring blind men with guide dogs. Dignifying the work of service-animals may not be the point of these narratives, but their consistently positive portrayal of these creatures waxes heroic, even saintly, throughout twentieth-century popular culture. These stories reflect no simple progress of modern animal agency in human company.

Early examples enlist dog along with disabled man as comrades in a more general fight against social oppression. As the political struggle for disability rights gains ground, the stories change so that the dogs come to serve these tales more as symbols than as actors. This narrative history suggests that, though certainly appreciated by their owners and advocates for disabled people, service dogs gain this broader public affection (even beatification) at the expense of inspiring more profound changes in views of human–animal relations, in this case as enabling civic life.

Bringing these stories together here, this chapter explores how they raise representational concerns about the interrelations of textual and political forms. Theirs is a rare history, which at odd moments synthesizes critiques of rights-based politics that now seem the separate provenances of disability studies and animal studies. And it remains rooted in the kinds of intimacies that these human–canine pairs share—consistently referred to in guide-dog literature in terms of irreducible partnerships or "working units"—that not only prove difficult to model in story and image but also confound conventional notions of rights relationships as negotiated by and for individuals.

In short, these stories open up yet another unsettling dimension to Hearne's provocative question: How may a human enter into a rights relationship with an animal?[3] Her concern is that animal-rights politics misses the point that training can maximize animal happiness, that movements to abolish training give such creatures the "right" only to be unhappy. Apart from raising the obvious question of how anyone knows when she (or anyone else) is happy, Hearne's argument uncovers some limiting assumptions about agency in training and social life that even haunt critiques of ableism and speciesism.

Service-animal histories attest to the ways in which the exercise of some human rights requires animal assistance. For folks who make their way to the polls with the help of a dog, this intense, highly specialized training relationship most obviously creates conditions in which the political viability of rights models extends beyond individual bodies, at least in principle. The ADA affirms that some people rely on service animals in order to hold jobs and otherwise contribute fully as citizens, that is, that their rights are predicated on the kinds of mobility that come only through constant companionship with a service animal. However, in practice, the struggle to exercise these rights reflects ongoing questioning about what happens to the human subject of these rights when a disabled citizen exercises them only through partnership with a dog, questions that are modeled through guide-dog fictions. What I want to highlight here are some particular elements in their narrative patterns that illustrate more specifically the problems of identification and imaging in rights-based approaches to social justice.[4]

Starting in the 1930s with Baynard Kendrick's formative mystery-novel series that features a blind detective with the first fictional Seeing Eye dog,[5] and continuing through film and television representations, including the 2005 ABC television series *Blind Justice*, guide-dog fictions have led the way in making public life for blind citizens more widely possible. They do so primarily by depicting such folks as gainfully employed, if often in exceptional circumstances. Given that in fiction as in fact stories of people working with service animals are few,[6] their rarity alone would seem to make such narratives visionary. But the same elements that unify American guide-dog fictions also link up with reactionary trends in identity debates that have unfolded in recent decades, mitigating their transformative social potential.

Again and again, these fictions tell stories only of white men blinded as adults, who are rehabilitated to professional careers with the help of German shepherd guide dogs. In these ways, the stories directly reflect the influential history of blind American Morris Frank, who brought Buddy, the first dog trained with modern guide methods, to the United States from Europe, and subsequently founded The Seeing Eye, the first guide-dog school in North America. The success of Frank and other activists certainly can be measured by the social support for service animals and working disabled people alike that has grown (again in principle more than in practice) along with this small but persistent narrative strain. As the urban dog-person fantasies of blindness indicate, acceptance does not necessarily entail understanding of these agents of change. So it seems well worth examining how this precise profile of service animal and user persists long after Morris's time in the literary and more broadly cultural imagination, and, more important, how it changes through very different stories of social justice.

In stark contrast to the biography of Frank—who was, by all accounts, a social extrovert whose guide dogs enabled him to run an insurance company along with the nonprofit Seeing Eye—the fictions imagine their central human characters as alienated. Working increasingly on their own and as detectives, the fictional guide-dog users make it their job to pursue justice but not always to uphold the law. In the beginning, this difference allows the blind man to assert intellectual superiority: Kendrick's early and more didactic fictions contrast his insightful blind detective, who efficiently enlists the help of both guard and guide dogs, with the obtuse lawmen via one running "sight" gag that shows the police detectives unable even to keep straight which kind of dog is dangerous. But the increasing loneliness and especially defensive aggression exhibited by such characters links them to all-too-human problems.

Indicating their broader purpose in changing sighted people's perceptions of what exactly blind men and guide dogs can do, the early stories proceed from the assumption that human society has to change fundamentally in order for the guide dog (and along with her the blind man) to work. Although in different ways, Kendrick uses these tales to pursue Frank's own objective, namely, "to mold the world to [his guide dog] Buddy" rather "than Buddy to the world," in order ultimately to "advance beyond" social limitations through their world-forming work together.[7] But the ways in which visual media adaptations of these narratives reframe this objective in exclusively human terms indicate why such ideals remain elusive.

Although often directly based on Kendrick's fictions, later film and television stories drop the difficult questions of cross-species representation. More precisely, they give up the struggle to account for the special sense of interdependence that characterizes the impaired-unless-canine-assisted experience in favor of using this relationship to symbolize a more personal struggle, the identity conflicts of a suddenly disabled white man working amid failing justice systems. The narrower focus on the blind detective's wavering authority by the end of the twentieth century makes his mission all the more precarious, not the least because it brackets off the more complex bodily and social understandings made possible by his work with a guide dog. Instead of enabled or expanded by association with a dog, this character violently defends a sense of self that he sees as threatened on multiple fronts, indicating what is at stake not simply for assistance animals in the institutionalization of disability rights but more broadly for alienating disability from species discourses, blocking off the latter as a sort of final frontier.

Theories of animality as encompassed by (even fundamentally repressed within) human identity certainly account for the conspicuous absence of animal questions from these debates in recent decades for reasons detailed in the introduction, but the blind-detective stories beg more exact accounts of what happens when human identity problems come to displace multispecies concerns. Examined in this context, the guide-dog fictions' symbolic retrenchments of human identity tell a more explicit story of the difficulty of developing a politics based on proliferations of multiple interspecies forms, and more startlingly perhaps of the human individual as itself a fiction, here produced through companion-species relations. The mixed achievements of disability rights that accrue in and around these representations arguably reflect the multiple and often menacing roles of animals in the histories and theories of disability. More problematically, in this particular case they have begun to create new and more formidable obstacles to modeling shared human–animal forms of agency.

Before analyzing these texts more carefully, I should clarify that "animal" and "disabled" refer to a broad range of bodily configurations. Each of these terms anchors powerful points of contrast to the singular sense of self-in-the-world as the norm whereby individuals are represented as the baseline for membership in the community of human beings, let alone as subjects of rights.[8] When this privileged sense of individuality is approached instead as a relationally produced effect, rather than an essential quality or fundamental element, it affords a glimpse of a much longer history in which animals have worked with (and against) people with disabilities (PWDs).

In making this connection, I do not want to downplay the damage done by the historically stigmatizing associations of disabled and other people with animals, but rather to pinpoint how the humanist subject becomes produced through these connections. Often they are forged within the extremely volatile medical and biological discourses in which animal proximities threaten the so-called normal human subject with metaphorical no less than bodily harm, even as they become means of representing the experience of being human. Primatologist and popular ethologist Frans de Waal cannot simply cure philosopher Thomas Nagel's celebrated pessimism about knowing what it is like to be a bat by pointing to studies that show how "some blind persons [use] . . . echolocation," in other words, by redefining blindness as a condition enabling people special access to the experiences of animals.[9] By looking at patterns of representing blind men and service dogs, what I want to suggest instead is that historic (mis)perceptions of animal proximities to subject forms become altered only through painful moments in enduring struggles to assert forms of species and social agency that defy the very terms of such comparisons.

Part of the problem is that animals serve as catalysts for the ways in which disability becomes understood (and often feared) as a potential identity for everyone. After all, it was a fateful fall from a horse that changed overmounted actor Christopher Reeve, "one day Superman, next day a quadriplegic," into what disability theorist Lennard J. Davis calls "the most dramatic example of this quick-change act."[10] As Davis and others argue, moving beyond this fear-based politics of otherness involves learning how to read human (and I would add animal) agency as potentially compromised as well as re-formed in these contexts. No simple alternative to disability identity politics, these reformulations of social agency across species and other boundaries marking the human subject require a thoroughgoing interrogation of the ways in which power operates not only through the disciplinary regimes focused on the body but also the biopolitics of multiple and intersecting populations, joining others in becoming differently enabled publics.

This is perhaps the most important lesson of the textual history of service dogs. Like the first Seeing Eye dog users who inspired them, guide-dog fictions directly confront the negative image of a blind man led astray by (and consequently like) a dog, a popular trope of the pitiful or repulsive "cripple" in European painting from the Renaissance onward that was replicated by celebrated artists, including Tintoretto, Rembrandt, and Gainsborough. As early advocates like Kendrick and Frank well knew, this negative linkage draws powerfully on the growing fear of disability as dehumanization that accompanies the rise of the Enlightenment subject.

This fear ultimately imperils the institution of modern guide-dog training methods well into the twentieth century, even among leaders of prominent institutions for the blind.[11] While earlier representations arguably set up guide-dog fictions to walk thin lines between exploitation and critique, these narratives promote forms that blast away at the grounds of victimization, and so have the potential instead to develop mutually informing (and not mutually exclusive) discourses of disability and species with profound implications for the politics of mixed-species social life. If, as I will argue about *Blind Justice* in the next section, some recent examples suggest that the dog is simply a prop for the wounded white American serviceman's reclamation of his rights, then they do so only by abandoning the goal of structuring a story in such a way that a man and dog together can become the agent of justice.

Bookending this chapter, then, are very different examples that sustain a complex vision of contemporary service-animal politics. In all of these narratives, achievement hinges on shifting perceptions, as much of police/guide dogs as of enabled/disabled citizens. In this respect, a greater significance may lie in these stories' lack of resolution, in their ongoing dramatization of rights that can only ever be realized through cross-species intimacies. Rather than focusing on their failure to engender new subjectivities, my aim is to bring attention to their compelling case for a more integrative model of social agency, one that opens perspectives on the complex linkage of animal and disability rights histories as well as the partiality and incompletion that might be said to characterize any discrete human subject. While this linkage of textual and political representation presents its own difficulties, it also provides a way of accounting for how, with the help of service animals, disability identity—rather, people's enabled-with-dog lives—becomes heroic, and perhaps even more desirable. And this in turn reveals a complex emergence of intersubjective agency forms in modern animal narratives.

Identity Problems: Jim Dunbar and Hank

Fifteen years after the passage of the ADA, the short-lived television series *Blind Justice* in many ways seemed long overdue. Although it is not the only television show that deals with the repercussions of the ADA, it is the first one to be premised on the law's potential for social transformation. The series starts when New York City Detective Jim Dunbar (played by sighted actor Ron Eldard), who was blinded in the line of duty, wins his lawsuit to return to his job in law enforcement. And it encourages audiences to take seriously the logical premise of the blind-detective genre, namely, that blindness can be an asset to a detective. Each episode features surreal, subjective shots that pare down crime scenes to highlight significant elements, literally envisioning the kind of mental clarity that might come to a detective who is freed from the distractions of seeing many more irrelevant details. There are also precise limits to the ways in which viewers are encouraged to identify with this complex character. A Gulf War veteran and reformed lothario, Dunbar's consistently confrontational approach is linked to his own ambivalence about depending on others, even his German shepherd guide dog Hank, indicating profound anxieties about his special situation.

As an ADA story, *Blind Justice* at the very least seems an exception based on exceptional cases. From the start, the show found fans within the blind community, in part because it bucked a discriminatory trend in which people with disabilities rarely are envisioned as "productive" citizens, let alone as entitled to work with fair accommodations like Detective Dunbar.[12] Few as they may be, representations of the special kind of human–animal relationship that Dunbar and Hank embody significantly challenge notions of disabled people as stereotypically social parasites by distinguishing physical impairments from the environments in which they become disabilities. So this blind character, who moves about freely with a service dog, only becomes disabled when entering restricted private property, like a suspect's home in which absolutely no dogs are allowed.

These important distinctions are largely lost in American popular culture, in which disability is represented more often in terms of an individual's problems rather than as a shared social concern.[13] On this point, *Blind Justice* certainly breaks with these negative representational patterns, which some say fuel a sense of defeatism among disabled people[14] (a significant majority of whom do not work),[15] as well as a virulent backlash against efforts to change these conditions. Yet as a prime-time television drama, *Blind Justice* perhaps inevitably reflects even as it enters a cold cultural climate, beginning with the

Jim Dunbar (actor Ron Eldard) and Hank in a promotional still for ABC's *Blind Justice* (2005), a short-lived television series that exemplifies the modern narrative tradition of blinded white male detectives returning to work with German shepherd guide dogs.

incredible, socially progressive alternative to a trend in which very few actual ADA suits have been decided in favor of disabled plaintiffs, and quickly retreating to a debilitating stereotype of the disabled person as horribly isolated.[16]

Through these tensions, the show opens up many more questions about narrating disability, but it stops short of developing concerns specific to Dunbar's use of the guide dog. As Hank quickly devolves from rare service-animal character to plot motivation as valuable property (later episodes would involve his theft and recovery), Dunbar in turn emerges as a stock character of contemporary American television cop shows. With his constant and often physical altercations with able-bodied co-workers, crime suspects, even his psychiatrist, this blind detective identifies and internalizes disability as his personal problem, and, more important, as that which stands in the way of resuming the unquestioned authority that he enjoyed before he was blinded by a gunshot fired by a fellow policeman. The impaired-without-dog figure thus becomes reduced to a symbol of white masculinity in peril, and, if these aspects of the heroically wounded and socially disserved NYPD officer have a post-9/11 predictability, then they also begin to explain why Hank remains underdeveloped as a character.[17]

More present in the show's credits and advertising than in the show itself, Hank appears mostly to be a part of the furniture of Dunbar's new life as a blind man.[18] Even the few episodes that were aired depict none of the necessary training and little of the maintenance work involved in this kind of relationship, so from the outset Hank's dramatic role is severely limited. Dunbar's human partner even renders superfluous Hank's utility as a mobility tool when she learns in the first episode to guide the man by the arm and thereby to help him pass sometimes as sighted. With the success of the blinded white male detective riding on the outcome of sometimes violent conflicts that he as often as not initiates with other people, his canine companion may not be instrumental as service dog so much as powerful symbol. But what does this fictional dog signify?

Referencing the long and complicated histories of this kind of dog, the breed of this canine actor offers some clues. This casting choice itself might strike contemporary viewers as anachronistic. In the early days of modern guide-dog training schools, German shepherds were favored over all other breeds of dogs, so much so that the image of one in harness continues to be recognized as an iconic marker of human disability. The German shepherd's genetic problems (such as those associated with hip dysplasia) have led guide-dog trainers in recent years to opt instead for breeds like Labrador and golden retrievers, and consequently to put a different public face on the service animal.

The old associations still linger, possibly informing canine casting choices in the production of *Blind Justice*. But the complex symbolic value built into this role also illustrates problems with the conceptual split between disability and species as identity forms, and more specifically the German shepherd's idealization, as well as a sort of backlash against or denigration of this kind of dog in current philosophical and cultural debates.

Analyzing recent developments in disability studies, for instance, Rosemarie Garland-Thomson identifies the harnessed German shepherd guide dog in a magazine model's photo as her "mark of disability," and more significantly as the key element that makes this disabled person seem stereotypically attractive. For Garland-Thomson, the photo exemplifies a pattern in contemporary culture that she critiques as an "inadvertently progressive" form of "cripsploitation."[19] But is it the identity of the German shepherd dog or her association with the subject of disability that renders the dog-in-harness a sort of fashion accessory in this image?

Responding directly to Garland-Thomson's underdevelopment of the dog as a structuring element here, animal studies theorist Cary Wolfe asks, "[Rather than] . . . doing to nonhuman 'differents' what 'normates' have traditionally done to the disabled[,] . . . wouldn't we do better to imagine this example as an irreducibly different and unique form of subjectivity—neither *Homo sapiens* nor *Canis familiaris,* neither 'disabled' nor 'normal,' but something else altogether, a shared trans-species being-in-the-world constituted by complex relations of trust, respect, dependence, and communication (as anyone who has ever trained—or relied on—a service dog would be the first to tell you)?"[20] This question frames exactly what I expected to find in service-animal narratives, but my research has yielded a far more complicated struggle at the heart of these rarified forms. Embedded in the choice of a German shepherd dog as a partner for this model are stories of changing social conditions that have allowed these two together to become perceptible (let alone affirmed) as one of several kinds of working units.

Amid these varied roles, the conflicted iconic and ego-projection functions of this particular kind of dog shape literary and other media histories in ways that both reinforce and problematize the terms of subjectivity. This singularly human form anathematizes the more expansive, if much messier, shared forms of social agency made possible by service dogs occluded by discussions of disability and species in terms of the limits of human identity. A different sort of appeal to the figure of the German shepherd dog as embodying disability clarifies how contexts never simply reflect but more actively inform this problem.

Proposing a meeting point for traditionally oppositional disability and animal-rights agendas, philosopher Martha Nussbaum offers the example of a German shepherd using a wheelchair specially defined for dogs as "analogous" to mentally impaired adults and all children to illustrate "core capacities that form the species norm" in the human as well as other species, a concept of "central capabilities" that can "include particular interspecies relationships, such as the traditional relationship between the dog and the human" that in turn "defines the context, the political and social community" that makes provisions for such individuals.[21] This image of the dog as requiring (and in a way that makes it incapable of providing) mobility assistance serves Nussbaum's immediate interest in the dog as an object of human stewardship, "prudent guardianship," or "intelligent, species-sensitive paternalism," and more generally her assumption that "individuality" is a benchmark of social participation.[22] Here more clearly the failure to address this particular dog's iconic value along with any reference to service animals throughout her argument suggests how such relations boggle even the most well-intentioned attempts to challenge foundational thinking of rights.

This is not to say that these meanings are unchanging. Cultural perceptions of these particular animals' capacity for social agency shape and are shaped by the intersubjective and other relations through which they gain social value. And nothing makes this point clearer than the ways in which the iconic values of German shepherds come to include conflicted meanings in and around their representations as both guide and police dogs.

Rearranging documentary photos of an attack on civil rights protesters by police with dogs included in the May 17, 1963, issue of *Life* magazine, artist Andy Warhol's *Race Riot* (1963) encapsulates another sort of violent police story unfolding in tandem with these developments in the blind-detective genre. Initially created as part of his *Death in America* series, Warhol referred to these monumental (10' x 7') images as "the dogs in Birmingham."[23] His cropping and sequencing reinforce not only the animal presence but also a narrative of race and species that is more obscurely referenced by the single screen repurposed in the later series, *Little Race Riots,* which marks the structural shift in his work toward smaller images produced for nonhierarchichal compositions. While it is significant that (at least one screen of) the initial image persisted through this major shift in Warhol's work, the centrality of a particular canine image within the story of *Race Riot* also inscribes broader cultural shifts in media representations of as well as attitudes toward this kind of dog.

The same reasons that made German shepherds initially seem exceptionally suited as guides—namely, their size, physical versatility, and amenability

Andy Warhol, *Race Riot*, 1963, illustrates how German shepherds become part of the stories of white policemen in civil rights movements, and part of the forces of racist states in anticolonial movements worldwide by the end of the twentieth century. Copyright 2009 The Andy Warhol Foundation for the Visual Arts/ARS, New York.

to training—also made them the breed of choice in training programs for canine military and police work in the twentieth century. Although *Blind Justice*'s Hank (as represented by the canine actors playing this role) remains entirely in character as a guide, by the beginning of the twenty-first century his breed's history resonates with Dunbar's military and police service record, bringing to the role complex associations with racism and colonialism. In human terms, the show singles out the wounded white man as knocked out of power and clawing his way back with a vengeance. As an icon of besieged white manhood, Dunbar thus can be seen as becoming marked (or rendered visible) through the German shepherd guide accompanying his return to the police force. Although not explicitly developed in *Blind Justice*, the blurring of the roles of serving and protecting a particular kind of person has also become part of the German shepherd's breed history in the American popular imaginary, and as I develop below, this conflation most directly ties this show to prior visual narratives of service dogs.

Like *Blind Justice*, these earlier texts also focus on a white man, a heroic all-American guy adventitiously becoming blind as an adult, first in war and in later examples through criminal action. In each case, the character is never congenitally blind (or even blinded as a small child), which means in part that, though blinded, the man always has a memory of vision, making it easier to represent his thoughts through visual media and for sighted audience members to identify with him. But he is always blinded as the result of violence, and, in keeping with the popular fantasy of this kind of disability, he also is always depicted as remobilized with canine assistance. While this work does not always stay strictly within the law, the stories insist that he is consistently working for justice, troping the conditions of his own impairment ("blind justice") even as he complicates these metaphorical terms by relying on a German shepherd guide, who in turn is tactically paired (at times even fantastically conflated) with a police or attack dog.

Particularly when these stories involve multiple dogs, they work like detective fiction more generally to recast questions of authority in terms of modern cultural conflicts between forms of identity and community.[24] Identifying criminals remains the key to solving crimes in these stories, but the detective's own identity as hero derives from his reliance on others. Dunbar's human partner may come to displace Hank, but in earlier blind-detective stories, several people as well as dogs are explicitly enlisted to serve in different capacities that assist and complement the performance of these working units. Equally important to the earliest of these fictions is their framing of these relations squarely within the conditions of modern urban life, and of the detective's reliance on several others. For his entanglements in multiple codependencies contribute to a sense of these intersubjective relations with dogs as extending, rather than limiting, social power in the interest of justice.

Superman: Duncan Maclain and Schnuke

The idea of blindness as a surmountable hazard to canine-assisted detective work is the unabashed premise of Baynard Kendrick's *Last Express*, the first of a series of twelve mystery novels and four short stories published between 1937 and 1961, featuring Captain Duncan Maclain, a character imagined as blinded in action in World War I. More than just a reworking of the author's wartime experiences, Kendrick's own account of how he conceived of this blind detective fixes him firmly as a product of war. While still on active duty, Kendrick visited a former schoolmate in St. Dunstan's Lodge, the charity hospital for blinded soldiers in London, and there was astounded to meet another serviceman who accurately detailed Kendrick's convoluted, multinational, four-year military record simply by "brailling" his uniform.[25] Years later, while researching the histories of famous blind people, Kendrick returned to this experience as he attempted deliberately to create not the first blind detective, but rather the first realistic one, whose feats could be duplicated by any equally clever and diligent sighted person.

More specifically, Kendrick was frustrated with the former schoolmate's (who was by then also his roommate) miserable obsession with the first fictional blind detective, Max Carrados, and saw the man's alcoholism as driven in part by "his inability to duplicate the utterly impossible feats of Ernest Bramah's overdrawn character."[26] This set Kendrick on a search for historical examples of successful blind people, among them novelist Henry Fielding's step-brother John, the vision-impaired judge known as the "Blind Beak," who pioneered policies for handling juvenile offenders and police administration. Eventually he contacted Helen Keller's teacher, Anne Sullivan, who fatefully advised him to use this knowledge himself in his own work as a fiction writer. And so, he recalled, against the demoralizing power of figures like Carrados, "The idea of Captain Duncan Maclain was born." But to flesh out this character, Kendrick concluded, "Maclain needed mobility."[27] Pursuing a realistic mechanism, the author was led to research and include another first for fiction, the Seeing Eye dog character Schnuke, introduced as the product of guide-dog training programs developed for war-blinded veterans in Europe.

Even within Kendrick's fictions, Maclain constantly calls attention to this peculiar history by crediting his rehabilitation to the help of The Seeing Eye, and he exemplifies this organization's ideals of blind people as model working citizens by taking full advantage of the tools of modern living, chief among which emerges the Seeing Eye dog.[28] Kendrick carefully constructs a positive image of Maclain by introducing him to readers as already firmly established as a world-famous private detective and sometime G-man, the bane of organized crime in New York City, and a handsome (if reluctant) blue-eyed media darling. The stories do not downplay the difficulties involved in achieving this position, but set them in the past, supplanting them with Maclain's tenacious struggle to clarify the dramatic difference that a guide dog makes in the blind detective's day-to-day life. The repetitions (sometimes verbatim) of what exactly the dog does for Maclain, especially of her dispelling despair when she enters his life, clearly aim to educate readers about the guide dog's social advantages at a time when prejudices against these "canine citizens" remained strong.[29] Although one measure of Kendrick's success might be the way in which the Maclain series enters directly into historic changes for disabled Americans, another might be seen in its visionary assertion of this particular intersubjective relation as a crowning achievement of modernity.

A key feature within this series—and one that contradicts many theories of companion species in modernity—is the central assumption that dogs trained through the Seeing Eye methods are integrated as (and not simply with) cutting-edge technologies. The novels are saturated with descriptions of the urban and urbane gadgetry that makes the blind detective's independent life not simply possible but more attractive, even futuristic. Amid frequent references to the air conditioning, artificial ice cubes, and automatic elevators of Maclain's Manhattan penthouse, descriptions of other machinery designed specifically to aid blind people, like talking books and record players lent by the Federal Records for the Blind program, Braille books and typewriters, and even Maclain's personal adaptation of the "detecto-dictograph" (a version of the early recording device invisibly built into his office to help him with casework), enter as harbingers of the future, not the stigmata of a crip.

Throughout the series, Kendrick is careful to update these technologies. These upgrades emphasize how Maclain remains at the cutting edge of modern technology, for instance, showing him in a later novel using a "Gray Audograph," a machine for communication among the blind that displaced the dictograph.[30] A single modern asset, however, remains supremely reliable, and it is the one showcased in an image that became the Maclain series icon. In this ultramodern landscape, the guide dog appears the most marvelous new technology of all, and more: together, blind detective and guide dog, "welded into a single entity," portend radical transformations to the social as well as material conditions of disability that the novelist Kendrick worked hard to bring about.[31]

Like most fictional detective heroes, Maclain proves exceptionally perceptive, and his blindness provides a motivation for vigilantly disciplining his own movements, memory, and senses, for instance, by training to shoot accurately at sound. So it is not a stretch when he himself articulates (even as he establishes) the operative assumption of *Blind Justice* and other stories in this genre, namely, that being blind is actually an advantage to a detective, if only for the most obvious reason that a blind man's constant questions procure information "without arousing suspicion."[32] Mobility would be his only problem, if not for faithful canine assistance, for the very "freedom to use his talents was placed in his hands" by working with his guide dog Schnuke.[33] With this kind of presentation, the Seeing Eye dog emerges as not simply another means with which the blind man gets along but more profoundly as the key to the blind detective's success, and with her Kendrick too moves beyond educating his readers about the realities of blindness and into advocacy for this new vision of disability as impairment effectively overcome with canine assistance.

Outlining a transformation that is as miraculous as it is unequivocal, the first novel clarifies that Maclain once endured "miserable days of bitterness when he felt that he was a helpless burden on his friends," and that these feelings "disappeared with the coming of" Schnuke. Language choices in passages

Series logo included on the title page of Baynard Kendrick's *Odor of Violets* (1941), the third novel in the series featuring blind detective Duncan Maclain, introducing the iconic image of a blind male figure and a German shepherd dog in harness.

like the following insist that physical rehab is only part of this experience: "Immediately, with the ability restored to him to come and go as he pleased, all of Maclain's highly developed talents were released[,] . . . turning the blind captain into a superman of intelligence and efficiency."[34] The frequently passive verb constructions in such descriptions cleverly sidestep questions about the dog's volition in changing the blind man's life. But they also suggest that her companionship enables him to be more than he was, perhaps even before he became blind, an interpretation that finds further support in the descriptions of the social effects of this transformation.

More than a mere mobility tool, the guide dog in these novels serves as a catalyst for social improvement, including the blind detective's good working relations with others. As the head of his combination home-office, Maclain captains a human–canine team that also includes married couple Spud and Rena Savage, who had befriended him long before his rehabilitation. These human companions also are important to restoring Maclain's sense of security—indeed, his unflappable confidence remains one of this blind detective's trademarks—yet these early novels insist that it is the guide dog who staves off the sense of identity crisis that seems to plague later incarnations of this character, like Detective Dunbar. As Kendrick clarifies, Schnuke does not serve as a substitute for Maclain's human companions and co-workers: "On the contrary, Schnuke drew the three closer together by dispelling bitter thoughts of being a burden from the captain's mind," a characterization that intimates that help from within the human community may never be enough to move beyond the conceptual limits of ableism.[35]

Although fictional, these descriptions of the difference that the dog makes to both the sense of self of blind persons and their social lives with others strikingly echo the much more recent sociological accounts of Clinton R. Sanders, who explains that people describe their guide dogs as "extensions of the physical self."[36] Such dogs do not simply enhance the abilities or self-confidence of blind people, but more complexly give them a consistent sense of "feeling 'complete' or 'made whole' because of their association with the animal."[37] The blind detectives' professional success while employing guide dogs becomes informed by this research, which also begins to explain the narrative trouble in subsequent guide-dog fictions with representing this sense of self as extending beyond the blind person's body.

Of course, this remains a most pressing problem for actual guide-dog users, who describe their own lives with dogs as having a particular impact on reforming workable personal and collective identities. The liberal humanist one-body-equals-one-self terms of representation often lead to frustration when the person tries to share this kind of cross-species experience with others who do not work with dogs. Sanders cites one blind interviewee: "People have often tried to find the human equivalent to the relationship that I have with [my guide dog] Winnie, but there isn't one. People ask me if she's my best friend, or if she's more like my child. *Winnie is my eyes.* What is your relationship with your eyes?"[38] In such moments, it becomes clear that the blind person does not simply identify with the dog, but rather feels through the dog as part of a shared bodily and agential experience that, as in the descriptions of Maclain, is extraordinarily empowering.

Moreover, these accounts complicate accusations of exploitation (another daily hazard that guide-dog users encounter from the general public) by elaborating how guide-dog relations enhance social operations like those imagined in fiction among Maclain and his friends, especially the Savages. For the informant, the practical advantages—improved navigation, canine companionship—are clearly part of what makes the relationship with the guide dog attractive, and, more important, contribute to the less tangible sense of these experiences as contributing to what Sanders characterizes as "changing social identity."[39] This kind of shifting perception of a self that is differently abled from the human body alone is in part what makes them so attractive to Kendrick's novelistic rendition (if not the to dog people's passing fantasies), and also so difficult to sustain in ensuing representations of these stories, especially as they move to visual media.

Kendrick's attempts to model these benefits through the Savages' reliance on Maclain's canine-assisted leadership for their own jobs may be most prescient because they demonstrate that the flourishing of these "uniquely interdependent, communicative, and emotionally binding" cross-species relationships has profound social consequences among what disability activists now term temporarily able-bodied people (or TABs) as well.[40] Yet the historic influence of this blind detective appears instead to involve a conceptual separation of the blind man from his dog. Maclain's guide dog Schnuke, always described as a Seeing Eye dog and a German shepherd, becomes a means of connecting guide-dog fictions not just to each other but even more directly to the media career of this kind of service animal in the United States, a parabolic journey that for Kendrick and others dangerously overshadows the problems of people with disabilities. Considering how the history of Morris Frank and The Seeing Eye (which in turn is inextricable from the modern breed story of the German shepherd) seems almost from the start to be one of conflict between disability and animal rights, I will take a closer look at how the series comes to connect the blind detective and his author more directly to the political struggles of blinded veterans, apparently at the expense of elaborating the even more complex relations that Maclain develops with multiple dogs.

Activists: Morris Frank and Baynard Kendrick

From the first novel in the series onward, Maclain credits his success explicitly to The Seeing Eye and its founder, Morris Frank, underscoring the historic changes that Frank at that time was still very active in bringing about.[41] The son of an adventitiously blind woman who himself was blinded as a teenager in a fight, Frank's public advocacy began with a correspondence sparked by a 1927 *Saturday Evening Post* article by wealthy American expatriate and German shepherd breeder Dorothy Harrison Eustis. Titled "The All Seeing Eye," Eustis's essay detailed her initial skepticism and ultimate "conversion" to the modern guide-dog training methods focused on this breed of dog, which extend and are informed by the long European war histories of institutions for the blind.

Immediately after World War I, a tripartite coalition of the German government, a war-blinded soldiers' association, and Verein für deutsche Schäferhunde (Society for the German Shepherd Dog) organized schools that for the first time in history used sighted instructors to train dogs and blind people to work together, pioneering the methods of guide-dog training that have been in use ever since.[42] With the aim of bringing this amazing feat to the attention of American audiences, Eustis's article, like so much of the publicity surrounding guide dogs in the interwar period, exploits the novelty of providing effective canine assistance for blind men. More precisely, the focus of her article is not rehabilitating disabled people so much as promoting the German shepherd's superior breeding (a term that signals the volatile admixture of eugenic technologies and bourgeois sensibilities popular at that time), and ultimately inspiring others to join her in cultivating the intelligence of such dogs through elaborate programs of selection and training.[43]

But dog breeders' responses to her article were by far outnumbered by those of many blind readers who wanted one of these amazing animals, including Frank. His letter appealed to Eustis for expressing a more encompassing desire to help in addressing the pressing need for guide dogs among blind civilians, and in 1928 she honored his request—chosen from among many others on account of Frank's suitability for both the rigorous dog training as well as tricky promotional work. Eustis brought him to Switzerland to train with a beautiful German shepherd named Kiss (whom Frank immediately renamed Buddy) with the hope of making them a hit with the American public. They did all this and more. In 1929, shortly after Frank returned to the States with Buddy amid a news media blitz, he began helping others like himself by starting The Seeing Eye foundation, but not without opposition.

Organized resistance came on two main fronts: from other nonprofit organizations for the disabled, and, more virulently, from animal advocates. Eustis, Frank, and their supporters anticipated that institutional advocates for the blind would hesitate to embrace the modern methods, especially because they self-consciously labored against the repulsive Old Master images of blind beggars attached to ineffective dog guides. They guessed rightly that germaphobic urbanites, too, would not welcome dogs back into areas like restaurants and shops, newly regulated by public health institutions that among other things had cleansed such places of the sight of live animals. But they were surprised to find that the mission they considered to be unequivocally emancipatory was challenged by others who saw (and even still see) its means as a form of animal exploitation. In the early years, their efforts were fervently opposed by animal-rights activists, who termed the training methods a rarified form of "cruelty," and even denounced the whole concept as animal "slavery."[44]

Through sometimes violent confrontations between animal activists and trainers on the street and eventually in European courts of law, these early guide-dog advocates learned quickly that publicity emphasizing the joys of working life with Seeing Eye dogs and their benefits to society as a whole would be the only way around a looming stalemate of animal and disability rights activism. This is in part why, immediately upon his return to the States, Frank traveled far and wide amid a carefully orchestrated media frenzy surrounding his demonstrations of the safety and efficiency of Buddy's guidance for both dog and man. Always accompanied by impeccably cared-for canine guides, he continued this work for nearly thirty years, remaining to the end a fervent advocate of, as well as stellar example for, the ability of blind people to improve their own lives along with those of others. While such work has helped to ensure that the mission of The Seeing Eye stays focused on helping blind people to become working citizens, it also has cultivated a sense of service animals as public spectacles, a problem that troubles not only Kendrick's protagonist but also the novelist's involvement with the Maclain series.

Wartime propaganda films of the next decade reflect Frank's efforts to mainstream blind workers with guide dogs, but, as was the case for women and African American workers, jobs for the disabled largely proved temporary, lost with the peacetime return of able-bodied white men.[45] And, in spite of high hopes in the early years for large-scale implementation, long-term studies commissioned by The Seeing Eye eventually demonstrated that, regardless of anyone's desires, only a small fraction of the vision-impaired public would ever be able to meet the emotional and physical demands of guide-dog work. Strangely, then, as the blind-detective fictions more broadly suggest, the most direct and enduring cultural legacy of Frank's efforts in the United States may be the growing public approbation for canine guides rather than the emancipation of disabled people. Serendipitously, however, The Seeing Eye also served as an inspiration for Kendrick's novelistic presentation of Maclain's disability in terms of a social (not personal) barrier, an impairment overcome with the help of the guide dog and others. This reconceptualization of disability more generally would prove pivotal in shaping effective political campaigns for disability rights.

Kendrick's work grew to involve public policy changes benefiting especially blinded veterans, who came to appear at least in the public imagination very like the blind detectives: largely as heroic white men, adventitiously blinded, and commanding social change in the pursuit of justice. By the 1940s, the Maclain series more directly entered into the rehabilitation of American soldiers blinded in World War II. On the basis of the popular and critical success of these novels, Kendrick was recruited first to give talks to newly blinded soldiers, and later to teach them creative writing. As part of the latter job, he was supposed to write an official history of the long-overdue (and by then centralizing and rapidly expanding) national rehab system for blinded veterans.

He instead produced the novel *Lights Out* (1945), which is narrated from the perspective of Larry Nevin, a more ordinary blinded veteran. Like the Maclain concept, Kendrick describes this book as an amalgamation of actual incidents, an attempt "to tell quite truthfully some of the amazing things [he] had seen" in his work with rehabilitation centers for blinded veterans.[46] Again, the story becomes far more complex in the telling. Serving as a sort of back story to all of the blind-detective fictions, this novel follows the soldier from the moment of his being blinded by a bullet wound in the line of duty through the process of learning to live with his blindness, which in Kendrick's vision of Larry becomes a struggle that is less about physical training and more about overcoming social prejudices, his own as much as any others.

Lights Out makes this mental journey explicit through extended depictions of poor, white southerner Larry's consciousness-raising. Especially poignant is this character's central dramatic confusion about whether to embrace "the brand-new world of blackness," in which he has befriended Joe Morgan, a similarly blinded black soldier, or remain "in the visual world" of segregation, in which Larry must continue to "see" Joe through racist stereotypes as his mortal enemy, an "ape man intent on nothing in life but marrying, or preferably raping, white women."[47] Although the novel's 1951 film version, *Bright Victory*, relegates this "racial subplot" to Larry's overcoming ableist prejudice, the novel more deliberately links these issues along with sexism and classism as interlocking forms of oppression.[48] To overcome the barriers set for him by anyone, in the end Larry must rid himself of all his own bigotries, which Kendrick aligns here as barriers to democratic society.

The first of the Maclain novels suggests such a connection by likening the blind detective to Jewish lawyer Max Gold as "two men at the head of their chosen profession—a place reached by the most obdurate refusal to ever consider handicaps," even as it in other ways falls back on then-current patterns of racial stereotyping.[49] But *Lights Out* extensively links the viability of working blind people to a more thoroughgoing social critique, modeling the postwar rise of disability activism through the political organization of wounded veterans. Still more directly, it is informed by Kendrick's role as the only nonblind adviser to the Blinded Veterans Association, founded in 1945 specifically to promote their own welfare. He was the only sighted person ever to have been elected to its board of directors, and he served as its honorary chair.

So it is not a far stretch to imagine *Lights Out* in this context as calculated to spur a political struggle that culminated in the U.S. Veterans Administration establishment of the first comprehensive Blind Rehabilitation Facility in 1948. In keeping with the VA's policies, however, the novel imagines Larry soldiering on in peacetime without canine assistance. This raises again the specter of division between animal and disability activism that Seeing Eye advocates earlier tried to stave off through public education, a problem that I will address more explicitly through the question of whether Maclain needs one (exceptional) or several (complementary) dogs.

One or Several Dogs? Schnuke and Dreist

Kendrick's literary biography ostensibly moves away from dogs as his work grows more deeply entwined with the disability activism of blinded veterans. The Maclain novels that he continued to produce, however, complicate this movement by imagining in greater detail the complex dependency of the blind detective's success on his involvement with multiple working canines.[50] What positions the Maclain series as influential in gaining acceptance for service dogs are its attempts to teach readers about animal training as much as vision-impaired life, and more specifically the careful distinction between the kinds of working dogs that assist the blind detective. Again, the plots often hinge on Maclain's ability not only to work skillfully with Seeing Eye Schnuke but also to switch her as needed with his police dog—or, in today's parlance, "police service dog"—named Dreist.[51] Like much of the descriptions of Maclain's actions in the novels, didactic clarifications of the different training and temperaments of these dogs aim to account for the particular means with which people might achieve such exceptional lives in modern industrial societies.

Echoing the popular terms of Eustis's influential *Saturday Evening Post* article, which would only begin to be sorted out scientifically in the 1960s, distinctions between dogs in the early novels reflect confusing ideas about breed genetics and training roles. Characters (and presumably readers) have trouble understanding that Schnuke's presence offers Maclain no guarantee of protection. Such audiences may end up still more confused by the repeated explanation that, though visually interchangeable with Dreist, she is a "German shepherd dog" and not "a trained police dog" like him.[52]

Patterns in metaphorical descriptions elaborate better the sense of the Seeing Eye dog as an organic technology, coevolving with the man in modern society, as opposed to the attack dog, who seems merely his tool. Schnuke is "gentle as a lamb," in contrast to Dreist, described mechanistically in almost every novel as "dangerous as a loaded gun."[53] In one standout description, Schnuke, as "the Captain's eyes," appears part human (or a human body part) in contrast to Dreist, who is objectified in terms of modern implements of violence: the police dog is "a weapon, not a pet," "a rocket from a bazooka," even "a brown bundle of German dynamite."[54] Reflecting the growing efficiency through complementary placement in training programs for these kinds of dogs,[55] explanations that relate their different temperaments to training methods eventually displace breed rhetorics in accounting for the key differences between guide and guard. Yet this initial alignment casts a long shadow over ensuing fictions of the guide dog.

Kendrick's ostensible message is that a dog's looks can be deceiving. Along the way, a related lesson emerges in the series: that different training methods inform the ways in which each dog serves a separate set of the blind detective's needs, namely, protection and mobility, a lesson that proves far more difficult to visualize. Although the novels carefully explain how Maclain best handles only one dog at a time, selecting each canine companion to suit a specific purpose, at least one cover image depicts an extraordinarily rare (if superheroically alluring) scene in which Maclain uses both dogs at once. Adding to the confusion is the apparent visual similarity of both dogs, which again allows for the "trick dog" switch often occurring at the climaxes of the stories. Criminals never recognize the difference, much to their chagrin, but readers are prepared by such descriptions to recognize that it is never the German shepherd Seeing Eye who lunges ferociously at Maclain's would-be attackers. Increasingly plausible descriptions of these successful maneuvers correct misleadingly idealized images, like the dust jacket featuring the fantastic (and anachronistic) scene of Maclain handling both dogs at once, used to market the series in the early years.[56] More significant still, they echo the multiple, complete-only-with-a-dog sense of self that is articulated not only by canine-assisted people with disabilities but also high-level dog trainers.

If more shrilly articulated, the message yet remains consistent that these canine working partnerships complement rather than displace human ties. By mid-series, Maclain protracts his engagement to beautiful, sighted, and famous designer Sybella Ford following the onset of different fears of being burdensome that Schnuke for once cannot dispel. He ultimately marries Sybella, who jokingly yet repeatedly accuses him of delaying their nuptials because he is instead "married to" Schnuke.[57] Yet it is clear that the woman neither impedes nor replaces the bitch when she joins the team as a provider of another kind of organic link, one that keeps the blind detective himself from permanently "turn[ing] into a cold, unfeeling, thinking machine."[58] Ever more complexly, people and dogs are integrated into a social network represented by the blind detective's success.

This sense of canine–human social complementarities becomes even more precisely foregrounded by the inclusion of details about day-to-day kennel operations. Also building in a growing racial consciousness by the 1960s, one of the last novels includes the significant detail that Cappo Marsh, who across novels incrementally outgrows the stereotypic aspects of his role as Maclain's black chauffeur (and often, like Schnuke, intelligently defies orders only to save Maclain's life), also proves a highly skilled dog handler of both Schnuke and Dreist. No simple kennel maid, Cappo is the "one other person living besides Spud and himself who could feed those dogs and handle them" and live to tell the tale.[59] Trainers and dogs alike emerge from such narrative developments as skilled, mature individuals, all learning to work together for a common good.

The ruptures of Maclain's relations with his dogs make painfully clear that all of their success hinges on these human–canine bonds. Such losses not only devastate the man, triggering returns of his self-doubt, but also potentially end his career as a detective by testing his commitments to justice systems. Autobiographical accounts clarify that one huge risk inherent in gaining the benefits of a dog's vision is a far "more terrible darkness" the person feels when the dog dies or is retired from service.[60] Intensely moving human–animal narratives in their own right, firsthand stories focusing on this aspect

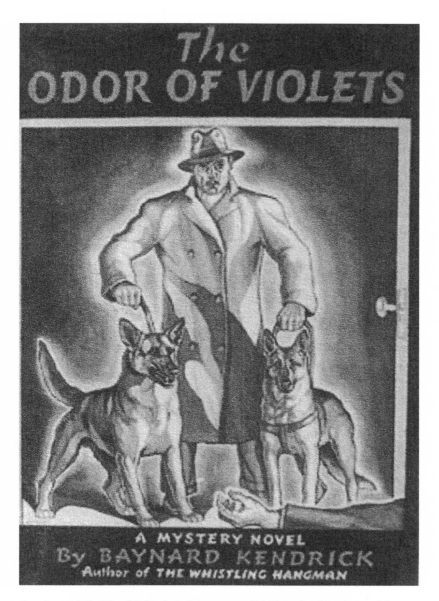

The ODOR OF VIOLETS

A MYSTERY NOVEL
By BAYNARD KENDRICK
Author of THE WHISTLING HANGMAN

Cover image of *The Odor of Violets*, featuring a rare—and highly implausible—image of the main character simultaneously working with both a guide dog and a guard dog. This ideal was realized only in two scenes, both in later novels in the Maclain series.

of the relationship surfaced frequently in my research, often like military or police service-dog stories in the form of a tribute to the deceased dog. For readers with this vivid narrative context in mind, Kendrick's multiple fictional attempts to represent these relations forming, foregone, and forged again with new dogs provide a plausible explanation for the wavering of the detective's confidence.[61]

Fans of the series learn along the way that, given dogs' drastically shorter working lives, Maclain's dogs realistically need to be replaced "every eight years."[62] This situation provides still another pretext for the ongoing confusion of the two dogs, even among his friends, as the series advances. Maclain allows that it is "a little matter of self-deception and also of sentiment" that compels him to give the ensuing dogs the same names that were bestowed upon the initial pair, in fact as in fiction, by The Seeing Eye.[63]

"Sentiment" here becomes complicated further by the dangerous conditions of detective work. While Maclain usually tries to deliver criminals to justice, meaning to the custody of law enforcement officials, he seeks revenge in kind exclusively for the (sometimes successful) attempts to kill his dogs. What is more, he acts as though motivated not by a sense of self-protection for his "eyes" or proprietary interest in his "bodyguard," but rather in each case by what is for this normally cool character an estranging sense of overwhelming passion, a self-endangering love that in dog-training literature signals a successful working relationship achieved through a crucial shift in worldviews.

This kind of understanding proceeds not from a hard-boiled force of (human) will, but rather through the studied development of mutual vulnerabilities. Vicki Hearne illustrates how this kind of love emerges exclusively through intense training processes, narrating her own experience of training a dog for high-level tracking work as "moving with some trembling" from a more familiar sense of being smitten or "head over heels in love" toward a much deeper commitment to trust her dog, as she puts it, "into an area where I will be wholly dependent on the dog's integrity to get the job done."[64] Likening this shift to a quantum leap or metaphysical mutation, she tries to convey how successful dog training is a misnomer because it requires of the person a kind of trust characterized by an openness to learning from the dog, which has no truck with desires for dominance.

Given the ease with which people who apparently do not share in cross-species training underestimate its demands, it is no small wonder that so few people make it through exceptionally rigorous programs like guide-dog and police service-dog training. Successful training in these circumstances means that the user's life depends on whether she can demonstrate the kind of love that requires people both to give dogs direction and at pivotal moments to honor their dogs' leadership. In training manuals and less formal narratives like Kendrick's novels, demonstrations of this ideal behavior are triggered by the guide dog's "intelligent disobedience" or refusal (no matter what the command) to bring the guided person into danger.

Such traits also are in keeping with what Sanders describes as the "liminal character" required of high-level police service-dog training, which likewise requires a smart ambivalence—here between the "dog's potential dangerousness and his obedient predictability." This trait also characterizes Maclain's Dreist, who, like Schnuke, proves capable of calculating choices that at times compel the dog to override human orders for their mutual benefit.[65] The descriptions of each of these canine characters (along with their same-named replacements) doing this, again and again, to save Maclain and their other handlers, often in the process endangering their own lives, glimpse the very special human–animal bonds at the heart of these stories, even as they risk misrepresenting them, especially to the dog-loving public.

The risk of misperception is always a serious hazard for people working with dogs in public, and one that Kendrick increasingly addresses in his later novels. In what might otherwise seem a five-page tangent from the plot of *Blind Allies* (1954), readers learn that, for "a quarter of a century," Maclain's favorite topic of conversation has been the irrational fear of German shepherd dogs, which he likens to that of the sighted for the blind.[66] Here Kendrick emphasizes that through his work Maclain intentionally serves as an example through which others can learn, and that clarifying the safety of carefully managed dogs like Schnuke and Dreist in and to the public remains central to this pursuit. This proves a motive for revising the initial breed argument to emphasize training, specifying, for example, that only "weeks of work by the dog's prospective owner [make a] . . . German shepherd overcome his natural gentleness and become a police dog, thereby giving his owner even more protection than a gun."[67] Beyond the novel series, though, these explanations of canine intelligence also portend their eclipsing of the human intelligence initially conceived as unleashed through these working relations.

Like Frank before him, the fictional blind detective is aware that dog guides prove an irresistible media spectacle, but in later novels he expresses profound (and profoundly self-reflexive) skepticism about how this attention both benefits and hurts people like him. In *Reservations for Death* (1957), Maclain sarcastically accounts for public disbelief of his own achievements as tempered by faith in farcical visions of canine genius ("grist from some lying reporter's machine"). Schnuke, he self-deprecatingly jests, "can read the name on the door of the lawyer's office I want. . . . I have nothing to do with it[, just as Dreist] shoots at sound with his left hind leg[,] . . . so he can save the life of that zombie with him, who's blind and hasn't any brain."[68] The increasing references to other detective fictions—including in this novel the television series *Dragnet*—make it hard not to interpret this comment as also a reference to unauthorized film adaptations, whose detectives Kendrick insisted "in no way resembled the Duncan Maclain of my book[s]," and whose canine–human relations become conspicuously diminished, even as their German shepherd dog characters steal the show.[69]

Film and television versions of Kendrick's novels preposterously collapse guide and police dogs into a single role played consistently by German shepherd dog actors, exacerbating rather than resolving confusion about what exactly the blind-detective's dogs are doing. Examining how these developments still more directly relate to cultural changes, I suggest that they set the stage for the blind-detective stories' retreat into human identity problems. For the guide dog's ability to serve as a catalyst for social transformation seems in many ways blocked by the assertion of white, male identity as augmented by the presence of German shepherd actors like Hank of *Blind Justice*. Whereas Frank and Kendrick worked to promote independence and fair treatment for the working blind by realistically representing Seeing Eye dog capabilities, their fictional counterparts in the blind-detective stories of film and television increasingly are cast with superdogs, representing disability as a personal problem.

Superdog: Hollywood's Maclain and Television's *Longstreet*

For their decision to write disability out of the film adaptation of his first Maclain novel, Kendrick unequivocally lambasted Hollywood studio executives: "Scared to put a blind man on the screen as a detective, Universal released *[The Last Express]* in 1938 starring Kent Taylore as a sighted detective in possibly one of the worst c-minus pictures ever made."[70] With this start, it is amazing that Maclain ever made it to the screen with his impairment. Kendrick understandably despaired of getting his message through to Hollywood.

One lucky break came via sighted actor Edward Arnold, a fan of the series whose "father had been blind for the last twenty-five years of his life."[71] Arnold lobbied hard to bring the blind-detective character to the screen, and eventually he played Maclain in two film adaptations of Kendrick's novels, and to wide acclaim. Much as these more accurate cinematic renditions might appeal to efforts to normalize disability, in visual media the superior crime-fighting skills of disabled man and dog translated all too readily into the superhuman and supercanine abilities that are the stock-in-trade of the star system.

To be fair, these film representations seem to reflect as much influence beatifying service-animal narratives. Published a year before Kendrick's *Last Express*, the very first example of these fictions, *Beowulf: A Guide Dog*, tells the implausible but not impossible story of a German shepherd initially "fully trained as a police dog," who, through a series of traumatic incidents, which includes witnessing the shooting death of his original handler, is retrained successfully by Guide Dogs for the Blind (a parallel organization to The Seeing Eye) to assist his final owner after he suddenly becomes blinded.[72] Writing under the pen name Ernest Lewis after he lost an arm in an auto accident, Ernest Blakeman Vesey crafted this and other animal-centered novels through fact-finding adventures chosen to be physically demanding, like dog training and arctic travel, in part to demonstrate that his work was not impaired by his disability. And in this case the details of the fictional Beowulf's training—for instance, the clarification that the Guide Dog trainer, who "usually selected bitches for training between the ages of 1 and 2 years," saw Beowulf's sex and age "not as a definite bar" because "temperament" is key—also clarify exactly how this dog's unusual story depends on modern training methods.[73]

However inadvertently, this highly unlikely story of a dog successfully functioning as guard, then guide, seems to cast the mold that the Maclain fictions are made to fit in their translation to visual media, straying from the didactic intentions of both authors. There are many possible reasons why the dogs of blind detectives rarely act in character on film and television. While the plot-driven interchangeability of Schnuke and Dreist in Kendrick's novels might provide a rationale for the blind detective's dogs' depiction as German shepherds in other stories, this breed choice also aligns them with Rin Tin Tin, the original (and then-contemporary) canine media star, whose popular films famously saved RKO Pictures from bankruptcy. This paragon of dogdom remains a cultural icon, and, following Beowulf's trajectory, a rare German shepherd character now used to promote public support for children's assistance animals.[74]

In the Maclain adaptations, such figures more precisely inform the displacement of realistic representations of cross-species interdependence. Reinforcing even as they reflect the misperceptions common among "members of the sighted public" of the animal guide as an all-purpose "superdog," the visual emphasis on the one guide dog in the novels' cover images and series icons still more directly sets in motion the reduction of canine roles in film and television versions.[75] These presentations revert to Kendrick's original plan—which the novelist scrupulously corrected after consultations with Seeing Eye staff members—to make Maclain's guide dog provide him with protection as well as mobility, fueling the novelist's ire.

Two of Kendrick's novels were made directly into the films *Eyes in the Night* (1942) and *The Hidden Eye* (1945), and among their most striking departures from the original concept is that the dogs of the more accurately portrayed Maclain (again played in both by Edward Arnold) become reduced to one incredible creature. Setting the trend for future blind-detective stories, these films feature a German shepherd named Friday, who (more like Rinty than Schnuke or Dreist) unbelievably serves as guide, attack, and tracking dog. Like the animal, Maclain is envisioned on screen as an extraordinarily gifted and far more isolated individual, only with more devastating consequences for representations of disability.[76] As if his superior detective and blind shooting skills are not enough, the filmic Maclain also demonstrates his physical prowess by expertly using judo to overpower both sighted colleagues in his everyday training sessions as well as criminals resisting arrest, an expertise in martial arts that along with the lone German shepherd superdog becomes a characteristic of blind-detective stories in visual media.

In later versions, the character of the blind detective reduced to a single German shepherd companion changes in ways more obviously reflective of cultural developments. None of Kendrick's subsequent novels made it directly to the screen, but the characters and concepts of these books provide the basis of the critically acclaimed 1971–72 television series *Longstreet*. In the series' pilot, the title character, an insurance investigator (played by sighted actor James Franciscus, a handsome blue-eyed man like the fictional Maclain), avenges both his wife's murder and his own blinding with the aid of his guide dog Pax, yet another German shepherd. Although the covers of reissued editions of the Maclain novels in the 1970s clarify *Longstreet*'s basis in these stories, within the show the explicit connection appears only in a brief credit line, making it seem likely that the direct link was lost on most viewers. Instead, what seems significant about the return here of a blinded white man and German shepherd dog are the ways in which they incorporate historic shifts in identity politics.

In the same way that the inception of the Maclain novel series quickly follows the founding of The Seeing Eye and, in turn, its film versions come hot on the heels of the unprecedented success of blinded veterans' lobbying efforts to reform VA policies, its televisual revival appears shortly after a major political victory for disability rights more generally, the 1968 passage of the Architectural Barriers Act, the first major piece of legislation to promote specifically the legal rights of disabled citizens, which paved the way for the ADA. *Long-street* therefore emerges in a cultural moment in which the canine-assisted blind detective more than ever before seems poised to lead the charge for disability rights. Instead, however, the series develops man and dog in ways that align them with reactionary forces then coalescing around a more explicitly militant image of German shepherd dogs.

In an era in which rights movements for women and traditional minorities were spurred by protests of the U.S. involvement in the Vietnam War, it seems significant that Longstreet develops his skillful use of physical force through a plot line featuring martial arts film star Bruce Lee, who appears in a cameo role as the blind detective's self-defense instructor. While moving away from the racial stereotypes that especially trouble the early Maclain stories, Longstreet's friendship with this Asian character is premised on the disabled white man's newfound vulnerability. Perhaps more important, it is motivated by the blind detective's increasingly self-conscious sense of defensiveness, rather than the political alliances against interlocking oppressions explicitly featured in *Lights Out*.

From the start, the television series gives him several motives to enter into the kinds of violent spectacles featured in the Maclain films. More like *Lights Out* and *Bright Victory* in narrative form than content, Longstreet's story starts with his becoming blind, only here through an explosion set up by criminals that involves the concurrent murder of his wife. Whereas bitterness (if not always vengeance) is quelled for Maclain by working with Schnuke and eventually finding a wife, the guide-dog magic cannot mend the shattered life of Longstreet, who uses the dog instead as a tool for pursuing revenge. Bracketing off potential social transformation, this lonely and reactionary blind detective's story stalls out on the spectacle of wounded white manhood, a story that seems to culminate in *Blind Justice*.

In this earlier show, the capacity for the guide dog to transform the blind man's sense of himself becomes further obscured by the continuing confusion of the dog's guiding with guard work. In spite of his peaceful name, Longstreet's Pax continues in the cinematic tradition of fantastic hybrid guide-attack dogs. A contemporary parody of the series in *MAD* magazine titled *Longshot* insists that viewers had become more skeptical (if not knowledgeable) about the limitations of canine abilities. Here the German shepherd partner again attacks on command, only with a bungling lunge for the throat of the blind detective rather than his adversary. With this clever twist, the "sight" gag for once backfires, and in ways that emphasize growing conflict in the cultural meanings of this particular breed within and beyond blind-detective fictions.

Longstreet (the television show adapted from the Maclain novels) follows the film tradition of combining guiding and protective work in one impossible "superdog," and so becomes ripe for parody in *Longshot*. Courtesy *Mad* magazine, no. 153 © 1972 E.C. Publications, Inc. All Rights Reserved. Used with Permission.

Using this particular kind of dog to illustrate its overall questioning of authority, the parody also resonates with what had by then become ambivalent American attitudes toward German shepherd dogs, who by the early 1970s, along with white men in uniform, waver between roles as iconic American war heroes and instruments of racist states.[77] Narratives reflecting on these histories, like Romain Gary's memoir *White Dog* and its suppressed film version (in which the eponymous canine stray once trained to serve and protect only whites by lethally attacking only black people is identified by breed type as a rare white German shepherd), underscore how this connection increasingly requires no elaboration. In this context, the filmic blind-detective stories' couplings of violently impaired white men with the iconic value of this kind of dog might represent anxiety about (if not nostalgia for) social power as vested in a certain form of human identity.

As I suggested earlier, this growing symbolic complexity may begin to explain why, though more realistically portrayed as just a guide dog, *Blind Justice*'s Hank is at once portrayed by a German shepherd and relegated to the landscape of Dunbar's life. Images of Hank in harness complement shots of the detective practicing martial arts in the show's credits, suggesting empowering alignments of bodies across species lines. Yet the narrative underdevelopment of their apparently positive relationship in lieu of Dunbar's troubled human ties seals the visual reduction to personal at the expense of social justice. Rather than celebrate or despair of its demise, I want to turn to one last example that suggests how the blind detectives' ultimately debilitating legacy of stereotypes in other ways might be perceived as motivating a concurrent return to the problem of representing multiple forms of social agency through changing stories of service animals and people with disabilities.

Hearing-Ear Solutions: Sue Thomas and Levi

Maclain, Longstreet, and Dunbar are not only the sole blind characters but also apparently the only disabled ones in their respective narratives. Increasingly drawn into physical confrontations with adversaries and even colleagues as the tradition grows, their attempts to overcome the pitfalls of disability identity prove anything but smooth or complete. In spite of these limitations, the relationships at the heart of these fictions clarify how service animals trouble the triumph of human identity, particularly when they are enlisted to pinpoint the identities of criminals. Their constant pairing with guide dogs, though not always realistic or central, suggests further that the problem may not be with the representations of oppositional human identities in flux so much as with the philosophical and political models that they are enlisted to serve.

A pivotal moment in *The Odor of Violets* (1940), a novel in which Maclain breaks up an international spy ring, and the basis of the film *Eyes in the Night*, emphasizes how the detective's work hinges on cross-species working relations. In the following passage, the irreducibly human–animal subject of the guide-dog relationship conceptually transforms the conditions of disability into more explicitly (if mythically) enhanced ability: "He had no eyes, but he could shoot with the devastating accuracy of lightning at the most infinitesimal sound. He was blind, but it was the implacable blindness of Justice. Duncan Maclain and his dog, pitted against a world full of fools; no more a man, but a killer out to destroy the God of War's machine."[78] The dog here is Schnuke, the pioneering fictional Seeing Eye, and the superdog qualities imputed here (like Maclain's superpowered hearing elsewhere), if interpreted literally, signal a singularly absurd moment in a series that labors hard to discredit this kind of howler.[79]

In the spirit in which it is offered, however, I read it as a prophetic vision. Particularly in light of the complex and comprehensive critique of social oppression that Kendrick develops throughout his novels about blind men, this passage conveys a dawning sense of the dog as transforming the blind man into an agent of global justice. And both together are poised to flesh out a new world of possibilities for these relations beyond problematic aesthetic, philosophical, and political histories of representing disability.

Disability studies scholars have been provoked in recent years by treatments of blindness as a trope for insight, insisting instead on the historical and cultural specificity of such meanings. From this perspective, it becomes important to question, for example, how Derrida's conclusion to *Memoirs of the Blind*—namely, that the conventional Western linkage of human knowledge and the power of vision can be ruptured by reconceptualizing the eye not as an appropriative tool but as an expressive/reflective mechanism of imploration—perpetuates, even as it purports to critique, certain limiting notions of embodiment. But the involvement of guide dogs stakes out further grounds for critique.

Derrida and his disability studies detractors alike assume that the human subject remains the primary reference point, a position displaced by the range of social agency forms emerging through service-animal narratives. While the philosophical questions raised by this line of inquiry are huge, most relevant to this discussion are the ways in which deconstructive readings of this trope connect this blindness/insight pattern, as Paul de Man argues, to "a constitutive characteristic of literary language in general,"[80] and I would add of service-animal narratives in particular. This approach to literary representation offers a means of registering the phenomenological aspect of blindness, its productive relations with insight, and, more to the point, their disfiguration, or imbrication, in productive fictions of norms, orders, and even continuities.

Reframing discourses of disability, as I suggested earlier, as interlocked with species discourses in the service of oppression suggests only one way in which they might be put to different purposes. Literary narratives might then be seen as negotiating all sorts of differences of and between terms for species and disability. For instance, Davis argues that, from the eighteenth century onward, medical science has created the norms against which disability is measured, through his close reading of the failed "treatment" of the club-footed stable boy Hippolyte in Gustave Flaubert's novel *Madame Bovary.* He concludes that medical narratives not only reinforce the prevailing cultural assumption that "to have a disability is to be an animal," but also that this example shows how a novel's form and (dys)function are "intricately connected."[81] An other-wise minor moment in Flaubert's novel thus reveals how by the nineteenth century species discourses do not just symbolize or reflect but more actively adjudicate these norms of the able-bodied human subject.

While critiques of this equation of the human form with social power require further elaboration, the more immediate task is to recognize other (here cross-species) forms of social agency that factor into (and are factored out of) this equation. The stable boy thus appears inextricable from the animals whose proximities, materially and conceptually, structure his life. Before his failed treatment, he serves as a social figure not simply aligned (metaphorically, physically, productively) with horses, but as an embodiment of social agency intimately shared among animal lives. Along with Hippolyte dies a sense of life as successfully eked out around the demands of animal companionship, destroyed by the medical attempt to re-form this boy as human subject.[82] In extending this model to guide-dog narratives, it would seem that so much depends upon whether the animal serves as a medical prosthetic, an enabling device, or a transformative agent of biopolitics.

Describing a sense not of subjectivity but rather of social agency that emerges through cross-species relations as a sum that is greater than its human parts, the kinds of narratives of canine-assisted life sketched above at times likewise exceed the conventional notions of human being that even theories of disability as a social condition leave in place. The difficulty of conveying this sense may indicate an inability to reconcile different species-specific senses of self in visual narrative, a point to which I will return in ensuing chapters.[83] And it may also contribute to broader problems with what human beings (or human ways of being-in-the-world) require of other species. The passing fantasy of dog owners who would like to think of themselves as above the law, in all senses, reflects how ideals of human transcendence work to obscure the problems of coordinating bodies with shared and trusting intelligence, including the culturally specific formations of intersubjectivities and their diminishment that paradoxically inspire them.

The difficulty of representing the affective work embodied in intersubjective relations suggests another way of approaching the failures of *Blind Justice*. The show was abruptly cancelled in mid-season, with no public explanation from the network and before the few episodes that focused on Hank were aired. More curiously, in the few that did, the possibility for the blind detective and dog to work together in a complex relationship seemed clear to viewers, who complained that the dog remained underdeveloped as a character.[84] While this kind of response speaks volumes about popular desire for guide-dog fictions, it also gestures toward the emergence of service-animal relationships as changing (and challenging) disabled narrative subjects in the twenty-first century.

In many ways, the far more popular Canadian American prime-time television show *Sue Thomas: F. B. Eye* traces other trajectories for service-animal narratives. Airing for four seasons from 2002 to 2007, this show remains the most successful series produced for the PAX channel (later renamed the Independent, now ION, network). Brought back briefly on the cable network

Animal Planet, *Sue Thomas* clearly also presents a different kind of disabled detective–guide-dog relationship.

This series is based on the biography of a profoundly deaf FBI agent and her hearing-ear dog Levi. And it stars Deanne Bray, a severely deaf actor who, like the actual Sue Thomas, was encouraged by her parents to learn to speak and to read lips. Just as it was for the historical Sue Thomas, lipreading is the fictional character's superior crime-fighting skill. Useful for eavesdropping on conversations at a distance and translating surveillance videos with no sound, her ostensible disability plausibly becomes indispensable to the agency, which moves her from a low-level fingerprint-analysis job to a position with an elite surveillance team.

Familiar problems of guide-dog fictions surface in this series as well. *Sue Thomas* presents the disabled person as an instrument of a repressive system, here more clearly a detective with a service dog enlisted in government service. The show promotes a questionable, if familiar, ideal of the working disabled through an attractive white person with a breed dog fighting for justice, on the side of a system that historically only grudgingly changes in response to disability (never mind women's or animal) rights activism. Unlike such contemporaneous examples as *Blind Justice*, it deliberately addresses some of these limits. In the first episode, Sue's description of Levi to someone who does not understand why she has a canine companion references the ubiquitous association of service animals with blind people: "He's a hearing dog, kind of like a Seeing Eye dog. I'm deaf." And in many other ways, this series introduces some important differences within the fictional history of guide dogs.

The show focuses on a deaf woman, not a blind man, played by an actor who shares that disability with her character, unlike all the blind detectives of film and television. And she is assisted by a golden retriever hearing-ear dog, not a German shepherd Seeing Eye. Woman and dog are almost never depicted in physical confrontations. No characters appear chronically angry. Rather, their drama centers on whether and how they can all work together to improve social conditions, imagined here more often than not through workplace interventions. Resolutions to potential problems involve more comprehensive collaborations enabled by the receptivity to assimilating to deaf culture displayed by Thomas's co-workers (significantly a cast of multiethnic actors), who are shown learning and later gently guiding others to face deaf people when speaking, increasingly studying and integrating American Sign Language into their group discussions, even ones in which all participants are hearing, and trying to work around the problems of having a service animal in the office.

This canine character, much more so than his counterparts in the blind-detective fictions, has much to work with in this respect. Far from superdog fantasies, the character of Levi (played by golden retriever Jesse) is allowed at times to fall short of being a model canine citizen, at times becoming whiny and incontinent, even lost when he runs away (though almost always for very good excuses).[85] And, as the show progresses, the hearing-ear dog actor is visibly and realistically aging, reinscribing Maclain's multiple dogs in the genre by subtly bringing attention to the more sobering realities of these relations, including the inevitable need to retire dogs from service. In these and other ways, the show returns to the early work of the Seeing Eye and Kendrick's novels in inspiring people to reimagine human and animal interests as integral components in a vision of social justice that defies the model of rights-based politics.

One amazing episode of *Sue Thomas* clarifies further how narrative can play with the identity limits accruing along with the disability rights histories built into these texts in order to change perceptions of service-animal relationships. Jesse's ability to grin (a baring-teeth canine expression that does not signal aggression, uncannily like a human smile) becomes the premise of Sue's teaching Levi to growl while grinning on a sign command, a gesture in which she uses her hands to mimic biting jaws next to her own mouth. This gesture-vocalization combination is introduced as a gag, and for those who know dogs it looks downright silly. But if you run up quickly to a dog doing this, you could fall victim to the gag, as the criminal suspect does in the episode's climactic chase sequence. In this context, it is tempting to read the "trick dog" as a commentary on the blind-detective genre, but even more might be seen in this narrative development.

Predictably, this sequence reinforces the notion that the impaired-without-dog agent is superior FBI material, but it also introduces some important points about how a human enters into a rights relationship with this kind of animal. One is that service training is an ongoing project, involving individualized or situation-specific interactions that work to develop existing abilities through cooperation (some might say communication) for mutual human–animal benefit, or, in plain speech, to keep training in order to figure out how best to live together. Perhaps unlike any other narrative in this genre, this episode thus illustrates the kind of training procedures that Seeing Eye historian Dickson Hartwell characterizes as necessarily "complicated and apt to vary in some particular with each dog."[86]

And another point to be made here concerns the limitations of this kind of work that run contrary to high (and often unrealistic) expectations for these relations between dogs and disabled people. Levi can act protective—at least, fake it—but he will never be *that* kind of police dog. And Sue can use him to play with these fantasies in a narrative process that also acknowledges how people like her must work within and around these limiting factors in the pursuit of justice for all. While this sort of exchange could be read as providing a basis for the desirability of impaired-without-canine-assistance experiences, such aspects of this hearing-ear fiction also insist on some harsh realities that defer fantasized alternatives or even simple additions to the ethical conflicts (let alone everyday inconveniences) of pursuing political rights.

Considering especially the self-descriptions of blind people working with guide dogs, I am tempted to say that these representations of highly specialized cross-species relations at their best show how intersubjective forms transcend the terms of human identity, asserting an irreducibly social unit instead of an individual human as a more fundamental basis of action. But this would only dodge the more troubling aspects of the history outlined above of their literary and cultural representation of a very specific human identity, of their circling inward toward congenitally able-bodied, if adventitiously blinded, white male detectives working with German shepherd dogs in situations in which rights are often violently suppressed. Instead, I can only say (with a nod to the Maclain novels and *Sue Thomas* especially) that such stories demonstrate how all forms of humanity could use the help of animals in the ongoing struggle for democratic power sharing among differently embodied agents. Chapter 2 discusses in greater detail these hazards for people and animals mutually identified through working partnerships, in this case girls and horses involved in jumping sports, providing a parallel case study in which intersubjective relations provide professional opportunities still more deeply in conflict with struggles for social change.

Chapter 2   Velvet Revolutions: Girl–Horse Stories

Slike abc's release of *Blind Justice,* media conglomerate NBC's decision to air segments of the 2008 Olympic equestrian games in prime time was a first for television, also one that found most enthusiastic support within a small community defined by rare historic achievements. Since the twentieth-century reinvention of the Olympics, modern dressage, show jumping, and cross-country jumping—combined in the sport of eventing—have emerged as the only international athletic competitions in which women and men are allowed to compete on equal terms. Understandably appalled by dwindling coverage of these sports in recent years, fans cheered NBC's apparent reversal of this trend.

But because the network scheduled these prime slots exclusively on its Oxygen Network, branded as a cable channel for women, this decision proved no simple victory for gender parity. Cast alongside chick flicks and other programming typecast as "women's interest," this global achievement of gender equality in sport becomes harder to see, and along with it the significance of its mediation through animal bodies. Instead, it just seemed to many a no-brainer. Girls and horses have a natural affinity, right? Strange as it sounds, before the twentieth century, images and stories pairing girls and horses were as rare as hens' teeth.[1] And more bizarre still are the ways in which this abrupt shift involves a narrative pattern through which such achievements are both modeled and pushed to their limits.

Often in advance of their real-life counterparts, fictional female riders involved in jumping sports become precarious subjects of utopian imagining across the past century. More specifically, as fictions project the pathways of women's innovative and progressive entry into the highest levels of equine competition, they narrate a struggle to maintain cross-species partnerships within a whole range of nonhuman agency forms that are central to (if also imperiled by) these achievements. With far less plot justification than the

65

blind detectives, fictional horsewomen are cast increasingly on the defensive, victimized by a peculiar linkage of girlish love for horses with sexualized violence. Moreover, this strange situation both prompts and problematizes developments in visual narrative forms.

Women and more often girls together with horses are imagined in these narratives as confronting huge obstacles, and not just in show-jumping arenas and cross-country courses. Departing from the formula that has come to characterize horse stories more generally, in which a naïf finds true love with a rogue, the jumping-sport subset at the focus of this chapter emphasizes creative interplay with social and visual forms that cut across such hierarchical dualisms of relating and especially embodiment.[2] Such stories are primed to do so in part because the cultural and technological changes enabling the developments of modern competitive jumping—including innovations in saddles, riding styles, even underwear—pinpoint human and equine players together in world-forming movements, defying the terms of debate about the psychic significance of these cross-species working relations even as they become media spectacles.

From Sigmund Freud's case study of "Little Hans" onward, psychoanalytic interpretations of fascination with horses as a childish diversion reduce animals to perverse substitutes for adult human sexual agents, nowhere more clearly than in attempts to account for the "horse-crazy girl."[3] Eclipsing older, militaristic associations, women's rise to power in equine sports implicitly becomes the target of sociobiological accounts attempting to recover the horse as phallic symbol through a sort of surgical strike against girls.[4] Typical in this vein, biologist Midas Dekkers's "bestial" theory identifies girls as the source of trouble. Dekkers posits horses as "consolation for the great injustice done to girls by nature, of awakening sexually years before the boys in their class, who are still playing with their trainsets when girls are already sighing 'Trigger' when they actually mean 'Simon' or 'Jeremy.'"[5] Such accounts raise huge concerns about the abuses of evolutionary rhetorics (after all, the historic novelty of such associations leaves no evolutionary time for the compensation of frustrated reproductive mechanisms). But this argument finds strongest opposition for its mischaracterizations of female desire and embodiment among women writing autobiographically about the horses in their lives.

Arguing that the sociobiologists' claims say more about the frustrations of heteronormative culture than the "consolations" of nature, these writers contend that presumptions about girl–horse and woman-horse attachments inform forceful (even deadly) intrusions of men. With laughter and anger, they float oppositional views, for instance, that working with horses sharpens defenses against sexual, violent, and other less clearly definable assaults.[6] Much harder to articulate, however, are the ways in which human–equine relations foster other stories of desire that inspire more than self-defensiveness about these at once threatening and alluring positions.

Other narratives are premised on a more fluid sense of intersubjectivity that defines "the elusive oneness with the horse" as "an intimacy which is both enacted through, and brings about change in, the body."[7] Such a story takes shape through the multiple elements of artist Kate James's piece *The World Is a Dangerous Place* (2004). James's art incorporates photography, textiles, and performance, here to make manifest the tenuous bonds formed between woman and horse. The more viewers know about horses, the more thrilling this piece becomes, because it centers on a potentially dangerous stunt, one that no person should attempt with just any old horse. Physically tied together by knitted and worn headgear, the actors involved are James and her "first love," an appaloosa mare named "Suckatash," calmly contemplating each other in a delicate moment that is premised both on their long-term relationship

Kate James, *The World Is a Dangerous Place,* 2004. Physically tied together by knitted and worn headgear, the actors, James and her "first love," an appaloosa mare named "Suckatash," calmly contemplate each other in a delicate moment. Copyright Kate James. Courtesy of the artist.

and, less clearly, the distinctly gendered story that makes jumping sports into women's television programming in the twentieth century.

To elaborate on this historical context further, this chapter focuses on the broader development of visual narratives of girls and women not simply making lives for themselves with horses but, more important, engaging directly with representational forms in order to transform equine along with other social spheres. Partly, this approach begins to account for why *National Velvet* so often is cited as exemplary. Vicki Hearne, for instance, lauds this narrative as enriching people's desires and imaginative engagements, and laments how it is being eclipsed through another pattern of storytelling that casts animals as absolute limits, as "insufficient and antisocial" barriers to maturity.[8] While my research makes me empathize all the more deeply with Hearne's point, her elaboration of this particular fiction falls into the problematically self-defensive pattern, capitulating to psychoanalytic rhetorics that end up positioning girls' bodies as battlefields:

> Our stories and legends about horsemen, whether they are historical stories of figures of genius or children's tales of effort, courage and sacrifice for the sake of horses, are allegories about what it is to know what interests you, which is one of the reasons the passion for a life with horses is so powerful in this culture. It may also be one of the reasons (but only one—this is another subject) girls are so likely to become absorbed by the living allegory of horsemanship at just the age when their developing sexuality inspires the rhetorical forces around them to work harder than ever at distracting them from what they're interested in.[9]

How these relations take shape is indeed "another subject" altogether, one that raises huge questions about discursive histories and embodiment: In what ways are "rhetorical forces" used to target certain cross-species relations? Under what conditions do horsewomen elude or overcome these forces, for instance, in sporting arenas like those of the Olympics? And at what costs do representations of the mutual interests, the intersubjective relations—or as the best of these riders term them, "partnerships"[10]—enabling these achievements, become "children's tales" and, specifically, girls' fictions?

The increasingly aggressive ways in which girls are being sold out in these contexts, so often at the expense of other stories about their own bodies, along with those of animals, make this last question particularly pressing. Plugging "plastic pony doll" into a search engine while looking for a contemporary point of contrast to James's piece, I immediately turned up the "Struts Fantasy Fashion Model Horse Runway Magic Sydney" doll, a toy marketed in

2008. Intriguingly, the image appears most frequently in feminist blogs and Web sites that (again registering humor as well as outrage) characterize this product line as peddling "whorses." The stories built into such objects may defy the evolutionary biologist's wildest dreams. But as an indicator of a trend in horse-toy marketing away from the realistic, niche-market Breyer dolls (fast becoming expensive collectibles for adults) and toward Hasbro's more widely available My Little Ponys (a product line morphing into cheap, sexualized, even literally toxic toys),[11] the whorses prove problematic as well for further displacing the potentials lofted by James and Hearne.

Following the latter thread, this chapter elaborates the narrative history surrounding *National Velvet* in order to address much broader social concerns about the precarious establishment of the professional feasibility of particular kinds of human–horse partnerships. Like the association of guide dogs and blind men, novels and films that focus on the growing connections between horses and female jump jockeys (or riders in equine competitions that require jumping over obstacles) gain tremendous sentimental interest in the twentieth century, and this in turn contributes to the conditions that limit their viability. Depicting lives often enriched by the company of nonhumans, these textual representations also consistently depict girls using visual technologies, at first

Advertising photo for "Struts Fantasy Fashion Model Horse Runway Magic Sydney" doll, a toy marketed in 2008 in a product line ridiculed as "whorse" dolls in feminist blogs and magazines. Playmates Toys, Ltd.

on the road to fame and fortune and later to recovery. Set amid more broadly changing conditions, stories of girls in competitive jumping sports appear all the more clearly to offer tantalizing as well as terrifying glimpses into the processes whereby animal narratives negotiate forms of species and social agency throughout the past century.

Sporting Fields and Lasses

Stories of female jump jockeys can be challenging to read against the terms of identity politics in part because they are premised on human–animal relationships. Seen as just another example of a traditional companion animal gaining a new life in a modern working role, horses may pinpoint a peculiar sense of social cohesion for white female riders, a group that thereby seems narrowly defined against all men and traditional minorities. So, for instance, the 2000 inclusion of Kathy Kusner, the first woman inducted into the Horse Racing Hall of Fame (who, like all but two other inductees, is white), might strike some as further evidence of an erasure of the history of black male jockeys, who in the nineteenth century dominated the sport.[12] But closer attention to the specificities of these developments reveals how identity politics flag only one of many ways in which competitive arenas position horses to serve as transitional animals in industrial cultures.

For centuries the powerhouses of transport, industry, and war, by the twentieth century horses persist largely as pets or sporting vehicles, figures of leisure and wealth, and with consequences for people as well as animals. Like Seeing Eye dogs, horses may gain visibility as specialized tools. Yet, in the process, modern living is made to accommodate their increasingly specialized needs, perhaps nowhere more visibly than in the contemporary equipage of horse keeping, such as the various forms of headgear juxtaposed in Tim Flach's photo montage *Masks—Fly Net—Eye Surgery Mask—Lycra* (2008). Such changes prompt rethinking of the basic structures of relating underpinning them. Illustrating the utility of Jakob von Uexküll's ethological approach to biology (which builds categories based on affinities, not filiation) to elaborate Spinoza's ethics in practice, Deleuze and Guattari famously note, "A racehorse is more different from a workhorse than a workhorse is from an ox."[13] Moreover, the historical shifts of the twentieth century that favor racehorses, not workhorses, entail profound transformations in the daily lives of our own species consequently losing what was once a primary source of direct contact with large animals.

By the twenty-first century, these contacts have become not only rarified but also highly mediated. Starting with radio and newsreels and continuing

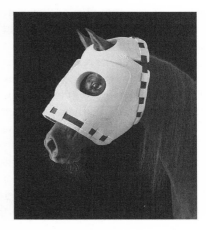

Tim Flach, *Masks—Fly Net—Eye Surgery Mask—Lycra,* 2008. Against theories of animals "disappearing" in modernity, the contemporary equipage of horse keeping indicates how modern living is made to accommodate their increasingly specialized needs. Copyright Tim Flach. Courtesy of the artist.

through satellite-enabled live television coverage and off-track betting operations, horse racing in part marks the growing economic dependence of sports on visual media, with ambivalent social consequences. From the 1920s onward, the widespread dissemination of these technologies enables horse races to become rare instruments for puncturing sharply class-defined barriers—encouraging "interest and participation from prince and pauper alike"—even as the architecture of racecourses worked to reinforce these same barriers.[14] Caught up in these processes, exceptional animal as well as human athletes become celebrities.

From Seabiscuit to Zenyatta (who in 2009 became the first mare to win the prestigious Breeder's Cup Classic race), fans of the large and lucrative sport of flat racing continue to follow contenders through news stories of come-from-behind victories and spectacular tragedies alike. With the future of racing becoming increasingly uncertain, such tales are charged with fears that the survival of the sport is at stake. So tempers flared among enthusiasts when a hard-used mare, Rachel Alexandra, was named 2009's Horse of the Year. To her opponent's fans, Zenyatta, her owners, and her trainer—widely reported as having deliberately chosen to enter his horse in far fewer races in order to keep her safe and sound—were robbed. Such emotions indicate how the racehorse as media star gains a strange relevance in urban environments, in which everyday contact with large live animals is highly sentimentalized even as it no longer seems feasible for most people.

And the most popular stories often amplify the stratification of the industry. Public interest swells for horse-industry outsiders, whether small-time operators or their unlikely prospects, because they beat the odds of what remains largely the sport of kings (these days, Saudi princes) and others who can afford to stake their claims on expensive bloodstock. That horse racing also became a conspicuous outpost of male chauvinism by the end of the twentieth century—its most prominent organizations licensed female jockeys and trainers only under successive threats of lawsuits—sheds light on the mystery of why in this period the association of girls and horses becomes so volatile, if not why it has become so prevalent.

A specialized subset of these narratives offers some more precise clues. Although steeplechase has a far more limited appeal outside the United Kingdom, fictions that connect these developments to this form of racing and the subsequently emerging jumping sports trace more precisely how these peculiar and in many ways unlikely cross-species relations move far beyond sporting fields. Often credited to networks of owners, trainers, buyers, breeders, and their breeding stock, achievement in these conditions requires more than any one body's efforts alone. Foregrounded in stories of girls and horses as athletic competitors, such relations become primary sites for thinking through the ways in which a successful training relationship offers an irreducibly social gain, but one that, if it inspires selfish interests, then does so only by risking collective tragedy. Because each entry always risks disability and death for horses along with riders, steeplechase racing and eventing make success appear all the more awesome for underdogs even today, and so provide the setting for fictions of these intersubjective transformations and their frustrations, perhaps nowhere more apparent than in *National Velvet*.

Earlier narratives clarify the cultural conditions in which women riders come to represent at once sexual and professional threats. But *National Velvet* marks a turn in ensuing fictions toward depicting the visual narratives through which girls and horses change the terms of competition, here in the most difficult horse race of all, England's Grand National steeplechase. Particularly in the novel and film sequel *International Velvet*, released two years after women riders finally were allowed to compete in the Grand National, it becomes clear that the kind of visual narrative play at the heart of these texts cuts both ways. In these stories, girl–horse competitors are increasingly imagined as disfigured and killed, intimidated and erased from the very playing fields on which simultaneously their historic counterparts are gaining ground.

Reading them together in this chapter, I want to argue further that these texts, which narrate the breakdown of the subject even as they explore a broader range of possibilities for intersubjective forms, offer glimpses of a longer "Velvet revolution," one that concerns what Raymond Williams terms "the long and difficult revolution of the mind," or the provocation to think dialectically about cultural formations.[15] Although the violence and brutality accruing in stories and images of cross-species relations temper their utopian envisioning, such representations also clarify an important difference between women riders, who make history even as they endure backlashes that jeopardize their futures, and paired girl–horse teams, who become "exemplars of the coming community."[16] No actual woman rider has yet won the Grand National like the fictional Velvet, but in the decades following this novel's release the accumulating stories of female jump jockeys' other successes with horses against tremendous odds likewise concern a more resonant "experience of astonishment" regarding the potentials for narrative processes as well as mixed-species communities.[17]

Led by "horse-whispering" fantasies, recent trends in training discourses that advocate "gentling" in favor of "breaking" might give the impression that equine sports have become kinder, gentler arenas of cross-species engagement with the rise of what proponents call natural horsemanship or, more accurately, "horsewomanship" methods in the twentieth century.[18] Yet the final-frontier status of steeplechase for women riders, who have been grudgingly included only after the successful gendered integration of eventing and, before that, show jumping—"both of which sports had evolved in more emancipated times," according to female jump-jockey historian Anne Alcock—speaks to the endemic sexism of horse racing, at least in the English-speaking world.[19] Although important in its own right, the story of women's achievements on these sporting fields is only a piece of the larger puzzle of girl–horse associations with sex and gender politics.

Instead of deciding finally whether these narratives work more to strengthen or to disrupt patriarchal order, I think it is more important to consider their implication of jumping sports and visual technologies as key points of intervention into the work of individuals, cross-species partnerships, and, rarer still, multispecies communities. In part, these aspects explain why, long after its economic utility expires, the horse persists largely as a family pet and girls as the stereotypic stewards of horsey things. More suggestively, however, these stories also configure the often startlingly violent conditions within which cross-species relations become a breeding ground for idealized forms of intersubjective social agency.

Slaughterhouse Beginnings

The first best seller to focus on the potential for female athleticism in cross-species relations, Enid Bagnold's novel *National Velvet, or The Slaughterer's Daughter,* published in 1935, imagines an unlikely pair together triumphing in the Grand National steeplechase. Although marketed today as "the classic story of a girl and her horse" (as the cover of the 1999 Avon paperback edition declares), its author insisted, "This is a book for grown-ups not children."[20] And it has become a touchstone for the more recent victories of adult equestriennes like "the American National Velvet" Joy Slater Carrier, the first female jump jockey to compete in steeplechase's two toughest races, the Grand National and (as two-time winner) the Maryland Hunt Cup.[21] Such characterizations overlook the novel's argument against just this kind of emphasis on the human athlete alone and its far more influential role in working with horses to create more than just media spectacles.

Even in literary discussions, the novel remains overshadowed by the film version of *National Velvet,* largely because of its formative role in the careers of young celebrities. Velvet was Hollywood studio queen Elizabeth Taylor's first of many top-billed performances, securing the young star's rapid transformation to film icon. In an image found in the studio after his death, Andy Warhol repeats a still close-up of Taylor on the horse in the film in his *National Velvet* (1963). Likely produced in the same year as *Race Riot*, this image represents another exploration of story and media forms—according to the authors of Warhol's catalogue raisonné, "selectively masking and overlapping impressions of the screen" to emphasize "repeating patterns of verticals"—that both simulates the flickering quality of film and anchors the visual narrative that the artist created (though never publicly exhibited in its entirety) of Taylor's life.[22]

In Warhol's story as in much commentary on the film, the beautiful child takes center stage, and her association with the horse is ancillary. This effect of the film leads literary critics to rail, "Velvet is not a young Elizabeth Taylor."[23] As I develop below, Taylor's identification with this role significantly contributes to the stereotyping of horsey girls as sex objects, and even imperial subjects. Yet Warhol's treatment prompts further consideration of the differences between narratives that emerge through biographical pictures, like his source photos of Taylor as they first appeared in *Life* magazine, and the speculative "genealogical portrait" of which *National Velvet* becomes the first part.[24]

Bagnold's title character remains a reluctant media darling, and one who finds that gaining personal recognition as a star is a limit, not a goal, in her vision of fame. Success in this story involves not just training for physical ability but, more precisely, cultivating an intersubjective mind-set, a framework through which the girl–horse connection precedes and exceeds any individual's achievement. Intriguingly, she and her horse alike are seen first as ugly individuals; only through their working partnership do they become attractive. Depicting such intimacies as clearly imperiled by the terms of media stardom, the novel also adumbrates the fitful relationship with film media forms that has come to characterize modern animal narrative traditions far beyond the sporting histories of women riders.

Especially in the novel's first edition, the only version illustrated with Bagnold's then-teenage daughter's line drawings, a range of potentials for imaging technologies supports a complex vision of social transformation via girl–horse relations. The story opens with a scene in which the eponymous girl, Velvet Brown, plays with her paper cutouts of photos and prints of famous race horses. More than just toys with which she pretends to ride, these repurposed media images prove tools with which she "dreams" into being "stories" of how a girl can "be a famous rider."[25]

And these pictures have stories of their own as well, even in the novel. Bewildered later on by her own transformation to the famous steeplechase jockey "National Velvet" in newspapers, film, and even advertising, she preserves

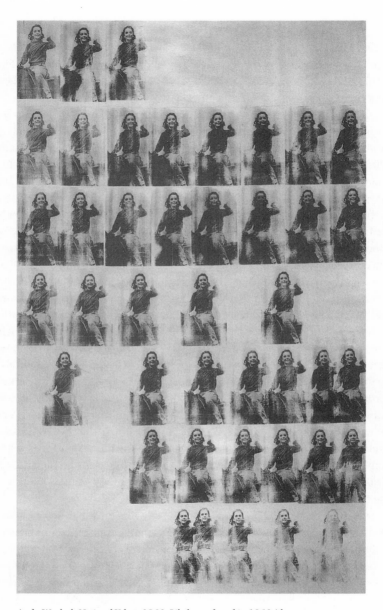

Andy Warhol, *National Velvet*, 1963. Likely produced in 1963 (the same year as *Race Riot*), this image—composed of repeated silkscreen prints of the same still of child actor Elizabeth Taylor on horseback, taken during the making of the 1944 film *National Velvet*—echoes the flickering quality of film and anchors the artist's visual narrative of Taylor's life. Copyright 2009 The Andy Warhol Foundation for the Visual Arts/ARS, New York.

her dreams of glory for her one amazing horse by refusing outright all plans to sell her winning animal to filmmakers. This is a strange moment, particularly when it recurs in the novel's 1944 film adaptation, and one that indicates what gets lost amid psychoanalytic reductions of horse love to girlish perversity, never mind its purported cure in writing animals out of scenes of desire.

One measure of the transitional nature of *National Velvet* is the absence of the subtitle, *The Slaughterer's Daughter,* from both the film and all subsequent editions of the novel. In no small measure, this shortened version reflects the increasing influence of urban-industrial perspectives on Velvet's family and their village slaughtering–butchering business (both housed under the same roof) as at best quaint, and at worst "gruesome."[26] The novel's contemporary reviewers, however, praised these very details in terms of realism, a striking interpretive difference that suggests how sensibilities have changed now that slaughter yards and their animals are no longer seen as local fixtures in industrialized societies (a point elaborated further in chapter 4). Far from contrasting these traditional relations with more equitable ideals of animal companionship, the novel presents the daily interactions central to this family business as a foundation for their successful realization.

National Velvet takes place in rural England between the world wars, a time and place in which automobiles were fast becoming the primary modes of transport, and horses in turn were morphing into the visible trappings of leisure. The novel depicts these animals emerging as playthings for tourists to rent, children to show, and wealthy foreigners to collect. As horses become repurposed, knowledges gained from living with them in turn are rarified, for some, even lost. This sensibility emerges through the novel's early descriptions of small-town life, which include the lack of horse sense in "tripper-riders" or day-trippers on holiday from London.[27] These inexperienced riders fall from their rental horses with such regularity that locals who know the likeliest spots to spook horses can wait there to collect tips for reuniting riders with their mounts.

Typical of this changing world, the family slaughterhouse/butcher shop uses a motorized van but still keeps an old pony to send the kids out on local deliveries.[28] Because the Brown children use the pony for leisure riding as well, she serves as another kind of transitional figure in a household teeming with bodies and conflicts. Along with people and pony, the Browns' various dogs, canaries, rats, and (as Velvet comes into possession of them) horses all depend on the family business of killing animals. A "togetherness" shared across species, families, and communities is thus intricately interconnected with Velvet's eventual National victory with the horse descriptively named "The Piebald."[29]

Another elision in the textual history of *National Velvet* speaks more directly to this dynamic. Like the subtitle, the novel's original illustrations, which spell out the kinds of everyday engagements so crucial for the success of the girl–horse team, were left out of all subsequent editions, in spite of favorable mentions by its initial reviewers. Drawn by Bagnold's only daughter, Laurian Jones, and "always considered an intrinsic part of the work" by the author, these images do not depict scenes from the narrative so much as document the sort of creative interplay with animal images that becomes so crucial to narratives of girl riders' success, and later their resilience.[30]

The presence of piebald horse figures among these drawings suggests a way of reading the images literally as records of this kind of girl–horse play traveling across fiction and life, even generations. Added to a herd of horses and ponies collected for her children's amusement, the author's own horse, a piebald gelding named "the Pie," apparently inspired his fictional namesake. This creature was known for his strikingly bad looks and knack for jumping, and (according to Anne Sebba, Bagnold's biographer) inspired the plot that moves the author beyond an otherwise "dry discussion of the female–equine relationship" or, as the author later put it, the spectacular girl–horse "collaboration."[31] Yet these line drawings include several horses (varied in size, markings, and body type), often depicted together with other horses as well as dogs and humans. As sketchy impressions celebrating more than recording pony-mad girlhood, they add to a sense of Velvet's paper-horse play in the novel as bodying forth lives shared across species.

Again the novel opens with a significant scene, in this respect, in which Velvet "canters" home on one of her paper racehorses, which she has meticulously cut from magazines, newspapers, and (Velvet's secret shame) library books. At every level it seems that the purpose of this initial description is to situate the girl as an integral part of a multispecies world: the "Hullocks" surrounding their village are "like the backs of elephants . . . , like a starlit herd of divine pigs"; her sisters are like "golden greyhounds"; her father audibly washes down the adjoining slaughterhouse floor, with its bloody signs of another day's work; the nameless black dog tied in the yard barks incessantly; the house dog Jacob "wriggle[s] and grin[s]," while the yard spaniels "press against . . . knees" for attention; and even the dinner that awaits her return exudes a "smell of liver and bacon" into the open air.[32] Approached on all sides by touches, smells, tastes, sights, and sounds of animals, Velvet preoccupies

Line drawing from the first edition of *National Velvet* by Bagnold's then-teenage daughter, Laurian Jones. Her drawings were dropped from subsequent editions of the novel. Used by permission of HarperCollins Publishers.

herself with constructing an as-yet-unrealized potential in this scene, a sporting life with horses that she imagines through visual media.

Called to account for these equine fantasies, Velvet provides fodder for the psychoanalysts when she concedes her own rejection of her own kind. "I don't like people . . . except us and mother and [the family's hired hand] Mi. I like only horses," she says, embracing her role as a misfit, though not a disconsolate one.[33] Yet this statement also reflects a cultural moment in which women riders were perceived as threatening gender ideals, particularly in light of her sister's response: "Pity you weren't a boy."[34] This apparently well-meaning sentiment, echoed again and again by others, even Velvet herself, indicates how this character's androgyny operates as one among many components of her social estrangement (if not that of all horsey girls).

More surprisingly, narrative descriptions of her "boy's face," layered in discussions of her horse-racing aspirations, also adumbrate and justify her later successful passing as a male jockey in the Grand National—and a man described as a "Bolshie," an "Esthonian," and a "half-Russian" at that.[35]

Providing the plausible excuse of a language barrier for Velvet to remain silent through the pre-race formalities, his unstable national identity also serves as a glaring reminder of the then-recent Soviet Revolution. The ruse thereby allows her plausibly to ride her own horse to victory, while also extending a range of revolutionary qualities to the transformation of girl and horse alike throughout the novel.

From the inauspicious introduction, descriptions of their appearances in animal terms cast Velvet's physical difference within the family as a hideous variation on the natural beauty of the other Brown girls. Against her sisters, Edwina, Malvolia, and Meredith—again the "golden greyhounds," even "gazelles," all with faces like "antelopes"—the awkward Velvet, with "all them teeth," sticks out like a monster, "like a fairy wolf gone blond."[36] The ugly duckling in a family teeming with animal life, Velvet seems well aware of her need to change games. "I don't ever want children," she says, "Only horses."[37]

This self-consciousness begins to explain why Velvet, unlike almost everyone else in her world, sees potential in a horse that others regard as worthless. Although the anachronistic quality of boyishness is one point of overlap in these girl and horse characters, the horse more clearly is presented as a thwarted sexual being. Certain aspects of The Piebald's appearance—he's "thick-necked" and, for an unworked horse, remarkably "muscular" when Velvet gets him—initially suggest that he is a stallion, and later get attributed to his being either "gelded late" or "not clean gelded."[38] But it is their "terrible" appearances that provide the most obvious visual association between the girl and The Piebald, whose name as a description of his color virtually announces that he is a combination of "carthorse and Arab," and so more like the early stock of this breed than a true thoroughbred.[39] Never minding appearances and instead pursuing what their extraordinary bodies can do together, Velvet sets out on a course for greatness, which also stems from her own athletic genealogy.

Unflattering comparisons with animals align Velvet with her mother, Araminty, who self-identifies as "fat," and is described consistently in terms of a big animal (for instance, as "elephantine" and like a "sea monster"). Bagnold's fictions more generally use this attribute to cultivate a sympathetic vision of the maternal body, connecting corporeal "greatness" with a tender vision of human animality, but she exploits a more literal advantage of fat for this particular character, who is introduced as "an enormous woman who had once swum the [English] channel."[40] Velvet does not share her mother's looks, in part because of her "problem" of constantly vomiting. But her body type likewise offers a singular advantage in her chosen sport.

While more recent critics take this aspect of her physique to mean that Velvet is anorexic, the novel's situating of skinny little Velvet amid an incessant parade of traditional English food like head cheese suggests a more plausible explanation of how Velvet maintains the weight and strength of a world-class jockey (not to mention a love for animals amid the daily practices of slaughtering and butchering, literally in her own backyard). The girl's weak stomach thus might be seen as introducing a "micropolitics" regarding mass consumption writ large by her uses of and by visual technologies, a dynamic that more broadly has come to characterize the complex relations with media and marketing that proceeded across girl–horse fictions in the twentieth century.[41]

Descriptions of Velvet riding with steady and delicate hands show how her sensibilities extend beyond simple visual identification. She may begin by toying with print media images of horses, but she later learns to ride well by using techniques that exploit these physical and mental points of connection with animals. She wins the formerly unmanageable Piebald in a lottery, and as she begins to train him, others comment on her soft touch as an entry point to working with him. Mi, for instance, accounts for the young equestrienne's unlikely success as a result of "handling him gentle," which means knowing when to make "a decision for her horse's good," such as forfeiting a competition, even at the risk of "throw[ing] away her own honors."[42] Echoing current stories of Zenyatta and contrasting those of her rival Rachel Alexandra, who is seen as far more typical of the racing industry for having been sold at the height of her career and subsequently raced until she lost heart (or no longer showed a keenness for competition), this complex understanding becomes the basis for the fictional girl–horse partnership's mutual "accomplishment," which assumes a smooth and strong "silken cooperation," and reflects more specific twentieth-century developments in riding and training technologies from which such stories proceed.[43]

Unlike earlier girl–horse fictions, there is no obvious shift away from physical intimidation and toward internalized discipline, no Foucauldian narrative of subject-formation in either girl or horse.[44] Like natural horsemanship today, Velvet's approach to training as the cultivation of genial qualities echoes instead earlier riding and pet-keeping manuals, which by the turn of the twentieth century proffered a new suburban ideal of gentle horses (marked especially by their fitness even for girls to handle)[45] and helped to put into more general use the social and practical means by which women become contenders and then winners in jumping sports. Albeit very subtly, the novel thereby references a wide range of historic changes that make way for these sporting revolutions, if not more generally for women to make lives for themselves with horses.

Feminine Underpinnings

The oldest and biggest online horse game, *Horseland* enables users virtually to manage stables, breed horses, and design 3D jumping courses, in short, to imagine becoming equine professionals. Since its inception in 1994, 6 million users (mainly girls from ten to twenty-two) have subscribed, inspiring an animated series of the same name broadcast by media corporation CBS since 2006.[46] Pitched to young female audiences, television shows like *Horseland* and *The Saddle Club* (2001–3) depict equine industries from children's perspectives, and not surprisingly there is little if any mention of the ongoing struggle for women to make a living from owning, training, and riding horses. The inclusion of boy characters in strictly ancillary roles indicates further that these dramas are centered on girls and horses. But how did horses become such a girlish passion?

While profound, these associations are anything but natural. The obvious absence of girls from images and stories of riding before the twentieth century instead indicates how such narratives are informed by very specific changes in animal practices. To clarify the shifts that lead up to and follow from *Velvet's* story, this section takes a brief tour through the literary histories of women riders that inform technological and cultural changes in jumping sports. Beginning with nineteenth-century stories that figure foxhunting female characters jumping (or "leaping" in the older parlance) horses over obstacles as sporting and sexual spectacles, I chart a long—and, yes, bloody—struggle for acceptance for women riders in sports like steeplechase, often prefigured in fictions of foxhunting.[47]

Unlike girls, women who ride are a staple of literature, and in fiction as in history ride to hounds. So, in the Walter Scott novel *Rob Roy* (1817), Diana Vernon enters the story directly from a foxhunt, more startling in her French riding habit than as a member of the hunt. Such figures of affluence seem cast in the mold of Sophia Western, whose father spends 60 guineas (a small fortune then for a country squire) on a horse for his daughter to ride to hounds alongside him in Henry Fielding's novel *Tom Jones* (1749). And they evince a tacit agreement that aristocratic Englishwomen always have been entitled to hunt. But the problem with reading them as the fictional foremothers of today's professional horsewomen is that the hunt does not become the scene of great drama for these minor figures as it does for their major male counterparts.

This problem comes to a head in the mid-nineteenth century, as can be seen through a quick comparison of Anthony Trollope's hunting characters. In a minor episode, the title character of *Phineas Redux* (1873) delightedly accompanies his beautiful foreign friend and former sweetie to a meet ("now she was a woman who could hunt"). But in an earlier novel, *Phineas Finn* (1869), this setting is introduced as far more significant for this particular hero, who becomes fast friends with his future rival by saving him from certain death in a foxhunting accident (the fate realized by the less lucky patriarch of Trollope's novel *Ralph the Heir* [1872]). Such scenes reinforce the prevalent nineteenth-century stereotype of foxhunting as a young man's sport, making it all the more incredible that from this period onward other novelists would use foxhunting to stage women's sporting and social triumphs.

Historians of the chase often observe that the enclosure of the English countryside in the eighteenth century set the stage for foxhunting to become an exciting and popular sport. What often go unnoted are the cultural conditions surrounding the British Enclosure Movement, which, peaking between the late eighteenth and early nineteenth centuries, often is seen as creating a new population of landless poor migrating to cities as the workforce of the Industrial Revolution. With these changes to the landscape, anyone following hounds also had to be able to take horses over fences, walls, ditches, and other obstacles that were suddenly legally required to separate fields from roadways, and at gone-away speed, factors that virtually reinvented the sport as a man's world.

Riding aside was the only practical option at the time for women, and it involved dangers ranging from the annoying to the unthinkable. Women around the world wore skirts in order to discourage the chronic condition then known as "thrush" and later identified as *moniliasis* or yeast infections before innovations in the later nineteenth century (including piped, clean water and central heat) made personal hygiene conditions less conducive to these and other skin ailments once collectively suffered under the term "the itch."[48] But in fast-paced equine sports like foxhunting, this otherwise practical fashion sometimes proved lethal. Particularly because heavy, draped skirts carried over from Regency period fashions into later styles of riding habits, they became all too often a means by which girls and women might be dragged and killed by horses.

A slow evolution followed from these deadly habit skirts, which were made of thick material and designed to conceal the feet, even to touch the ground from the horse's back (in the style of the flowing purple habit so famously envied by Jane Eyre). The next iteration was the slit or "safety" skirt, which, for its lightweight material meant to rip away in an emergency, was lampooned in a *Punch* cartoon in 1860 as the "fig leaf."[49] This then led to the short-lived (and by all accounts extremely uncomfortable) split skirt, and finally to the introduction circa 1900 of the backless or "safety-apron" skirt, which has become the formal convention for sidesaddle riding ever since. Along the way, as renowned sidesaddle rider and author Lida Fleitmann Bloodgood explains in *The Saddle of Queens* (1959), women's customary "complete nakedness under a concealing mass of petticoats" begins to explain why otherwise competent women riding aside in the earlier decades of the nineteenth century required a pilot, or male attendant, whose job it was to secure her moral if not physical safety.[50] The authors of women's riding manuals often included careful instructions regarding pilots and other devices to quell fears of appearing indecent, which they thought was the primary reason that women would refrain from riding.[51]

The question of decency was a factor that may have limited the participation of women in the early years of foxhunting, but by no means was it a deciding one. Until the invention of the modern sidesaddle around 1830, which features a "hunting horn" (a "leaping head" or third pommel), and the later addition of the balance strap, galloping and especially jumping aside were precarious ventures at best. What is more, women writers of these handbooks from the 1850s onward temper their encouragement of mastering these more thrilling and dangerous skills with the insistence that stockings and pantaloons and eventually breeches or trousers be worn under skirts "both for modesty and comfort."[52]

Although instrumental in implementing clothing changes that later prove crucial, the early riding-manual writers contributed in other ways to defining foxhunting as a man's world by advising readers against actually following hunts. Rather, they encouraged women and girls to ride out to the hunt meets that precede the chase but to refrain from joining the hunt itself. Clearly it would take more than just the innovations of saddlers, clothiers, and riding-instruction manuals to make foxhunting a desirable leisure pursuit for women. And in their absence, the culture of the sport quickly became decidedly masculine, in ways that curiously prevented some while encouraging other opportunities for integration.

Contradicting present popular perceptions of foxhunting as elitist, the sport emerged as one of many forms of riding that appealed to "a more (though by no means thoroughly) democratic recreational equestrianism," one that offered an affordable alternative to the kind of *haute école* riding typically studied in residence at far-flung academies.[53] In an era in which steeplechases were run from one church steeple to another, increasingly reliable train services began to bring weekend warriors and their mounts into the countryside to ride in races organized by publicans in the interest of boosting business. In between races, these thrill-seekers began to ride alongside the landed gentry, who allowed them to cap with (or pay a daily fee to ride as nonmembers of) clubs that, at least in the early days, appeared to favor performance as much as breeding in man and mount alike. By the mid-nineteenth century, these dashing young fellows cultivated a broader culture of risk that thrived amid the absence of women in the field.

A peculiar form of holiday home, hunting boxes first cropped up as the haunts of prostitutes and countryseats of courtesans, supposedly unknown to (more likely just disregarded by) foxhunters' female family members. Although occasionally a trailblazing titled woman would hunt her own pack in the absence of her spouse, as did the Marchioness of Salisbury starting in 1775, the few foxhunting wives and daughters of masters were the exception that proved the rule that riding to hounds was a man's sport. Other women entering the field faced strict social barriers that are elaborated in novels featuring female characters breathtakingly leaping horses over obstacles after hounds.

Especially for nonaristocratic young women, opportunities for developing high-level sidesaddle skills came with strings attached. Professional training and riding jobs through the nineteenth century were unequivocally male-dominated (as they remain now in much of racing), and social stigmas attached to the few jobs open to women guaranteed limited participation. "Pretty horse breakers" was a euphemism for prostitutes hired by dealers to parade horses for sale in city parks and avenues. Like car-show models in the twentieth century, their job was to attract attention to themselves (and away from their mounts' defects), for which they were provided with expensive, tightly fitted riding habits. Highly sexualized, pretty horse breakers in fact and fiction nonetheless became associated with the daring and athleticism required of cross-country riding to hounds, leading a precarious way to the greater involvement of women in sport riding by the end of the nineteenth century, as one historic example indicates.

Although born in poverty in Liverpool, Catherine Walters, known better by her nickname "Skittles," was the most famous and successful pretty horse breaker of the Victorian era, eventually becoming a wealthy courtesan who foxhunted with exclusive clubs from the late 1850s onward. In spite of some initial controversy, members of these clubs accepted her presence in part because the celebrity jockey Jem Mason (who rode the horse named Lottery to victory in the first Grand National) agreed to serve as her pilot, and more important because her stylish beauty and horsemanship were universally admired, even showcased in Edwin Landseer's portrait *The Shrew Tamed* (1861). Astonishing in their own right, the entrées into foxhunting of Skittles and other racy equestriennes also chronologically follow that of the fictional character Lucy Glitters, the paragon of female excellence in the hunting field, whose small but significant part in the comic British country-life fictions of Robert Smith Surtees traces the other main route then open to professional equestriennes.

Perhaps the most intrepid horsewoman in fiction, and, as Surtees's sarcastic narrator says, "tolerably virtuous," too, Glitters makes her entrance in *Mr. Sponge's Sporting Tour* (1852) as an accomplished horsewoman whose feats in the field ultimately make her seem irresistible to the title character.[54] Riding in a habit borrowed from her friend Lady Scattercash, Glitters stops the show when she enters the field, "looking beautiful on horseback, and for a time rivet[ing] the attention of our sportsmen."[55] Unlike all but one of them, she proves capable of keeping up with their pack in full cry. And so this chase scene ends with the hero, Mr. Sponge, filling in as master and Glitters as whipper-in to bring the fox to ground. Presenting her with the brush, Sponge cannot help but declare his love and proposes marriage to Glitters at the conclusion of their first hunt together.

Returning in *Mr. Facey Romford's Hounds* (1865), Glitters (now Mrs. Sponge) again temporarily fills in for errant hunt staff, only this time as part of a sneaky plan to conceal the viciousness of her mount (a horse that the eponymous master is trying to sell). Again whipping-in generations before any nonaristocratic women took such important leadership roles in foxhunting, Glitters leads even the master over the worst obstacles, and so inspires the ordinarily timid men of the Heavyset Hunt to enjoy a great day's sport. Back home, however, their wives deride her incredible performance: "'What! they were to have pretty horse-breakers down in the country were they?' the ladies exclaimed[,] . . . and stimulated themselves into a grand phalanx of resistance. 'No pretty horse-breaker' was the cry."[56] Yet the particulars of this character's story more plausibly account for her abilities.

Readers are informed that earlier Lucy Glitters's skills and habit alike were honored by her "taking part in the monster steeplechase at the Royal Agricultural Hall at Islington, . . . to the great admiration of crowded audiences."[57] She has been working, in other words, "in a circus," which for riders in nineteenth-century Europe meant not the traveling big-top pageantry with three rings and elephants but rather an urban entertainment fixture that has all but

Let me by then, said Lucy.

Engraving of Lucy Glitters in the hunt field in Robert Smith Surtees's novel *Mr. Facey Romford's Hounds* (1852). Perhaps the most intrepid horsewoman in fiction, Glitters goes where male foxhunters fear to tread. The caption: "'Let me by, then,' said Lucy." From the collections of the National Sporting Library.

disappeared, featuring daily individual performances of extremely skilled riding in the *haute école* tradition showcased in a single, permanent arena.[58] As was the case with pretty horse breaking and stage performance more generally, taking part in such work effectively compromised a woman's respectability. Nearly always viewed "as object of the male gaze," literary equestriennes foreground the social risks to which contemporary horsewomen's manual writers allude, and which novel writers have exploited ever since.[59] Literary figures like Lucy Glitters, moreover, register deep ambivalence toward the varied attractions of these professional riders, and show how a special exception began to be imagined through their capacity for demonstrating astonishing jumping skills, particularly by the end of the century.

Similarly assuming women's competence at the highest levels of professional and sport riding, Finch Mason's short stories of the 1880s more deliberately attempt to defend the integrity of female riders. As its title suggests, "The Queen of the Arena" stands out for its sympathetic revision of the narratives of Skittles and Glitters, as well as its more direct implication of aristocrats in arbitrating these developments. A generation after Queen Victoria's example confirmed the gentility of women's pleasure riding, the Empress Elizabeth of Austria bucked trends barring women from jumping in continental countries—for "usurpation of the masculine role," not just for incurring risk of physical damage—by vacationing in England and Ireland expressly to ride to hounds. Attempting to draw attention away from rumors of her sexless marriage to Franz Josef, at home this queen of her own arena "even vied with the great circus rider of the day, Caroline Loyo, who, hiding a three-pommelled skeleton under her ballet skirts, appeared to be executing the most complicated airs bareback."[60] Concerns about whether more ordinary women, who in increasing numbers were capping (again, paying to ride occasionally as nonmembers) with foxhunts, could gain rather than lose respectability by performing such feats proved easier to resolve in fiction.

Exploring such possibilities, Mason's titular queen starts as a foxhunting girl, but when her wealthy father is bankrupted, she runs away to London on her favorite horse in order to relieve everyone of the burden of supporting her. Unable to relinquish a passion for the chase, she eventually is followed from a foxhunt and discovered performing her "Daring Hunting Act" in the circus

The Queen of the Arena.

"The Queen of the Arena," drawing of the title character from a story of the same name by Finch Mason, c. 1880. The "Queen" performs in a circus that featured daily performances of highly skilled riding in the *haute école* tradition. From the collections of the National Sporting Library.

arena by her true love. They marry and return home to hunt together happily ever after. While the inverse seems true of the heroine Gwendolyn's story in George Eliot's novel *Daniel Deronda* (1876), whose successful feats in the fox-hunting field lead to her matrimonial doom and effective banishment from the hunt, together such stories indicate a growing concern with female fox-hunters as social creatures, not just spectacles. For Gwendolyn, finding a husband means avoiding the necessity of employment, and so leads some-what anachronistically to her removal from the sport that by then was secur-ing historical connections across royalty, pretty horse breakers, circus riders, and more ordinary folks, leading eventually to gender parity in some equine professions. Much more can be said about how the foxhunting field emerges as a transitional space in fiction, where girls and women become sexually objectified even as they stride toward equality, but here it is important to note how such treatments depart from other contemporaneous narrative patterns of representing women with horses.

Literary histories of women's sentimental fiction point to this period as marking a turning point in the symbolic values of horses, often at the expense of developing more empowering narrative relations between female riders and horses. As anticruelty concerns gained popular support, equine charac-ters came to articulate not only antislavery critiques but also the concerns of women's suffrage. For instance, horses in Anna Sewell's wildly popular novel *Black Beauty* (1877) describe their suffering at the hands of "ruling-class-male protagonists" in terms of both slavery and rape.[61] In this highly charged symbolic landscape, equestrienne images all the more clearly signal women's and horses' transformations into political subjects, even as changing atti-tudes in industrial societies favoring horses as pets and girls as athletes were making them all the more common.[62] More to the point, this symbolic align-ment obscures how and why women at the time came to embrace riding, especially the field and jumping sports in which they gain recognition in the next century.

Offering some clues, Irish fiction writer and pioneering female master of foxhounds E. Œ. Somerville reflects on the roots of this transition in poetic nar-ratives of the hunt in which foxes and women migrate from their eighteenth-century roles as villains (the latter for detaining manly hunters in the bedroom on hunting mornings) to more heroic parts.[63] These transformations become "noteworthy" because in them "the position of the fox is advanced no less than the wife," whose real-life counterpart in the later nineteenth century "as likely as not, insists" on joining her husband in the hunt.[64] Casting her own experiences as indicative of broader social changes implemented of necessity by World War I, Somerville offers a rare, firsthand observation of how "lady-masters and lady-grooms" came to serve "a positive national need" by taking up the work of men in training and otherwise providing "cavalry remounts" by participating in foxhunts.[65]

This claim is supported by Somerville's having kept a literary agent who also assisted in her brisk horse trading, and more generally by hunting diaries of the period. The obsolescence of mounted soldiers by World War II would have made these victories hollow, except that refinements to their training became the basis of modern jumping sports, which in peacetime drew new audiences and participants. And it is the condition that Somerville recognizes as securing these changes, namely, men and women both "riding astride," that becomes the focal point of sexualized associations of girls and horses and its mounting tension with the growing visibility of women's achievements as trainers and riders.[66]

By the beginning of the twentieth century, all commentators seemed in agreement that sidesaddle—a style that requires riders to arch their backs and open their chests to remain balanced—was the only feminine way to ride. Disagreement centered only on when to begin instruction. With warnings that "little girls are apt to grow crooked," and thus suffer "incurable disfigurement"

Photo: *Elliott & Fry, Ltd.*

THE WEST CARBERY FOXHOUNDS AT DRISHANE, 1908

Irish fiction writer and pioneering female master of foxhounds E. Œ. Somerville, the figure mounted aside and leading the West Carbery Foxhounds in 1908 in Drishane, County Cork, Ireland. From the collections of the National Sporting Library.

if started in sidesaddles—as did lifelong sidesaddle rider Somerville, whose coats had to be tailor-made with one shoulder higher than the other—manuals for horsewomen began to advise the delay of instruction in this style until girls became teenagers and therefore sufficiently coordinated to learn its complex fundamentals.[67] To prepare, they argued, girls must ride astride in childhood.

Sidesaddle rider and manual writer Betsy Skelton recalls (and regrets) burning old pony-sized sidesaddles in the early twentieth century, for their rarity now reflects how, "after about 1900," it became the case that "no little girls rode sidesaddle until they were young ladies."[68] The many heated debates of the period never resolve the question of whether disfigurement was caused by the saddle itself or by poor instruction in its use. But their constant return to the feminine appearance of women in sidesaddles speaks volumes about why fictions strictly cast girl characters in positions that would remain controversial for adult women training (let alone riding) hunters and jumpers long into the twentieth century.

As early as 1887, Hawley Smart's *Cleverly Won: A Romance of the Grand National* imagines a farmer buying an unlikely steeplechase prospect, whose ability is proven by his foxhunting daughter—"a pretty girl with a good figure in that most becoming of dresses, a riding habit."[69] True to fictional type, the girl first demonstrates the horse's ability by leading the hunt in a long chase sequence. Schooling the horse gently before and after the latter's first steeplechase experience, the girl talks her father into entering the talented horse in the Grand National, the race that she (like Velvet two generations later) perceives as the greatest of all jumping competitions. And her honor remains unimpeachable.

No pretty horse breaker or circus rider, this English village girl's boldest move is to get her would-be sweetheart to serve as jockey for the big race by agreeing to marry him. As in Surtees's and Mason's stories, the social riskiness of women entering into these roles appears tempered by conclusion with blissful matrimony, in which men ultimately assert leadership as sporting masters and winning professionals. Subtly but more innovatively, this girl's success as a trainer implies that she skillfully rides astride as well as aside. By the twentieth century, fictions deliberate in greater detail the changing social and technological conditions of riding for girls and women as they progressively assume greater roles in these and other sports.

The switch to riding astride was triggered by the invention of the balanced or (more properly) "forward seat," the innovative technique developed by Italian cavalry instructor Federico Caprilli, who is thereby credited with inventing modern competitive jumping sports. According to Vladimir S. Littauer (the White Russian officer who became a refugee to the United States and later a foremost instructor and author popularizing this technique), the implementation of this style among female riders was greatly assisted through the efforts of physical-education proponents in women's colleges who guided the next generations of "outstanding professionals" in equitation.[70] Significantly, he gives credit to "girls rather than . . . women" riders for bringing about the most dramatic improvements in jumping sports from the fictional Velvet's era onward, more specifically for fostering appreciation for the "elegance" and "smoothness" now expected of horseshow riders.[71]

Although this account seems to disprove older assumptions that girls mature to elegant riders only through sidesaddle riding, it also indicates how sidesaddles were no simple hindrance to the progress of women jump jockeys. In sharp debates coming to a head in the 1920s, even the harshest critics were hesitant to claim that girls or women could ever compete with men as riders.[72] Such overtly sexist prejudices, expressed by men and women alike, were dispelled only by the generations that followed, the girls who started and continued riding astride, and so became trained in the forward technique. As Littauer explains, these girls pressed to be allowed to ride alongside their male counterparts in competitive sports, and with further-reaching implications for professional riding.

Once more, clothing secured changes in these stories, for, as with many other sports, elastic-banded underwear did much to enable this transition. Girls like Velvet, whose families either would not abide or simply could not afford girls' jodhpurs, breeches, or other specially designated riding pants, were thus able to join the sport in their everyday skirts and what Velvet's mother calls "strong knickers."[73] Following the course of earlier technological improvements, greater ease of access also brings more direct encounters with social barriers, obstacles that regardless of girls' skill levels they cannot clear cleanly on horseback. The next sections explore the changing frameworks of gender and sex within which these struggles erupt in order to clarify further how the success of *National Velvet* casts a long shadow over the more specific conditions of realizing human and equine athletic potential, especially as their motivating desires are writ large on the big screen.

Girl Dreams and Bedroom Scenes

Responses to the film *National Velvet* frequently stray from the novel's concern with how Velvet's dreams center on intersubjective formations. These discussions more often focus on how "rapturously attractive" Elizabeth Taylor epitomizes the horsey girl's appeal, even (along the lines of Dekkers) "an odd sort of pre-specific erotic sentience."[74] One Taylor biographer even explains it in terms of a queer pedophilic appeal: "the peculiarly androgynous English innocence of the girl who loves ponies with a boyish passion and sets racing the hearts of men who can see themselves teaching her to transfer her affections to them."[75] The novel too inscribes this kind of response, only among admirers of the newly National Velvet. In spite of her family's misgivings about her marriage prospects, Bagnold's ugly girl likewise fans the flames of this peculiar desire on horseback; after she becomes famous, she receives "marvelous love letters from strangers, and boys at school, and workmen."[76] Recalling the sociobiological debates with which I began this chapter, these masculine desires for girls and horses together seems far more predictable than their own passions, which run further afield.

Despite the many practical claims of experienced riders that girl–horse relations promote self-esteem, positive body images, and other defenses against sexual assaults, *The Big Book of Lesbian Horse Stories* (2002)—an anthology of pulp fictions published from the 1950 to the 1980s—illustrates how equine fictions tell a different story of desire that explicitly concerns women's sexual along with professional fulfillment by the end of the twentieth century. Such stories may be crafted to appeal to niche audiences, yet they proceed from a narrative focus on adolescent bodies on the move, not (yet) settled into identities, that resists pigeonholing. In this context, *National Velvet* gains significance for offering a foretaste of the power of libido or erotic desire to destabilize identity and body image alike.

Describing her photograph series titled "Being and Riding," which features female human models, tack (saddles, halters), and plastic horse toys, Deborah Bright explains the creative appeal of "a girlhood attachment to horses" for herself as a queer adult artist: "[H]orse-craziness might represent a more anarchic place for young girls to inhabit, where contradictory erotic and social forces (power and gentleness, hardness and softness, wildness and control, danger and pleasure) can be reconciled in a body, a horse body. For those of us who have never settled comfortably into a two-gender world, such memories have talismanic power."[77] Such accounts position girl and horse bodies together on queer offensives, and in ways that begin to explain *National Velvet*'s apparently more lasting appeal for female audience members. Casting the image-making aspects of the novel and film in a new light, Bright writes wistfully of harnessing the "deviant passion" along with the talent reflected in the horse images that are characteristic of young women's art-school application portfolios, a desire that betrays "their membership in a subversive sisterhood."[78]

Queer cultural theorist Elspeth Probyn affirms this sensibility, and more, by pointing to the film *National Velvet* as an example of how horses become conduits of lesbian desire: "I am, of course, far from alone in thinking that there is something wonderfully thrilling about the movement of women on women on horses. . . . The desire to become-horse is unmistakable in scenes that show Liz [Taylor] in her bed repeating and caught up in the motion of riding, her arms stretched forward, her legs straining."[79] Glossing Deleuze and Guattari's comments on "becoming-horse," Probyn moves beyond Bright's notion (and, for that matter, those of the men cited above) that girlish passions can be leashed by others. Through her discussion, an idea of desire as a productive force begins to explain the power of this film in terms of its ability to redefine images of embodiment, showing how body images can be made to do more than contain identities, to serve more expansively as mechanisms of connectivity or "hyphens" between desire and the social.[80]

I want to venture further that narratives of human–animal performance require this kind of distinction between forms of identity and social agency, and in doing so can model desire as a productive and immanent force and in turn an understanding of social power as incitive. Deleuze and Guattari describe this kind of social agency as taking shape through all sorts of "becomings," providing a way of accounting for how movements between bodies (even though they lack the stability of singular identity forms and remain largely imperceptible in political domains dominated by individuals, like the novel form) may therefore be specially enabled to make social impacts. Their critique of Freud's "Little Hans," a boy pathologized as experiencing a severe horse phobia, pinpoints the affiliations of child and horse in resistance to the analyst's imaginative restriction of desire to filiative forms, and therefore as illustrating the transformative power of affect.[81] Hans's story becomes significant not for sorting out appropriations of other identities, for explaining how to pretend or learn to be something other, but rather for its more sweeping decenterings of all the bodily components of such alliances, a characteristic that I see emerging in more sustained ways through the female jump-jockey fictions.[82]

Such stories of becoming in Deleuze and Guattari's sense do not automatically transcend species differences; rather, these implications can be developed in strictly human social terms. On the one hand, like Bright, Probyn's description of her own childhood response to *National Velvet* provides an example of how girls' creative involvement in their own representation inspires others to begin the kind of play with image making to realize dreams otherwise deferred, for instance, by heteronormative prejudice. Yet, on the other hand, Probyn's writing about the film comes to concern how filmic girl–horse interactions "aid and abet a certain structuring of femininity, social class, and the establishment of a structure of feeling of young girls' sexuality, even as they may be put to work to deterritorialize these structures."[83] And I find further support for this argument in certain aspects of the source novel and sequel, raising further questions about how these texts both emphasize and challenge developmental sexual norms, and at what expense.

Resisting reconciliation with the terms of identity, all of the novel's heroine's words, thoughts, and actions move toward achieving a sort of greatness with her horse that sustains no hierarchies (let alone progression) of platonic, filial, and sexual desires. In this context, the girl's bedroom horseplay can be seen to challenge a *bildungsroman* narrative structure. The film version of this sequence downplays the more obvious masturbatory elements of Velvet's play-driving, keeping her clothed and quiet about what she thinks she is doing, only to send a more specifically erotic message about horses as psychosomatic "transitional objects."[84] This is the moment at which the film's Velvet declares that she chooses horses over boys, but her sisters and father (and, presumably, viewers with those racy "hearts of men") understand this in psychoanalytic terms as a disavowal.

But there are ways in which the novel reflects on image-making processes to engage what psychologist Kenneth J. Shapiro terms "kinesthetic empathy," a process that he elaborates as formative for dogs and people learning to live together, and that I extrapolate is a pretext for extremely complex kinetic relations like working with guide dogs and competing on hunter-jumper-type horses.[85] Without this perspective, it becomes difficult if not impossible to read this particular working partnership, so forcefully charged by fictions of female riders of the previous century, apart from egos and icons. The "horses" in the film's version of the bedroom scene remain offscreen, projected into and by the young actor's upraised legs, which Probyn initially interprets as expressing "a reaction to puberty" and later "the desire to become-horse."[86] In the novel, however, such meanings become further destabilized by Velvet's mother's simultaneous musing that The Piebald presents her daughter with a different "suit" altogether.

Araminty is the character who comes closest to articulating this difficult and necessary notion that embodied desires construct the human as a social creature, and moreover through her reflections on athletic experiences calls attention to the importance of image-making practices in mediating these knowledges. Mistaking at first the appearance of the horse in terms of a "suitor" for her daughter, and later her daughter's clandestine Grand National plans for an attempt to elope with Mi, the mother listens to her and learns to think of the horse as something other than a sexual practice-mount. Relieved to discover that "her shining Velvet" is just heading off to ride in what can be a deadly event, and "not all messed up with love," Araminty recognizes the aspirations for glory that she once pursued as a swimmer, and awards them by underwriting Velvet's preposterous plan with the prize money from her own girlhood victory.[87] In this passage, the story references the broader female athletic genealogies through which female jump jockeys emerge, and more precisely introduces the more difficult aspects of image-play through which they proceed.

The description of Araminty's famous Channel swim adumbrates the sense both of interspecies accomplishment and its violation, to which Velvet along with her fictional and historic descendents later attest, even using an equine metaphor to elaborate a terrific sense of lost potential in being made spectacles. Misunderstanding of what otherwise could be a world-changing collaboration follows from media reports of the performance strictly in terms of an individual's lone achievement. She reflects: "It was for Dan [Mi's father and Araminty's trainer] that she had done it. . . . She had never thought of the crowds on the beach, the cameras, and newspapers. . . . She and Dan could have opened a new world together, he directing, she enduring. She could have been a great mare whom a jockey rode to victory. . . . [Instead, s]he had been exposed in front of thousands, dripping, huge, shapeless, tired."[88] The knowing chuckle (or horrified gasp?) invited by this figure of the male trainer "riding" the girl athlete betrays how reductions of such collaborations to strictly sexual terms jeopardize their professional and social development into intellectual and physical intimacies that produce more lasting effects.

The curious choice of a riding relationship to figure these shared sensibilities among people underscores how revolutionary connections get forestalled by the focus on the one athlete, presented here as media spectacle amid the representational (non)histories of becomings. Rather than distinguishing the distinct roles of athlete and trainer, Araminty's firsthand account of their relationship in terms of this cross-species connection emphasizes complementary actions, movements, and performances ("he directing, she enduring") in which achievement inheres in responsiveness, in what happens between the two. Thus the novel foreshadows how the girl makes her own triumphant girl–horse story by repurposing images, eventually those of her own high-performance relations with her horse, and becomes betrayed in the process whereby she becomes a media star. But Velvet valiantly takes up her mother's burden of resisting reduction to a singular image as winner, and so Bagnold's fiction clarifies further how photographic mediation operates as an ambivalent mechanism for producing and reproducing subject forms, forestalling—even as it adumbrates—intersubjective and other potentials for agency beyond human individuals.

The setting of the big event, the racecourse at Aintree, on which the Grand National has been run for over 150 years, pointedly builds into the narrative frustrations with, especially, photo-realism as the standard of representation. Because of the extreme length and irregular shape of its course, the Grand National to this day cannot be simulcast from one position but requires multiple commentators and cameras posted at several positions to narrate the emergence of winning riders and horses through the requisite two times around the course. Even before the advent of television, the multiple mediations of this and other horse races connect the stories that unfold on the racecourse to broader audiences through cinema, radio, and even music-hall re-creations. While historians more recently have traced the effects of this ongoing mediation of horse racing especially via radio for the development of national identity,[89] the trend toward increasingly realistic representations obscures how such races profoundly challenge attempts at authoritative storytelling. Whether for riders, horses, stewards, or audience members, the experience of the National becomes filtered through communications technologies, enveloping and reconfiguring the race as it is run, just like the dense fog surrounding the novel's National, as well as the fictional race's most obvious historical precedent.

Velvet and The Piebald's Grand National win shadows the 1928 upset victory of amateur rider W. P. Dutton and his mount, Tipperary Tim, a 100–1 long shot who ran among "42 horses, the largest field that ever started during the first 89 years of its running," and that year proved "the only horse not to fall" on the course and one of only two who finished it amid severely limited visibility because of the thick fog.[90] Historian T. H. Bird writes that, because of their "poorest credentials," Tim and Dutton's unprecedented clean and victorious round had an immediate and "disastrous" effect for the sport: "Everyone who owned a steeplechaser that could walk aspired to win the Grand National," in Bird's estimation greatly augmenting "the rubbish with which the field was cluttered."[91]

Just as The Piebald's ugliness inspires much commentary in the novel, Tim's "tubed" forelegs and "parrot-mouthed" appearance garnered much of this sort of attention at the time.[92] But the ambiguous referent of "rubbish"—whether poorly conditioned or ill-bred horses and riders—in Bird's characterization indicates the intricate imaginative ties between class and physical qualities, and, more to the point, cultures and genetics in "breeding" that were blasted apart by this historic upset, and, more important, its narrative legacies for other bodies that likewise were previously unimaginable as winners. Bird observes that even the "placing" stipulation added in 1931—allowing as entrants only horses who previously had finished first, second, or third in a three-mile steeple-chase—did not, as it was intended, work to reduce the size of the field.[93] However, this revision of the race's rules informs Bagnold's clarification in a note added to the original text (and also curiously absent from reprints of the novel) that places the race run in the novel before 1931, bringing the novel's story closer in history to Dutton and Tim's win than to the novel's publication date. Bagnold cites the National Hunt Rules to explain that, before 1931, "it was not necessary for a horse to have distinguished itself 'by being placed . . .'— and for all that I can find in the Rules a zebra could have entered, provided he was the proper age."[94]

And the fictional image of a girl in the winning jockey's seat intimates even more widespread social changes. Pointing to the crowds gathering around their house following the news of Velvet's and The Piebald's surprise victory, her sister Meredith's questions signal these broader political resonances: "Are you sure it is only about Velvet? . . . It isn't a revolution?"[95] And it clarifies how media coverage can help to make or break this Velvet revolution. The winning girl's face appears everywhere, first in cinema and later on all sorts of "Velvet Novelties," clarifying how she becomes grist for the machinery of marketing.[96]

Although speaking much later in the century, the few actual women jockeys who have ridden in the National confirm that this media omnipresence, fed by a fixation on their "different" bodies, has proven the most hazardous aspect of their experience, making it all the more difficult to imagine a young girl enduring this kind of exposure.[97] Like other women athletes, Velvet finds this aspect of fame estranging, and solidarity with her mother provides the only means of sustaining the intimacies that inspired it. In a rare, long speech, Araminty challenges her husband's plans to cash in on their daughter's fame by selling The Piebald to eager filmmakers, and again appeals to the rhetoric of horse training to explain that as parents they must work instead to "keep her going quiet," intimating that there may be greater things to come.[98] Araminty's experience has shown that more than just the immediate, physical connection between the winning girl and horse are at stake in this transaction, only words seem to fail to express it.

Girl and mother alike speak haltingly here, and on behalf of an emergent sense of community, in Velvet's case elaborating a complex sense of serving as an exemplar for something other than individual triumph. Uncharacteristically she stutters in her impassioned speech to persuade her father not to sell out, trying to explain that what she wants instead is their names to be added to "roll-of-honor books where they put down the winners and call them the Immortal Manifesto."[99] In so doing, she makes a funny sort of reference both to the cumulative effects of these winners and at the same time to one exemplary horse, the historic Manifesto, whom Mi describes as the "Greatest National horse ever was" because he completed the treacherous race an unprecedented eight times and won it twice.[100] By a slip of the tongue, Velvet indicates that all National winners become *the* Immortal Manifesto, even as they provide yet another example of irreducibly collective achievements. In this vision, the intersubjective relations of girl and horse become enmeshed in a process of becoming something more than winning individuals in a long Velvet revolution that kicks against any resolution into a singular star performance.

Once again, imaginative engagements with animals make plain how girls spin stories of their own bodies as differently empowered, as Probyn puts it, metaphorically approaching them as a kind of "swapping ground for different imaginary maps and cards of what one is becoming."[101] This accounts for the central concern of horse films like *National Velvet* with female strength, and for the ways in which horse narratives more generally sustain queer visions of desire. While I agree that such stories concern displacements and rearrangements of power forms, their increasing emphasis on competition, particularly the ways in which gendered rivalries come to involve not just sex but also violence, betrays a more profound ambivalence concerning media and intersubjective agency, at least in the female jump-jockey tradition.

Recalling as well the description of her mother's estranging experience of notoriety, Velvet's linkage of photography, identity, and containment in the end clarifies why the girl needs the horse out of cinematic pictures and in her life. The violence of separation and individuation may be forestalled in *National Velvet*, but the narrow escape of girl and horse here portends a darkening theme in ensuing narratives that move them away from steeplechase courses and into scenes of Olympic riding, only in part to reflect historical changes. While women jump jockeys have made tremendous strides in the past century, they remain in the minority as steeplechase riders. Much earlier (if also incrementally), girls trained in the forward-seat method and similarly sporting "strong knickers" entered the arenas of show jumping as part of a long and difficult revolution leading to their current prominence in Olympic riding competitions.

Velvet to Violent

Reflecting on the consequences of her breakthrough career, Pat Smythe, the first woman member of an Olympic equestrian team, pointed in the 1950s to two factors as interrelated: first, that "television has turned show-jumping from a minority sport into a nation-wide entertainment," and, second, that the public's "enthusiasm for show-jumping has automatically led to an emphasis on women riders."[102] Fifty years later, with the Oxygen Network's prime-time Olympic coverage of these events, this televisual connection seems all the more stunningly to contrast the spectacularly doomed affairs of girls and women on horses in Hollywood films. Whether through sequences featuring spoiled girls killed by their mounts, for instance, in *Gone with the Wind* (1939), psychotic women killing their horses as in *Marnie* (1964), or the pair killed together, as in *Giant* (1956), the attractions of female and equine characters prove fatal with surprising consistency in big-studio-era film versions of novels. *National Velvet* thus comes to seem all the more an exception that proves a rule that becomes more brutally enforced by the turn of the twenty-first century.

More recent examples like *International Velvet* (1978) and *The Horse Whisperer* (1998) posit girls riding horses as literally and figuratively becoming moving targets, most often when they are seen off the sporting field. Together they are imagined in these texts as threatened, mutilated, even killed. Possibly such depictions represent a backlash against the anticipated and later growing successes of women riders competing against men during this period, or even an acting-out of broader hostility toward girls for, among other things, turning riding into "a girl's sport."[103] Such interpretations, however, obscure important continuities in female jump-jockey narratives. Among the most prominent recurrences are the narrative structurings around visual media play that maintains in these unlikely circumstances a sense of the shared benefits of cross-species life, one distinguishing feature of Bagnold's novel that persists in stories of girls entering in equestrian competitions. Such texts respond to a growing sense of cross-species intersubjectivity and other bodily reconfigurations of agency as far more deeply imperiled.

In these ways, the narrative history of female jump jockeys counters arguments that, as bikes, planes, and especially cars become the favored vehicles for asserting power and independence, representations of women on horses no longer appear threatening so much as escapist.[104] According to this line of thought, "field sports, fishing, and above all horses" thereby come to signal nostalgia for the power of the landed aristocracy.[105] Following women's progressive entry into these sports, however, the more recent and virulent linkage of girls, horses, and especially sexualized violence indicates how this sort of retreat is not an option within Velvet's broader narrative legacy.

Just as a female jump jockey has yet to win the Grand National, an Olympic gold medal for individual achievement in eventing has yet to be awarded to a woman rider. Even getting to compete has been a battle that has turned in women's favor only in the last half-century. In 1911, the Swedish Olympic Committee turned down the application of horseshow superstar Helen Preece to compete in the pentathlon. At fifteen, Preece would have been the youngest competitor in the 1912 Olympics, but the committee instead refused her simply because she was female. With this precedent, the wonder is that girl riders even persisted, let alone eventually triumphed.

Preece's case notwithstanding, the substantial amounts of time and money required to train for Olympic competition effectively barred all but active-duty cavalry officers from this level of competitive equitation prior to World War II. Anticipating a flood of applications that would follow the disbanding of cavalry forces, a rule implemented in 1938 explicitly barred "Amazons" or women riders from competition.[106] Following a 1952 rule change, pressed in part by the renegade appointment of Pat Smythe to the British team in 1948, women were allowed to compete in dressage, which they have "dominated" ever since.[107] Following Velvet's lead, the ensuing battles centered on women's entry into jumping sports were fought in the pages of female jump-jockey fictions as well.

Young adult novels of this period reflect a growing awareness that, while women may be capable, girls have a long way to go in preparing to enter this kind of competition on equal footing. So even as late as 1955, Alice L. O'Connell's *The Blue Mare in the Olympic Trials* depicts girls rising to national- and international-level show jumping, only to conclude with the one girl who eventually qualifies for the United States Equestrian Team (USET) getting turned down by the overseeing committee in her request for a special exemption to ride in the Olympics. Like Velvet, this girl is primarily interested in her horse's glory, and so proves a good sport by lending the mare she has ridden through the qualification process to a boy who has proven not as good a rider, but nonetheless a good friend, so he can have a chance at winning Olympic gold. More clearly than her fictional or historical predecessors, this girl jump jockey also understands that she did not really have a chance, lamenting that "they ought to provide equestrian events for girls at the Olympics, just the way they've got women's divisions in the other sports. That's the only thing that doesn't seem quite fair."[108] Readers of course are encouraged to agree.

A generation later, this kind of resignation to gendered segregation is conspicuous by its absence from a similar story by illustrator and sometime novelist Sam Savitt titled *Vicki and the Brown Mare* (1976). Here the girl again rides to qualify an initially difficult horse for the USET—whose unlikeliness is underscored in an opening foxhunting sequence, in which the girl disgraces them both by proving unable to keep the mare from running down the master, causing him and his horse to fall—only this time she also trains the horse, following the pattern of steeplechase fictions. Judged a better trainer than rider, the team takes her mare, but Vicki herself is not chosen to ride with them. The happy ending awaits her meeting with the rider Jill Radnor, who wins the show-jumping gold medal with the mare, and who subsequently congratulates the incredulous girl:

> "I guess I didn't do too well with her," Vicki shook her head. "I could never ride her the way you did in a million years."
>
> Jill answered. "But don't you see? I could never have done what I did with her tonight if she did not have the education you gave her. You made it all possible."[109]

The development of competition itself as the goal has become more typical of a girl–horse (and still more recently woman–horse) genre in examples more true to the stereotype in which the girl finally learns to leave horsey playthings aside, meeting sexist expectations that she should love a man instead. So this female Olympic rider character's clarification of the important difference that the girl has made in contributing to a team effort becomes significant for its insistence on the same sense of an irreducibly shared victory that surfaced in Bagnold's novel, clearly implicating the Velvet revolution as inspiring notions of cross-species intersubjectivity, even community, that yet remain fragile. That is, in this instance, an all-female cross-species circuit indicates further that the sexual politics of these sports involve far more than simply letting girls ride.

Such narrative developments follow from the 1953 ruling that allowed women to compete in Olympic show jumping after 1955. However, it was not until 1964 that equal access was opened to the three-day eventing competition. Because the cross-country course is weighted higher in scoring, this last development made it possible for women riders to contribute more to team victories as well as to win overall as individuals. But this recent achievement of parity among eventers comes at a distinct cost to perceptions of human–horse partnerships, which is again the term favored by those at the top of this

Illustration from the 1976 novel *Vicki and the Brown Mare* by Sam Savitt, featuring the title characters charging out of control in their first foxhunt together, causing the master and his horse to fall. Used by permission of Bette Savitt.

game. As Smythe suggests, public interest from this period onward tends to focus even more sharply on the visual spectacle of struggling female riders, rather than this unique opportunity to cheer men alongside women (not to mention animals along with humans) as Olympic competitors.

Following the older chain of cultural associations of royal women on the cutting edges of equestrienne politics, the publicity surrounding Princess Anne's participation on the British Equestrian Team in the 1976 Montreal Olympics "put eventing on the map," in part because on the cross-country course she fell and got a concussion.[110] Like steeplechase, eventing is a risky sport, in which riders and horses always risk harm (the actor Christopher Reeve being an example of what can go horribly wrong, especially on the cross-country course). More clearly than the ruling of the same year that allowed women to ride against men as steeplechasers in the UK, or the decision in

1975 to open all international jumping competitions at last to female competitors, it is the example of this famous aristocratic woman injured at the peak of competition that highlights the conditions to which *International Velvet* responds.

National Velvet's long-awaited film sequel (1978), released simultaneously with a novelization of the screenplay of the same name by director Bryan Forbes, was poorly received in the United States, perhaps because it openly resists American girl–horse film trends by returning to the central themes of Bagnold's novel.[111] A jarring admixture of adventure and melodrama, *International Velvet* takes on even more by explicitly developing the sexualized violence that characterizes later twentieth-century developments of girl–horse narratives. Whereas Bagnold's Velvet and The Piebald find international acclaim along with carefully negotiated family support, their more contemporary counterparts endure a seemingly endless string of traumas. Leading into later narratives like *The Horse Whisperer,* which explicitly visualize the destruction of girl–horse alliances, the story requires its central girl character to use image technologies to craft as well as to recover a more workable future for herself and her horse. Thus *National Velvet's* dream-machine technique for writing alternate narratives of girl–horse possibilities mutates into a survival skill.

The new filmic couplings are as pretty as the old, but their burdens become infinitely more painful. Although the girl similarly wears a retainer that hurts, this is the least of her suffering. Initially conceived as a remake and written instead as a sequel to *National Velvet's* film version, *International Velvet* begins with the eponymous girl Sara Velvet Brown (played by Tatum O'Neal, who by then was already a child star) becoming orphaned by her parents' death, and consequently relocated from the United States to the UK to be raised by a stranger, her aunt Velvet Brown (a role written for the director's wife, Nanette Newman). The cross-national perspective might seem a peculiar outgrowth of a novel that, as one contemporary reviewer remarked, "seizes on the one thing that more than anything else has always held England together—a passion for sport and particularly for horse-racing"—except that in this respect it only adds to the complication of national-identity models through the development of a peculiar postcolonial narrative trope, that of the British horsey mother of international girls.[112] Thrust into this position, Velvet, imagined now as forty, divorced, and herself traumatically sterilized following a fall from a horse, moves from reluctant guardian to beloved "parent" of this deeply disturbed child by exploiting their affinity for riding.

This shared and transformative passion emerges quickly through depictions of the film's Sara drawing childish pictures of the horse to whom she becomes attached, and along with these images Velvet's old paper horses return in this film, only now as objects of her own adult musings about what new girl–horse partnerships will bring. The novel more clearly captures the sense of girlish engagement in these processes of visual storytelling by depicting Sara taking inexpert photos of her horse, "strange, blurred images" that she reveres and that others find unintelligible. By contrasting the girl's distorted pictures with the professional-quality images that an admirer takes of them while competing (a boy whom the girl fatefully scorns), the eruption of these image-making scenes brings into open conflict the different potentials for embodiment projected through these stories of female jump jockeys.[113]

In the film's most memorable sequence, the girl and horse narrowly escape being killed by drunken boys, inadvertently inspired by their friend, the girl's unwanted admirer (and sometime photographer). Perceiving her as snubbing their sexual advances, the boys pile into a car to chase after the girl on her horse, leading not only to her fall and concussion but also to the death of the boys in the fiery explosion of their crashed car. In his novelization of the story, also titled *International Velvet*, Forbes offers a weird psychological justification in advance of this sequence, one that is diametrically opposed to what people generally say about *National Velvet*: "There is something about young girls on horses that brings out the worst in people. Perhaps it is that, nowadays, owning or riding a horse is sufficiently out of the ordinary to suggest privilege, and of course when this is combined with beauty it arouses, in those who feel inadequate, emotions that are both irrational and violent."[114] While in one sense this sequence provides more traumatic plot motivation for Sara's all-consuming passion for competitive riding, in light of this passage it also explicitly figures how and when sexualized violence aimed at girls with horses becomes normalized. In this narrative, it certainly stands out as perversely apologetic amid other scenes that normalize the injuries and deaths of humans as well as horses.

The meager hope that the text as a whole seems to offer girls and horses is that they can work together effectively to create and sustain an image of themselves that escapes these twisted passions, in lieu of changing the terms of desire itself. Together, Sara, following in the footsteps of her grandmother and aunt, and her horse Arizona Pie (anachronistically conceived as the Pie's last foal) fulfill a strangely combined genealogical destiny as they earn a place on the British Olympic Equestrian Team. Again her choice of sport signals the ascendancy of women riders in eventing, where in greater numbers they own, train, and ride horses. But it also emphasizes how their configuration as celebrities jeopardizes the "intimate communications" shared by different bodies and species that are central to this kind of competition.[115]

Unlike Velvet, who wins only illegitimately (by the end of Bagnold's novel, she is tried and acquitted of fraud for passing as a male jockey), Sara rides against no official gender prejudice in the three-day event, which is, as a television sportscaster in the film informs viewers, "the only event in the Olympic games in which men and women compete on equal terms." As they gain notoriety, Sara becomes a primary object of interest for newspaper writers and, later, television reporters, who single her out from fellow riders and horses, even Arizona Pie, as "International Velvet." Deliberately mitigating this undue fame, the team captain initially assigns her horse to a male teammate. While invoking the recent history of sexism at the crux of O'Connell's *Blue Mare*, this response to publicity underscores how Sara in some ways rides under more egalitarian conditions than Velvet, even as it again implicates news media in cutting the female athlete out of the irreducibly mixed social landscapes supporting her individual appearance of greatness.

More directly echoing Smythe's insider's view, television becomes peculiarly implicated as the key apparatus in staging perceptions of the winning girl. Velvet and her boyfriend tune in to watch the awards ceremony featuring Sara and her fellow silver medalists (and also getting their first glimpse of the American gold medalist, whom their daughter will soon marry). For the first time within the film, this television broadcast frames all of the horses standing to one side on level ground as a point of contrast to the humans, who accept their medals atop stages of graduated heights, a sharp visual contrast with the announcers' egalitarian rhetoric concerning eventing. In spite of their claims about gendered equality in this sport, Sara is the only woman medalist on the field, and apparently the only one injured on the course, though this is perhaps because the story imagines her as the youngest-ever Olympic eventer. And as is the case with girl–horse narratives, at least up to the television show *The Saddle Club*, all of the riders are white.

This suggests another front on which, as director/author Forbes notes in the passage cited above, a certain kind of person gets set up on horses only to endure a peculiar backlash regarding horses as symbols in the social imaginary. Taking this diagnosis and subsequent casting choices together at face value, white girls would seem to lose coming and going, gaining in the social prestige of equestrian sports just in time to become targets of anti-elitist rage. This sort of critique resonates strangely with long-standing debates in literary criticism of the problems with equating identity and authority, and likewise at the expense of discursive analysis. But I am not sure that it is sufficiently complex to account for what happens across species lines in this particular representational history.

Ranged alongside earlier equine fictions and contemporaneous intersubjective examples like those of the blind detectives, what appears instead to take shape are more complicated and site-specific alignments of sex, class, ability, age, gender, race, and species, such that privileged identities appear all the more clearly to serve as partial means of deflection. These in turn are dubious insurance policies that individually offer protection for their holders against critiques as well as responsibilities, and collectively promise to cancel one another out—hence the importance of media interventions especially in more recent female jump-jockey narratives.

Intersubjective Dissolutions

Akin to *Sue Thomas*, the Australian-set series *The Saddle Club* uses a multiethnic and otherwise mixed cast in ways that change the exclusionary public image of desirable human–animal relationships, a stereotype that is strangely reinforced in media forms that target the same young audiences and ostensibly allow for more choices in image construction. A casual glance at gaming options like Nintendo's portable DS game *Horses* and its *Petz Horsez 2* (developed for the Wii entertainment system) reveals not only that these games idealize participation in eventing and steeplechase as the goal of human–horse relationships but also that participants must play through an unchangeably white-girl avatar. "Boys can play these games," my nine-year-old niece explained, "they just have to pretend she's a boy," then proceeded to demonstrate how easy it is to change the horse's color.

Such contradictions may stem directly from material constraints in marketing virtual worlds, yet they also reflect the ways in which these sports gain in popularity without forcing new terms for social achievement. The intersubjective narrative developments outlined here so far insist that girls do not simply become horsey, nor horses girly. Rather, these associations proceed tentatively, amid shifts in narration along with visualization of the modern relations of companion species and with material consequences for the lives of horses and people.

Despite some incredible gains, social limits to girl–horse bonding persist, and are most graphically asserted in stories that depict the intersubjective dissolutions of girls and women from horses. More explicitly than the guide-dog narratives, these texts emphasize the fragility of intersubjective relations across species as well as their material construction of different ends in cross-species companionship, again through narratives of image construction.

Linking them to a different sort of interplay in the fictional and social development of women in veterinary practice, this chapter concludes by suggesting that, in so doing, these texts also express a deeper ambivalence about the viability of professional or even civic changes that can follow from these particular partnerships between members of different species.

Acclaimed as its most significant feature, the dreamlike opening sequence of *The Horse Whisperer*—both Nicholas Evans's 1996 novel and the 1999 film based on it—features adolescent girlfriends tacking up their horses to take off together on a ride along snowy trails that bring them to their doom when they are crushed by an out-of-control truck. Spectacularly foregrounding the violence and hostility that surfaces in later twentieth-century narratives like *International Velvet*, the narrative imagines one girl–horse pair dead at the crash scene. The other pair survives, severely disfigured and disabled, as well as deeply alienated from each other.

Image making takes on a markedly different valence when, in the novel as well as the film, Grace, the surviving girl, stares at photos and video images of herself in riding competitions on her horse Pilgrim, which were taken before the accident. She then declares that she will never ride again. The girl's use of these photographic images creates a story of the dissolution of their relations, thus anchoring a counter-narrative to the central drama (announced by their symbolic names) of this Pilgrim's progress back to Grace.[116] For the novel's Grace, old horse-show photos appear to trigger this recognition (and immediate rejection) of their relation as a point of weakness, but the film's adaptation of this sequence instead introduces the more complicated idea that video conveys a sense of their shared strength as lost, and as presumably unrecoverable, at least from the multiply traumatized girl's perspective.

Showing Grace alone and crying as she watches herself on television, once happily in the thick of a jumping class on her now-unrideable horse, this sequence in the film cuts immediately to a confrontation with her parents (again featuring another English mother to this American daughter), who then beg the "horse whisperer" for help that turns out to be more effective sex therapy for the parents than professional animal training for the girl. In a narrative focused on the destruction and dubious rehabilitation of girls and horses, this use of the videos also introduces fleeting images of not simply nostalgia for one's psychological and bodily wholeness but, more important, a world-forming process distributed across and growing through bodies. Unlike the television broadcast in *International Velvet*, here the video-within-film segment gestures toward a greater set of possibilities in these relations than the trauma-recovery narrative allows, a reenvisioning of potentials for girl and horse that both precedes and exceeds such forms. How these technologies are used and for what narrative purposes seem the central concerns of the girl-horse narrative tradition, and, in this narrower context of jumping-sports stories, much seems to ride on a contrast between generating publicity and creating other sorts of distorted images.

This is not to say that girls use horses to transcend dominant notions of identity, nor that these visual narratives of their relations ultimately destroy such capabilities. Rather, these stories of cross-species intersubjectivity show the intimate ties of narrative and imaging practices, extending "the possibility of symbolic interaction on a non-discursive basis" into narrative processes that posit nonsymbolic action as the basis of competing discourses.[117] Current theories of and experiments with animal aesthetics suggest further why these particular examples push the limits of form.

As art historian Steve Baker says of Lucy Gunning's video short *The Horse Impressionists* (1994), visual narrative processes demonstrate how imaginative engagements with animals can foster a contemporary sensibility of aesthetic practices "as, and at the cost of, a letting go of identity and of certainty."[118] Gunning's video mimics a horse-show flat class or dressage clinic, only with no horses in the picture. Instead, it features women making horsey noises and movements with their bodies at someone's gait commands, then spontaneously dissolving their own performance via infectious laughter. Foregrounding the amateurish visual narration of interspecies and community forms that lead from the girl–horse narrative tradition outlined above to a more nebulous set of contemporary representations—exemplified by "Zenyatta–Starstruck (Lady Gaga)," a fan-film montage of images of the equine star set to the bisexual pop star's chart-topping song, created and posted to the video-sharing site *YouTube* by a girl identifying herself as Chelsey—this professional artist's video short brings me to an overarching point about the stakes of civic life assumed across very different narratives of cross-species intersubjectivity.[119]

From *National Velvet*'s girl-drawn illustrations onward, tension persists between the professional achievements to which girls aspire and the dilettantism that emerges as the guiding condition of their most formative relations with horses. Especially given the blatant sexism that continues to characterize the most lucrative horse sports, it could be argued that animal narratives might project more open-ended transformations from performance to social life most effectively through the fields of amateur sports. So the aspirations of girl riders might be seen as thwarted in Gunning's and Chelsey's pieces, which unlike James's, are premised on a relationship with a horse that remains at a distance.

Moreover, it could be argued that these desires appropriately are migrating now to the nonprofessional fields of canine agility, which is modeled after equine jumping sports. At its late twentieth-century inception, it was dominated by women handlers and canine participants regardless of gender. A decade later, despite Haraway's moving accounts of entering these competitions as a postmenopausal woman along with her similarly reproductively silenced bitch, it is clear that male handlers and dogs have begun winning at the highest levels, where professions are quickly developing and the potential for the gendered emphasis on winning sires, who, like racehorse stallions, stand to earn more bang for the buck in terms of reproductive potential, remains to be seen. In so far minimally lucrative dog-training situations like these, as Hearne, Haraway, and others have argued, bodies that barely understand each other have to enjoy what they are doing enough to want to keep returning to the "contact zone," building intensely shared lives together through relationships that likewise have to stay fresh through creative, mutual problem solving.[120] The hope is that they find broader support.

Fostering emergent sensibilities of agency in ongoing play that are so readily dismissed by those outside the fold, the developing narratives of canine agility posit these intersubjective relations against dismissive characterizations of them as sexually titillating or juvenile. But the overwhelmingly amateur status of participants makes it easy to sidestep the problematics of sustainability erupting within the longer female jump-jockey tradition, which extends through narratives of women at the same time entering other animal professions. Whether working as mounted police officers, as police- or tracking-dog handlers, even as inmates being trained as pet groomers in popular prison programs, many women seem to be finding ways of sustaining these engagements through their adult and working lives, but only in settings defined by trauma. Not surprisingly, then, it is in the fields in which they have made the greatest strides in traditional gender imbalance that they also promise the most radical transformations to these aspects of companion-species relations in the twenty-first century.

Most of the little horse-obsessed girls in my acquaintance learn to know better than to say that they want to be professional riders when they grow up, abandoning this option (along with princess) to embrace what has become for them a more realistic ambition of becoming a veterinarian. Following changing patient demographics, federal mandates for gender equity in sponsored veterinary schools, and the movement of the profession toward small-animal practice, female students and graduates have come to outnumber males by at least three to one in veterinary science now in the United States.

This gap promises to resolve the historic problem of male dominance in the profession, but it also appears to be contributing to looming crises in animal industries.

For this development coincides with a profession-wide shift toward private practice and away from industry jobs, particularly in laboratory science and meat regulation. When the predominantly older men filling these jobs retire, their young female colleagues opt out of careers that some understand to be at odds with their profession's goals. Whether this situation reflects more practical motivations, such as maximizing earning potentials to pay off the substantial student loans incurred in their training, or political commitments—for instance, to animal rights or feminist ethics of care—it also informs a dimorphic pattern of representing fictional male and female veterinarians.

Like the hero of Sara Gruen's *Water for Elephants* (2006), veterinarians in novels remain largely heroic men who stereotypically save not only animals but also women and children, in this instance from greedy and sadistic circus managers, reciprocally painted in the broad strokes of cartoon villains. Even realistic fictions tend to focus on male vets as the heroes who arbitrate animal medicine's historic shifts. Beginning with *All Creatures Great and Small* (1972), the best-selling fictions of Yorkshire veterinarians by James Herriot (the pseudonym of James Alfred Wight) and the BBC television series of the same name also reflect a clear divide between popularly endearing stories of "Herriotesque animal doctors" from the changing histories of their profession by the end of the twentieth century.[121] Because these stories begin in the English countryside of the 1930s, they nostalgically envision the growth of this profession out of its primary commitment to public health and the service of livestock industries and toward small-animal care. By and large in these fictions, which proceed humorously and haphazardly, the men of veterinary medicine steadily enable the ongoing adaptation of companion-species relations to the selfsame social and technological conditions emerging so critically at the time in the fiction of Bagnold and Kendrick.

Reflecting the autobiographical experience from which the author purportedly has drawn, the central cast of veterinarians remains all male. Yet as the series continues on into the 1950s, it also introduces the changing face of the profession. At least, a later episode of the TV series includes an anecdote about a young woman, fresh out of veterinary school, who takes a tour with the country vets to determine whether she should join them in livestock work. Although she demonstrates physical fitness and other aptitudes for the job, the sexual harassment of male farm workers proves too much, and she retreats to her original plan of taking over her father's small-animal practice in London, a narrative that again seems to be repeated by so many of her counterparts today. While veterinarians and veterinary students confront a host of other injuries and threats throughout the TV series, this lone indication of endemic sex prejudice is depicted as coming from the public, not shared among professionals, and exacerbated by relations with large animals like horses. The problem appears more complex in the 1981 novel *The Lord God Made Them All,* when Herriot discourages his daughter (and pointedly not his son) from becoming a vet, mostly due to the dangers inherent in treating farm horses, "the ones that regularly put the vets in hospital with broken legs and ribs."[122]

Fictional depictions of female vets remain rare, making it hard to generalize, but more recently another set of associations with violence and sex bogs down the fictional veterinarian Bev Shaw, who owns and operates the neighboring animal clinic in J. M. Coetzee's *Disgrace* (1999). A more bleak and hopeless commitment to day-to-day veterinary work hardly seems imaginable than this character's resignation to killing the countless unwanted dogs of her South African town, especially given how this practice informs her one emotional breakdown after having sex with the story's professionally and sexually disgraced main character, David Lurie. If men as vets seem less and less likely saviors in animal and human worlds, then this parallel trajectory suggests that women do not simply take their place as animal professionals as much as they transform it by using veterinary science as contemporary fictional girl riders use visual media, that is, to mitigate suffering by managing pain.

Intersubjective representations may therefore prove less important than creative responses to (in lieu of retreats from) the traumatic representational and actual situations in which women are finding themselves working with animals. The more hopeful elements of these stories insist on a tremendous potential for social transformation through engagements with animals across artistic and scientific professions, growing (rather than opposing) amateurish and professional knowledges through visually narrating intersubjective relations in ways that inform such transformations in modern professional and public life. As the projected directions of veterinary medicine indicate, these alterations involve more equivocal changes to the intercorporeal intimacies that define humans through relations with animals. So it is to these matters of life and death—more specifically breeding and meat making—that the next chapters turn.

Part II

Intercorporeal Narratives

Chapter 3 **Breeding Narratives of Intimacy: Shaggy Dogs, Shagging Sheep**

WOULD HE OR WOULDN'T HE? The question hovered over comedian Drew Carey's first performance on the weekday program *The Price Is Right* in place of Bob Barker, a prominent animal activist who retired in 2007 as the longest-running daytime game-show host in North American television history. The answer came at the very end, when Carey turned to the camera and repeated (as he continues to do) Barker's closing mantra, "Help control the pet population. Have your pets spayed or neutered!"

This media moment highlights the capricious ties between the intersubjective ideals and embodied realities of cross-species companionship. In a country where millions of homeless cats and dogs are killed each year, squeamishness, especially about castrating male pets, might be said to necessitate extreme mandates, like the zero-tolerance sterilization policies promoted by Bob Barker and others.[1] Breeders so far offer the only organized resistance to these and other legislative efforts to enforce pet spay/neuter practice, and in the name of potential lost revenues. Drew Carey's decision is significant not simply as a political act but as a signal at the urban-crossroads of animal advocacy and urban–industrial pet-keeping cultures, where "taking responsibility for" has come to mean surgically sexually altering the animals with whom we choose to share our lives. What is not so clear is how this position follows from historic alterations to the terms of sympathetic identification and sexuality, and these in turn from the histories in which bodies come to be cut to conform to these ideals.

Few narratives of cross-species intersubjectivity address this topic at all, and even those tend to do so obliquely. In chapter 2, I could not elaborate on the implausible regrowth of the gelded Pie's testicles in *International Velvet* because in the text this act remains tacit, unspoken, just as in *National Velvet* the initial circumstances of his castration are presented as unrecoverable, matters of idle speculation. In narratives of cross-species intersubjectivity, more often it is cuts and not spontaneous regenerations that flag some serious disjunctures in ideas of love and sex, of biological and social forms, making it so that another kind of story must be crafted in order to address these restructurings of bodies in human–animal partnerships.

For such interventions never simply preserve pets' love for people at the expense of sex among animals, and to elaborate this point, this chapter considers how the pet-memoir genre arises amid profound changes to the veterinary science, biomedicine, and popular perceptions of sex and sexuality. A century ago, spay/neuter technologies were developed not as a manifestation of sentimental concern for companion animals, but rather as an afterthought to eugenic practices. J. V. Lacroix's *Animal Castration*, a handbook published by the American Journal of Veterinary Medicine in 1915, bluntly observes that meat animals are altered to improve the quality of livestock populations. "Dogs and cats" and other animals "kept for pets or companions," in contrast, "are castrated merely as a matter of domestic convenience."[2] Thus, animal gonadectomies initially were implemented in order to control populations in ways that primarily served human self-interests.

Arguably this remains the case, but (as Carey's decision makes clear) public perceptions of these procedures now are colored by concerns for animal welfare. Many locate the turning point in the 1970s, when the activist work of some veterinarians was galvanizing much broader support, especially for neutering programs. Through deliberate alignments of veterinary with human medical rhetorics of preventive care—not to mention the response of both to post-Pill feminists' pressure to locate responsibilities for reproduction beyond female bodies—neutering was recast alongside spaying as ethically responsible treatment especially for puppies and kittens. In the last quarter-century in the United States alone, "the spay and neuter crusade" seems the single biggest factor in the drop from more than 20 million to around 4 million animals killed annually in shelters, yet such obvious gains accompany the more dubious rise of an "underground dog railway" that follows the old journey of runaway slaves from the rural South, where shelters remain overrun, to affluent Northeast suburbs, where demands for adoptable dogs outstrip local supplies, by some estimates as much as 10 to 1.[3]

This history begs the broader questions: Are the ethics of companion-species relations ever fixed? Is spay/neuter (as animal activists once characterized the use of guide dogs) just another modern "practical convenience" for humans at the animals' expense? And one that, as Yi-Fu Tuan ominously contends, "makes it possible for [owners] to forget the insistent sexuality of all animals"?[4] Just now, the sudden interruption of my typing by a kitten whom tomorrow I take to the clinic to be spayed makes it all the more pressing for me to ask: Whose interests do these alterations serve?

Science and philosophy alike afford no easy answers. Just as human–animal working units are sealed in loving-pair bonds drawn from multispecies multiplicities, even at a conceptual level, populations defined by their "unwanted" affections haunt all cross-species commitments.[5] Attending to them in practice, veterinary studies conclude that such procedures do not definitively lengthen the lives of the wanted so much as they effectively reduce populations of unwanted cats and dogs.[6] At the root of these problems lies an underexamined dynamic of wanted and unwanted companionships not simply between human and animal individuals but, more pervasively, between species.

To get a handle on these problems, this chapter deliberately moves away from the language of subjectivity (i.e., sexual identity) by situating it amid an even more queer spectrum of interspecies intimacies. Among comparatively promiscuous animals like cats and dogs (and, for that matter, humans), in which pair bonding is not a typical characteristic, assertions of sexual agency necessarily involve far more messily organized intimacies than intersubjective couplings can bear. Consequently, the sentimentalizing of intersubjectivity across these particular species reflects and informs a distinctly "unnatural" pairing, that is, of the ideal of monogamous heteronormative couplings among humans with the surgical mutilations of companion animals, who (like so-called aberrant or degenerate humans) are thus demonized for their sexuality even as they are spared the ultimate punishment administered to their unwanted brethren.

My point is not to argue that spay/neuter practices are bad or good, or that they are to be equivocated with increasingly controversial practices like declawing, tail docking, and ear cropping.[7] Instead, I want to question public perceptions of companion-animal gonadectomies—whether as an alternative to killing, such as in the blunt "Desex Don't Kill" slogan, or, as in the controversial "Hooters for Neuters" campaign, as a means of reconstructing human masculinity while helping animals along the way[8]—by situating them amid cultural problems that cutting reproductive organs out of bodies cannot solve. These practices may prevent pregnancies, but in so doing they also cut off aesthetic considerations of intimacy that might lead to an entirely different ethics of intercorporeal relations.

The more basic considerations of desire and the social get under way not in policy debates or animal science research but rather in a more speculative tradition that explores human and animal companionship through documents

Placard promoting spaying and neutering as the ethical solution to the problem of unwanted animals, displayed by the World League for the Protection of Animals at the Minding Animals Conference in Newcastle, Australia, 2009. Photo by the author.

of pet keeping. The few that I bring together here are distinctively crafted to expose the mechanisms by which gonadectomies or desexing surgeries become perceived as normative solutions for overpopulating pets (and, yes, some people) in modern industrial cultures. But, no less effectively, they also record how narratives of animal domestication change in ways that challenge a more widespread regulation of sex through identity forms.

Again, the rarity of such representations—rather, the profound absence of this theme from popular representations of companion species—may be the most remarkable aspect of their literary and cultural history. But this is not to say that animals are unequivocally desexed in the popular imaginary. As animal film historians and others have shown, sexy beasts have become a mainstay of wildlife documentaries, and they do so exclusively through depictions of heterosexual (or at least what are made to appear to be male–female) couplings.[9]

What requires further attention are the ways in which such texts create, even as they associate, wild-animal stories with natural/normate/healthy sexuality, and, more precisely, against a growing sense of domesticated animal representations (and, indeed, human–animal lives together) as queer. Cast amid a culture that demonizes all representations of sex, the appeal of the spay/neuter crusade appears all the more ominous. Material manifestations of the fantasy of pets as having none of their own needs, genitalia now are being digitally erased (comparable to the blurring of "the bits" from nude human images) in network television depictions of dogs and, even more bizarrely, ads for Royal Lipizzaner Stallion performances. Such examples of prudishness regarding animals appear so absurd as to be laughable, except that they also show how the modern linkages of wild-animal and heterosexual human sex edge out queer configurations of domestic relations within and across species.

Like the enclosure of livestock breeding from public view, more is at stake in these limitations of the bestial imaginary than protecting innocence.[10] Reformed in the androgynous fantasy bodies of inanimate stuffed toys or talking cartoon characters, the creatures who provide us with the most obvious points of social comparison, that is, the domesticates who categorically are shaped by and shaping sexual interventions across species and millennia, are rendered incapable of engaging in the very relations that have defined our histories as shared and ongoing. In such presentations, significant otherness—in Haraway's playful sense, fusing the current politically correct term for coupled people with a recognition of the differences as important considerations in all contacts between unlike bodies, human and otherwise—becomes occluded, with consequences for personal and political perceptions of bodily intimacies.

Posthumanistic perspectives again suggest overarching questions: What is "the threshold of sexual difference[s]?" And what exactly does it have to do with the thresholds of species differences?[11] In this chapter, I will suggest some provisional answers to this line of inquiry by elaborating how perceptions of sex and sexuality proliferate across the last century regarding humans and other animals. But my inconclusiveness reflects a more primary task, namely, to follow the queer history of people's life writing about intercorporeal relations as they arise in cross-species companionships.

A genre that emerged in the twentieth century and that consistently has been represented in best-seller lists ever since, the pet memoir possibly booms today for the simple reason that people generally outlive their pets. This kind of story outlines ways of dealing with death in the modern world, which in turn is increasingly defined by distances, especially from human corpses.[12] But the origins of this narrative form reveal concerns as much about sex as death in lives shared between pets and people, offering insight into the ways in which by the twenty-first century, animals become provocateurs of more complex articulations of sexual agency forms across the arts and sciences.

Poster advertisement for a performance of The "World Famous"® Lipizzaner Stallions, from which the animals' defining "bits" have been digitally erased.

Moreover, the complex ways in which their narrative processes are linked to—and at times deliberately unlinked from—those of intersubjectivity clarify that pet memoirs negotiate a politics of intimate spheres that defies public/private division. A brief comparison of two recent fine-art examples intimates further this range of potentials in documenting how animals live with people, one leading more clearly toward the intersubjective narrative and another giving form to a story of intercorporeality. Indirect representations of the principal parties to these affairs are central, as are more direct inscriptions of the signs of intimacy, to both structures.

The book *Man's Best Friend* (1982)—artist William Wegman's photographic memoir of his last years of working with his pet Weimaraner named (after the other art photographer) "Man Ray"—includes an image in which stories of human and animal couplings collide amid the polymorphous perversity of pet keeping. Set up as a quintessentially modern couple, the two Weimaraner dogs named in the title, *Ray and Mrs. Lubner in Bed Watching TV* (1981), ostensibly satirize the conventions of "breeders," human and canine alike. A couple of live animals contrasted with taxidermied beasts in this boudoir image, the central figures come apart, however, through the stories of death, sex, and spectacle surrounding this photograph.

The inscription of *Man's Best Friend* clarifies that Man Ray died shortly before the book was published. Read amid the stories that Wegman and others tell of their twelve-year-long relationship, the image becomes part of a larger memorial to their innovative human–canine artistic partnership. From their early days together, the man's focus on his pet dog led to explorations of potentials for animal aesthetic agency in film and video, and, however indirectly, to the artist becoming a breeder of subsequent Weimaraner dog models (Man Ray was neutered as a pup).[13] Although Wegman himself is not included in any of the book's large-format Polaroids, signs of their special intimacy abound, even in *Ray and Mrs. Lubner in Bed Watching TV*.

Like so many of the photographs in Wegman's book, this image captures powerful emotions in the dog Man Ray's eyes, and here none of it is directed at the other dog. Instead, his gaze is trained away, presumably on another significant other, the human artist who is behind the camera. Displacing the physical attraction that might bring these would-be canine partners to bed is a poignant sense of human–animal intimacy as all too briefly shared. Against the critical tendency in art history to avoid the animal in such images—for instance, by reading him as an ego-projection for the artist—the neutered dog's story with the artist enters into this bedroom scene as a complicated tale of building an intersubjective companionship that is subsequently lost

William Wegman, *Ray and Mrs. Lubner in Bed Watching TV,* from the artist's photographic memoir of his canine collaborator Man Ray (*right*), *Man's Best Friend* (1981). Copyright William Wegman. Courtesy of the artist.

and mourned. While elsewhere I have argued that Wegman and his dog Man Ray's partnership is instructive for theories of animals' aesthetic agency, here the tensions of species and sex gesture toward an intercorporeal intimacy that commands another sort of engagement with representational forms.

Taking an entirely different approach to visually narrating the intimacies of pet keeping, the collaborative artists Snæbjörnsdóttir/Wilson's book *(a) fly (between nature and culture)* (2006) literally follows random shots through Reykjavik, Iceland, to document how animals live in human-built environments. For many reasons, Reykjavik provides a unique setting for this project, a city where, for instance, until 1984 dog keeping was illegal and still remains formally prohibited.[14] And the complex structuring of this project—which includes survey research, educational outreach, even the marksmanship of ptarmigan hunters, more than I can elaborate here—deliberately works against representing the total life history of any one creature or partnership. Instead, *(a) fly* presents a collective snapshot of many lives converging in the capital of a country experiencing rapid rural depopulation throughout the second half of the twentieth century.

There is much more to say about how Snæbjörnsdóttir/Wilson's visualization of human animality complicates the urban animals-are-disappearing problematic that (as I argued in the introduction) for many defines modernist aesthetics.[15] However, I focus here on just one image from the *dwellings* section titled *Gátta & Skotti*. It is not unique so much as exemplary of how their project directly and critically engages with the ways in which domesticates of different species not only meet some of one another's (intersubjective) needs but also necessarily live around one another's (intercorporeal) desires.

Gátta & Skotti is part of a series of interiors showing the home lives of owners and pets. Specifically, it is one of several photographs centered on the areas chosen by the pets as their own lairs within people's homes. The camera angles are meant to approximate the perspectives of the animals. As in all the images in this section, the absence of bodies is striking, for artists along with pets and pet keepers all are kept offscreen.

This sets the stage for a different story from Wegman's, one that is geared more to transform ordinary patterns of seeing, in their words, to get us "to imagine ourselves as animal without being sure necessarily *what* animal," a presence that then seems "altogether suddenly darker, more chthonian and ultimately and permanently just below the skin" (8). Surface contacts and concealments are central concerns of Snæbjörnsdóttir/Wilson's work elsewhere with taxidermized animals, notably in *nanoq: flat out and bluesome A Cultural Life of Polar Bears* (2006). Alive, always getting onto (and sometimes into) others in close contact, skin and other bodily surfaces here too prove pivotal as interfaces between the embodied lives of individuals. And in *Gátta & Skotti*, skin also contains clear limits.

Pets and people sleep in separate beds in the same room, so close, yet so far. The shed clothes, hair, and dander that have so obviously accumulated over time in this image betray not only the intersecting lives of animal and human

Gátta & Skotti, from *(a)fly* (2006). This image is taken from the section titled *dwellings*, which envisions the "nests" or "dens" that pets make in human homes from the animals' viewpoints as part of the project's broader examination of the human–animal interface within the urban environment of Reykjavik, Iceland. Copyright Snæbjörnsdóttir/Wilson. Courtesy of the artists.

individuals but also distinct pet and person ways of relating that take shape within that most intimate of dwellings, a shared bedroom. The image foregrounds the guarded human–animal intimacies of pet keeping, and in this respect it is important to note too that not all of Snæbjörnsdóttir/Wilson's *dwellings* images are like this. Many more pets' beds, or nests, or dens (they're not sure about what to call them, either) appear in out-of-the-way spaces like closets, along with in-the-way places like living rooms, demonstrating the tolerance, even generosity, with which companion animals make room around the rhythms of human life. Focusing for a moment on the bedroom scene, however, indicates how the different agents populating stereotypically human scenes of sexual intimacy complicate notions of agency in the lives of companion species.

Putting Wegman's canine bedroom scene in conversation with *Gátta & Skotti* indicates a range of ways in which intersubjective and intercorporeal forms enter into the task of documenting—and before that looking at—

animals amid the illusory lives of individuals.[16] Although conspicuously absent figures of course remain open to symbolic and anthropomorphic interpretation, the images' central relationships—again, the intensities that Deleuze and Guattari locate "between the two"—proceed from embodied intimacies, notably triangulations that cast whatever pairings may or may not occur into the irreducibly social spaces of sexuality. Historically, it matters that these artistic renderings also incorporate fragments of lives shared by pets and people, and that in this respect they join in the literary lines of inquiry taken up in the earliest pet memoirs. For, amid the de/sexing regulative norms that increasingly define human–animal cohabitation, these everyday struggles of narrative and visualization are necessary, and necessarily ongoing, in order to foster any meaningful dialogues about (let alone deliberation of) sex across species.

On the more limited documentary history of bestiality, Wendy Doniger remarks that animals "share our sexuality, but not our stories of sexuality."[17] To show how this formal problem plagues science (no less than literature), and becomes tremendously compounded when intact bodies appear lusty and especially frustrated, in the next section I outline a minor literary tradition of queer animal biography. Often inextricable from gay, lesbian, bisexual, and transgender autobiographies, the pathways of this tradition illuminate the complexity of cultural conditions in which cutting pieces out of our loved ones, whether pets or intersexed humans, becomes the normative solution to the problems of variation that cut most deeply across culture and biology, notably today the dead-ended debates that pit (human) identities against (animal) behaviors in the so-called gay-sheep science controversies, with which this chapter concludes. And it is not in a bestial or other pair bond so much as in triangulations of humans, pets, and their same-species sex partners— emerging perhaps most obviously in the narratives of British writer and editor J. R. Ackerley—that these stories effectively sustain intercorporeal forms of social and sexual agency.

Queer life writing from the early twentieth century onward provides an intriguing record of people and pets involved in struggles with intimacy. Although less bluntly than narratives of human–animal bestiality (or stories that feature sex acts performed with members of other species), they likewise illustrate how the emerging tolerance of homophilic desire complements a rigidifying persecution of bestial desire in the cultures of urban industrialization.[18] Through comparatively tame descriptions of pets pursuing intimacies with their own kind against human attempts at intervention, this tradition effectively launches explicit critiques of breeding intimacies, broadly writ, that include but are never limited to professionally administered gonadectomies and matings.

(De)Sex? The Pet Memoir

"It has come to my ears that *haiku* poets have taken to using the phrase 'cat's love' as a means of indicating that a poem is concerned with the season of spring," notes the feline narrator of quintessential Japanese modern novelist Soseki Natsume's (the pseudonym of Kinnosuke Natsume) satire *Wagahai wa Neko de Aru [I am a cat]*, published in installments between 1905 and 1907.[19] Relentless here, as ever, in his derision of human artistic endeavors, the cat nonetheless concedes the material basis of the metaphor. He explains that, though he himself abstains, so many more of his brethren engage in this kind of "caterwauling" on spring nights in Tokyo neighborhoods "that sleep is well-nigh impossible."[20] Like so many more details, this fleeting narrative moment pinpoints a lost world as it transitioned into modernity, here Japan in the rapidly changing Meiji era of renewed Western contact, in which animal rites join with other expressions of desire to shape lives shared in urban spaces. Across cultures, other modern animal narratives reflect in greater detail how these conditions change for animal along with human sexuality in the early decades of the twentieth century.

Although often self-indulgently styled as mourning a beloved pet, some of the earliest examples now seem bizarrely explicit in their sublimated expressions of human sexual desires. Alice Kuzniar's discussion of the poems in *Whym Chow: Flame of Love* (1914) clarifies how the focus on the dead dog sublimates the queer passion shared by the authors writing together under the pen name Michael Field, who were aunt and niece to each other as well as a long-term lesbian couple. And it is hard to miss in another memorial to a chow dog, Marie Bonaparte's 1937 memoir *Topsy, Chow-Chow au Poil d'Or* (published in English in 1945 as *Topsy: The Story of a Golden-Haired Chow*), in which the author rejects as unmanned her once-beloved dog when he can no longer function sexually following cancer treatments. Against these, however, other pet memoirs like Carl van Vechten's *Feathers* (1930)—which offers a sort of backstory to his popular cross-cultural compendium of cat references titled *The Tiger in the House* (1921), and was published alongside a reprint of his edited collection *Lords of the Housetops: Thirteen Cat Tales* (1921)[21]— stand out for fostering critical perspectives on animal (and by implication human) sex as not only limited but also surprisingly complicated by the urban–industrial conditions of pet keeping.

This short narrative, intended in part as a warning against the temptation to seek a breeder's help in attempting to immortalize a beloved animal, describes how he inadvertently killed Feathers, the cat he loved best of all, by sending her "in the middle of the very hot summer of 1920, very stupidly," from Manhattan to Long Island to be bred at a facility where previously she had fought off the tom into whose basket she had been "dumped."[22] As narrator, van Vechten mentions here that he is married, but not that he is actively bisexual, an omission that seems to inform his persistence in sending Feathers to the breeder in spite of the cat's obvious resistance. Long after Feathers's death, this story is presented not so much as a confession of guilt as a testimony of love and loss. But other potentials creep in through its details.

Of the other cats described as inhabiting van Vechten's building at that time, he provides the most detailed depiction of the janitor's Tom, a former stray who regularly paid visits to other apartments, and, on such occasions, "preferred using the elevator to walking and would call out his floor in no uncertain terms" (6). This example seems frozen in time for so many reasons: no one stops the roving cat—indeed he seems rather to have conditioned the machine operators to do his bidding—and moreover, his claim on this modern means of pursuing company makes him all the more a character in the building community. Particularly because Tom is described as growing "languid and dandified," even "somewhat arrogant" in his newfound urban high life, his riding around among other sexually active cats (like the author's own dear Feathers) invites contrast with the failed fiction-writer-turned-gigolo at the center of van Vechten's best-selling fiction *Nigger Heaven* (1926), all the more so because the urban–industrial conditioning of Tom's promiscuity is presented as funny, not as a sign of social decay (ibid.). More important, this earlier novel's indictment of the failure to recognize how the problems with primitivist fantasies of sex extend beyond human racial terms and into all self/other ways of thinking about difference directly resonates with the central tragedy of *Feathers*.

And the effective removal of the object of bestial affection from the home of the then newly divorced and quickly remarried author in this strange little memoir resonates with that of another queer cat narrative of the period. The celebrated bisexual writer [Sidonie Gabrielle] Colette's contemporaneous divorce story *The Cat* (1933) features a volatile household triangle, in which a young modern bride fights the cat nearly to death for her husband's affection, losing on all fronts. Colette's titular feline, suddenly confined in a high-rise apartment with the newly married couple, pines for her freedom to roam the neighborhoods of her master's batchelorhood, to which cat and man together return following the human couple's divorce. Like *Feathers*, the limits of love

CARL VAN VECHTEN AND HIS TORTOISE-SHELL AND WHITE SMOKE TABBY PERSIAN QUEEN, FEATHERS
From a photograph by Harriet V. Furness

Frontispiece of *The Tiger in the House* (1936), captioned "Carl van Vechten and his tortoise-shell and white smoke tabby Persian queen, Feathers." Original photo by Harriet V. Furness reposited in the Beinecke Rare Book and Manuscript Library, Yale University. Reprinted by permission of the Carl van Vechten Trust.

in human heteronormative coupling are the focus of this story. And again a cat's wanderlust asserts social as sexual free agency all the more sympathetically in contrast to the multilayered complicity with the normative breeding systems that leads to *The Cat*'s temporary entrapment and Feathers's untimely demise. Through these explicit narratives of sex and pet keeping, modern living emerges as deeply ambiguous for the social lives of animals, and their repercussions for people become even more pronounced in the explicitly gay and lesbian pet memoirs of the next generation.

With the automobile becoming the greatest threat to urban free-ranging pets' lives, the wanderings of pet cats no longer seem their entitlement. Concomitantly, affection is conceived of as not prevented (among animals) so much as aided (between pets and people) by veterinary surgery, in pet-keeping narratives and practices alike, sealing the homebound fate of such creatures. But the deliberative presentation of neutering and spaying that emerges through postwar queer life writing indicates an acute dis-ease with instituting sterilization as a social solution.

A quarter-century after *Feathers* and *The Cat,* May Sarton's memoir *The Fur Person* (1957)—presented in part as a sort of back story to the cat who temporarily lived with Vladimir Nabokov while the latter wrote *Lolita* (1955)—takes the perspective of the cat to problematize ideas about neutering as fixing the fraught lives of animals and the humans attached to them. Concerned about their adoptive stray Tom's pugnacious struggles with neighboring toms, Brusque Voice (presumably Sarton herself) and her girlfriend, Gentle Voice, carefully deliberate whether it would be kinder to castrate him or let him be torn apart in his nightly brawls. In contrast, this onetime "Cat-About-Town," by this point seeing himself as a "Gentleman Cat," is presented as having no sense of what he will be made to sacrifice in order to "evolve" further into a "Fur Person."[23]

The limitations of the cat's viewpoint underscore the difficulty for people weighing and ultimately choosing their pet's sufferings: "It never occurred to [Tom] that what they were contemplating was to change his personality, . . .

Snapshot of the cat Tom Jones (a.k.a. *The Fur Person*) and human "friend" Judith Matlock ("Gentle Voice"), included in an Xmas greeting sent by May Sarton in 1956. Courtesy of the May Sarton Collection, Maine Women Writers Collection, University of New England, Portland, Maine.

to change *him*, in fact, into a believer in non-violence, a Quaker cat. . . . This was the meaning of the word 'altered,' which, with the word 'hospital,' haunted their conversation. And [he] knew these must be dangerous words because they always looked at him so commiseratingly when they used them, and gave him extra pieces of roast beef, as if they had told him a lie and were feeling rather guilty about it."[24] Ostensibly, this narrative ends happily ever after (it is, after all, meant to be read to children) with the castrated Tom thinking of himself as having "given up part of his cat self into human keeping," that is, to the couple committed to a Boston marriage, whose decision to neuter him spells the end of his desire to fight with other cats (104). Riddled with ironies for adult readers, the narrative thus tempers its own conclusion with the idea that this form of feline domestic bliss incurs tremendous human responsibilities in lockstep with unwitting feline sacrifices.

A modern author perhaps best known as the long-lived writer of old age, Sarton significantly presents neutering in this early memoir as marking the end of the formerly fierce fighting Tom's sporting career, after which the cat retires to a quiet, gentlemanly (rather, fur-person-able) life with the lesbian couple. Along with his feline circle of acquaintance, his capacity to share in people's lives arguably becomes diminished. Becoming a confirmed homebody, he no longer seems capable of inspiring "the prowling cat" who fatefully disrupts Nabokov's Humbert Humbert from his first chance at consummating his love for a young girl, a frustration that sets him on the fateful course to loving Lolita.[25] Yet, by exploiting the gaps between species perspectives, Sarton's narrative likewise develops the conflicts within ideals of sex and respectability structuring concepts of domestic life. Quite apart from the extensions of this theme through scenes of mass slaughter of unwanted pets that come to characterize later narratives—including the bloody cat massacre at the opening of Doris Lessing's memoir *Particularly Cats* (1967) and more recently the incineration of unwanted dogs' corpses concluding Coetzee's *Disgrace*—Sarton's *Fur Person* intimates how alternatives grow through triangulations in more personal writing.

A contemporary of Sarton, J. R. Ackerely wrote queer memoirs that to varying degrees focus on the relations of men and dogs, and in so doing come to exemplify how writers' reflections on their responsibilities toward their pets' sex lives lead to sympathetic engagements that transform stories across species. Ackerley's stories present this problem of pets' sex lives through a more explicit sense of queer camaraderie, in the process opening up still more complicated questions of culture, particularly of when and how sex acts among all sorts of social animals contribute to alternate formations of public spheres, which only gain in relevance today at the bleeding edges of queer and animal theories. Few writers capture the frustrations shared by people and dogs in modern urban settings with humor and sympathy like Ackerley, yet these aspects also suggest why half a century after their publication his narratives provoke such mixed responses, particularly with respect to human–animal affect. Less clearly developed in literary discussions of his work are the ways in which his attention to form in interlacing stories of sex, men, and dogs across his narrative writing contributes to both his past canonical marginality and emerging centrality through diverse developments, including queer critiques of modernism and popular dog writing.

Born the year after Oscar Wilde became the first public figure convicted of having committed sexual acts of "gross indecency" under the Labouchere Amendment, and dead seven weeks before parliament passed the Sexual Offenses Act decriminalizing sex between consenting male adults, Ackerley positioned himself as a homosexual writer during the most virulent period of sexual persecution and prosecution in England.[26] Illicit sex between men is a common thread through Ackerley's writing, and the strain, anxiety, and wariness characterizing these precarious intimacies, which he aligns with those of dogs in suffering from strangely modern forms of prurience, often says more about their larger cultural and historical contexts than about the "friendly hand" recording them.[27] Yet Ackerley persists as one of the wilier fairy godfathers of literary history because his campy, scatologically funny, and popular narratives consistently test all sorts of limits, most significantly formal ones.

Although his narratives are told from strictly human perspectives, like Sarton's *Fur Person* they frame more questions than answers about the urban-industrial conditioning of human along with animal sex problems. With disarming candor, Ackerley's stories of sodomite intimacies confront not just identity forms but also disciplinary habits of thinking of human subjectivity as the default form of social agency, an underdeveloped angle of Foucault's infamous claim that "the homosexual" first emerged as "a species."[28] In particular, the late narratives for which Ackerley is most remembered—the memoirs *My Dog Tulip* (1956) and *My Father and Myself* (1968) and the novel *We Think the World of You* (1960)—transgress multiple boundaries in depictions of man-loving men with canine bitches, united in their sexual frustrations. Around these pairings, these stories incorporate still more people and animals in ways that ultimately deprivatize the modern sensibility of the gay man's sexual anguish: aligned as companion species, troubled individuals come together as outlaws in integrative structures, unleashing desires that otherwise seem doomed in cold cultural climates.

In England at midcentury (where and when the stories are set), laws out-lawing human anal sex augmented a distinctively modern and urban prud-ishness concerning animal sex in public, what Ackerley complains about in terms of a "human conspiracy" against sexually active dogs.[29] And these strangely shared circumstances foster greater appreciation of all sorts of "sexual trouble."[30] Ackerley persistently weaves a mature version of the boy-and-his-dog tale—"a fairy story for adults," as he termed his novel[31]—that transforms this special zone of cross-species intimacy popularly distorted as unconditional "dog love" into a powerful means of countering the pervasive puritan mind-set that leads today to the more radical erasures of domesti-cated animal sex and genitalia, along with a whole range of intimacies shared across species.

Reading these narratives in reverse order of publication, I will outline a pattern in which Ackerley couples man love and dog love to exploit the slip-page between sodomy and sodomite, between defining homosexual identity and claiming social space beyond identity forms.[32] These stories of intimacies give rise not only to a sense of canine agency as constitutively different from that of the human individual but also to a cross-species notion of sodomite culture, founded on aesthetics of multiplicity rather than individuality. Chron-ologically, they may start with the gay man's fascination with "marrying" his bitch to a suitable dog-mate, but ultimately they work together self-consciously to tweak the attitudes reflected in such euphemisms for canine sex. Frustrated bitches are not simply symbolic manifestations of what literary critics take to be Ackerley's own "conflicted response to the construction of identity through sexuality."[33] Together these texts walk the dog along a thin line between re-cording gay male sexual frustration and validating all sorts of desires in for-bidding circumstances, ultimately positioning human–animal intimacy as a means of transport from liminality in a sexually repressive heterosexual cul-ture to centrality in promiscuously evolving sodomite cultures.[34]

Again, these are not salacious stories of bestiality; men and dogs do not have intercourse (or penetrative sex) together in these texts. Instead, in terms of what Michael Warner has called heteronormative culture, their treatment of sodomy highlights how heterosexuality's juridical, economic, and aesthetic structures extend beyond sex acts and, in this case, into nonhuman animal bodies and behaviors. Through their deliberately narrated reconceptualiza-tion of cross-species agency in dog breeding and gay male sex, these stories develop a structure that provokes further considerations of how human and canine intimacies define public spaces as well as identities. And together they loft a notion of sodomite culture that I formulate along the lines of what

Warner and Lauren Berlant together term a "queer counterpublic," that is, queer culture conceived as a subordinate (and explicitly not separate) sphere founded on "nonstandard intimacies."[35] Not quite partners in crime, Ackerley more specifically imagines the gay man and his pet bitch as queer comrades, whose stories converge in ways that ultimately depersonalize the overwhelming sense of failure to couple and otherwise measure up to heteronormative standards.

Moreover, Ackerley's triangulation of gay men, bitches, and their preferred mongrel (here meaning alternately human bisexual or canine mixed-breed) significant others provokes a reconceptualization of sexual agency as mediated through cross-species relationships that I designate "pack sexualities," a term that flags the context in which intersubjective become superseded by intercorporeal significances. Accounting for the participation of many agents in the production of identity forms in what they term "becomings-animal," Deleuze and Guattari use the figure of the wolf pack to extend Deleuze's earlier notion of "radical multiplicity" (in the Bergsonian sense, collapsing the one and the multiple) as a shifting, volatile alternative to the psychoanalytic compression of agency into the binary and hierarchic model of "self" as mirror opposite of an equally singular "other."[36] Elaborating the ways in which narrative enters these processes in the queer pet memoir, pack sexualities likewise provide a mechanism not simply for contrasting but more directly undoing these deadlocked pairings by incorporating a third agent, another body that not only witnesses sex acts but also helps to construct their significance in relation to packs that traverse deeply mixed communities and contexts. Ackerley's development of several bitches through these texts—respectively, named Tulip, Evie, and Queenie—and his continued resistance to the interpretive reduction of the individual bitch to a metaphorical or other representation of a "real" individual or historical animal are but a few indicators of the importance of animal multiplicity as a structuring device, one that (as again Deleuze and Guattari insist) profoundly disrupts the hierarchic dualisms of symbolic and egotistical representation.

In these texts, a mongrel, by playing the transitional role that triangulates a gay man's relationship with his bitch, both immediately destabilizes couplings and more generally promises to queer the autobiographical narrative, collapsing its animal margins on its all-too-human center. More than just a synecdochical human/canine figure denoting successful evasions of familial identity forms (proscribed by "the metaphorical father," who invokes the Law of the Symbolic), the mongrel grounds entirely different, affiliative relational structures in these texts particularly when dallying with "the metonymical mother."[37] He muddies distinctions of sexuality and pedigree alike, occupying (and thereby betraying) the spaces between identities and publics. An invariably male image of the social limits of hybridity, Ackerley's mongrel "hyphen" both enables and suspends interspecific (or cross-species) sodomite identity in these narratives.[38] And whether human or canine, he shares only fleeting sexual engagements with the gay man or his bitch.

In the end, he is always a rover. Observing each other's couplings with their respective mongrel partners, man and bitch remain together with each other, long after the mongrel's inevitably permanent departure. That is, the persistence of the cross-species relationship complements the elusive intra-specific sexual moment, and in other ways also disrupts the heteronormative privatization of sex between the two. Through this triangulated or pack structure, an image of a sodomite counterpublic, centered not on identities related to sex acts so much as on sodomite situated knowledges, begins to take shape across these texts.[39] The queer life narrative that caps Ackerley's career (and for which he is best known as a gay icon) illustrates best how dogs anchor these and other frameworks within which authors and artists use representations of sodomy to interrogate the biopolitical problems with identity.

Phantom Triangle: My Father, Myself, and My Bitch

Midway through his last memoir, *My Father and Myself,* Ackerley abruptly remarks that his Alsatian (or German shepherd) bitch Queenie, "about whom I have written two books, has no place in this one."[40] Openly defying critics who claimed that he "could not create imaginary characters and situations," in this passage Ackerley characterizes *My Dog Tulip* and *We Think the World of You* not as two volumes in his own autobiography (or in the biography of his dog) but as "books" that are "about" his bitch.[41] This terse claim begins to explain not only why he keeps the pet on a short leash, so to speak, in his family-focused history of queer England but also why he took nearly half a century to write it.

My Father and Myself is fueled by the allure for the son of the posthumous revelation of some of his father Roger's "undisclosed and ultimately irretrievable" sexual secrets, which "threw" the younger Ackerley's "own awareness of male sexuality into disarray."[42] In part to present this internal conflict more vividly and immediately to his readers, Ackerley holds Queenie in check through this narrative, disabling the bitchy vehicle through which his other narrators resolve conflicts between sexual identities and acts. And, against the momentary protest of the author, canine companionship proves important to this story, too.

While Queenie is overtly marginalized, several other dogs creep through this text, encroaching on privatized identities in ways that clarify the tenuous relationship between sodomite counterpublics and queer family histories. An anonymous "shaggy dog," who "eavesdrop[s]" on the bisexual "secrets" that were only partly revealed to Ackerley after his father's death, is the focus of one of the text's few photographs.[43] Sitting on a lion-skin rug next to the young Roger, the shaggy dog in this scene is being fondled by the man who for no documented reason bought Roger's freedom from service as a guardsman twenty years before his son was born. Lamenting his inability to learn the exact terms of the men's relationship, the curious son casts the animal in the position that he comes to covet, that of being near enough to learn whether the patron "picked [Roger] up, as I had picked guardsmen up" for sex.[44] The dog at least could see whether the father had been the sort of prostitute with whom Ackerley, sympathetically characterized by his acquaintance W. H. Auden as a "compulsive cruiser," spent most of his time and money as a young man.[45]

Ackerley casts the shaggy dog as a crucial component of this lost world, yet he carefully stops short of claiming that he actually knew anything about the human relationships structuring this scene. Whereas in the photograph the dog augments the landscape as part of the furnishings, in the narrative the dog takes the bitch's place in marking the distance between Ackerley's father's likely sexual relationship with the older man and the son's biographical attempt to extrapolate from these circumstances a means of identifying with him, in his words, "to drag [Roger] captive into the homosexual fold."[46] Unlike, say, the animal whose pelt provides the rug on which they are sitting, the shaggy dog marks an elusive entry point into the not-yet outlaw homosexual world of which Ackerley wishes his father to be part, an oppositional limit to Ackerley's knowledge of his father's sexual relationships with men. The long-gone canine thus enacts a transference in this story from the son's idle fascination with reconstructing his father's sexual identity to the writer's work in imaging forth their shared involvements in a queer counterpublic, a point to which I shall return later.

If the shaggy dog's presence signals an opportunity lost, so too do the leavings of his kind. Ackerley's account of a typical missed opportunity for direct and "interesting talk" with his father focuses on a random "dog's large turd, . . . which lay in the middle of the path in front of us," one afternoon in the Bois du Boulogne. Chatting about "[w]hich of the people passing along would be the first to tread on it," father and son together skip this chance for frank discussion and instead fill their conversations here, as ever, with "trivialities"

(109). Composing this narrative later in life, Ackerley materializes in dog shit the outcome of the profound contradiction between his youthful comfort with his own sexuality—"By the time I reached, with my father, the dog's turd in the Bois du Boulogne I was well into my predatory stride"—and his disinclination then to imagine his father as sexually, let alone homosexually, active (123). It might be fair to say that this random dog's bowel movement concretizes what the father's and other mongrels' movements leave behind for the son piecing together a queer family history.

Especially when the younger Ackerley comes to reflect on the special intimacy that Ginger (the nonbreed family pet of his own boyhood) and Roger share, he lays the canine foundation for the father's transformation from suspected sexual outlaw to confoundedly queer progenitor. This dog alone accompanied Roger on frequent trips out of the family house, which Ackerley later learned were visits to Roger's "secret orchard" or his surreptitiously kept second family. Again the dog, unlike the narrator, is privy to the comings and goings of the principals, but not exactly a witness to the affair. Ackerley's precise phrasing emphasizes the difference for the dog in this queer scene: Ginger, "since he was *our* dog, was also therefore another conspirator in my father's affairs, had he but known it" (161). In this complicated situation, the problems of claiming ownership of Ginger mirror those of owning Roger as a father, and their constant companionship in traveling to the secret orchard make them collaborators in transgressing domestic boundaries. In the larger story of Ackerley's irreducibly queer and animal narratives, Ginger points the direction for the son (and presumably his readers) away from alienation from Roger's unrecoverable sexuality and toward a new appreciation for lives shared in queer counterpublics.

Whereas the male mutt becomes tied to the straying father in this story, a breed bitch arrives at the end to help the son extrapolate this overarching aspect of this narrative from its queer sum of sexual acts. The nameless bitch, who "has no place" in this narrative, nonetheless joins the narrator in these last few pages to create a happy ending of sorts, in which Ackerley explains that the fifteen years with her, all the while struggling to write this book, were "the happiest of my life" (217). Her anonymous appearance, otherwise brief and puzzling to readers unaware of his other work, introduces the catalyst for the narrative conversion of the father from the queer progenitor–center to its mongrel "negative identity," that is, the marker of the space in between individuals and collectives that resists analogy, and insists instead that contradictions have still more formal functions.[47]

Concluding this genealogy with an appendix largely devoted to detailing his own sexual dysfunctions (premature ejaculation and, later, impotence), Ackerley makes surprisingly overt connections between his sense of his waning sexual activity with men and growing absorption with his bitch: "In this context it is not she herself but her effect upon me that I find interesting. . . . From the moment she established herself in my heart and home, my obsession with sex fell wholly away from me. . . . I never prowled the London streets again nor had the slightest inclination to do so. . . . It was as though I had never wanted sex at all, and that this extraordinary long journey of mine which had seemed a pursuit of it had really been an attempt to escape from it."[48] While this passage anticipates only to dismiss questions of a bestial sodomite relationship between the two, it also ventures a more startling insight into the operations of the gay man and his bitch's relationships with mongrels and, more broadly, the triangulated terms through which Ackerley's narratives flesh out pack sexualities. Assuming his readers' familiarity with his previous books and assuring them that he enjoyed sex more fully if less often when his bitch joined his life, Ackerley's appendix wraps up both this volume's search for hereditary sodomite identity in heteronormative culture (which ends with the failure of unrecoverable history) and his far more successful three-volume narrative envisioning of sodomite counterpublics.

This vision grows from Ackerley's equally intimate treatment of the problems of translating sexual action to the terms of agency developed in his two previous books, the novel *We Think the World of You* and the memoir *My Dog Tulip*, the latter embraced almost exclusively by fans of dog writing. Read together in this way, Ackerley's narratives confound a critical tradition that assumes that his canine bitches are foils for his narrators' manly love interests.[49] Sympathetically aligned in their doomed passions for mongrels, man and dog together leverage a shift from narrating the sense of self as a sexual failure and narratively structuring alternatives in triangulated cross-species agency forms. Especially in Ackerley's only novel, elaborations of the social milieu of sexual frustration grow from (rather than emerge from behind the screen of) the gay man's involvement with his bitch's sexual activity, clarifying how the pack structure of sexuality introduced in the still earlier dog memoir, *My Dog Tulip*, influences this understanding as bound up with human along with animal sexuality.

Pink Triangle: Myself, My Mongrel, and His Bitch

We Think the World of You offers a singular glimpse of the immediate circumstances that lead a reluctant gay man to share his life with a bitch, and consequently change his ideas about sex and sociality. In this novel, Ackerley's narrator, a white-collar gay man named Frank, gets over a frustrated love affair with his married working-class boyfriend Johnny by taking over Johnny's dog, an abused and subsequently grateful bitch, who is aptly named Evie.[50] As the novel opens, Frank's frustrations with his on-again, off-again relationship become compounded when Johnny is jailed for robbery. With Johnny's imprisonment, Frank's communications with him become dependent on the cooperation of Johnny's family, particularly Johnny's pregnant wife Megan.

Frank's hatred of Megan erupts throughout the story, evinced in his references to her as "that disgusting woman," "that tart," even "the treacherous little Welsh runt."[51] If this pattern of invective outlines at one level the limits to the reader's sympathy for Frank—after all, he is xenophobic, male chauvinistic, even arguably homosexist—then it makes all the more surprising the emergence of this negative identity as the means by which Frank comes to gain respect for Megan while moving beyond infatuation with Johnny. More precisely, once the bitch moves in with Frank, he begins to recognize parallels between Megan and Evie and learns to read all of their relationships differently, opening up new narrative trajectories for himself as well as others.

Textual identification of women with animals generally impedes more often than it elicits sympathy for either, and the problematic terms clouding Ackerley's use of this narrative device sharply limit the degree to which these and other triangulations can be exported to serve different ends. However, the canine terms on which Frank overcomes this tendency also trouble its putative roots in perceived rivalries between the homosexual boys and the heterosexual girls over the bisexual roving mongrel Johnny.[52] For this novel interlaces Frank's progressive disillusionment with Johnny, his limited development of compassion for Megan, and his growing passion for Evie, such that increasing involvement with the dog marks a clear break between his frustration with polarized sexual identities and his understanding of the broader failings of heteronormative culture.

Reading the novel in terms of productive triangulations rather than failed couplings foregrounds the ways in which Megan's change in Frank's estimation from a romantic rival to a model heroine derives from his increasing involvement with Evie, more specifically from observing the beloved Evie acting exactly like the despised Megan. Frustrating the rivalry model through which some literary critics read the novel as working strictly within a "rigid and conceptually restrictive hetero/homo binary," Evie is presented as making a difference not just in Frank's daily life but also in his conceptualization of the relational structures of agency.[53]

A still image from director Colin Gregg's 1988 film version clarifies the complex, shifting intimacies that structure the narrative and extend far beyond sexual partnerships. Frank (Alan Bates) stands along with Evie next to Johnny (Gary Oldman)'s stepfather and mother, his baby, and (physically closest to Johnny) his wife. Although Frank and Johnny's mother frequently commiserate that Johnny uses them to look after his loved ones (the one as dogsitter and the other as babysitter), this image underscores how mongrel and bitch remain at the margins of Johnny's extended family, a pattern of nonstandard intimacies that can only be broken by more intense and deliberate alignments of desire.

An integral part of Frank's reevaluation and abandonment of his interests in Johnny, the parallel positioning of Evie and Megan enables Frank to abandon his own doomed dependence on sexual couplings with Johnny. In this light, Frank comes to see Johnny instead as a mongrel, a temporary traveler across lives that are in the end happily shared between Frank and his bitch. Much as Frank may wish to define this sphere as separate, these narrative operations open up this space as integrally (if subordinately) linked to the heteronormative turf that Megan so passionately defends, that is, grounding a queer counterpublic.

Publicity still of the cast of the 1988 film version of *We Think the World of You,* featuring Frank (Alan Bates, *right*) standing with Evie and his boyfriend Johnny's (Gary Oldman, *left*) extended family.

While this interpretation might seem historically anachronistic, textual as well as contextualizing evidence supports it. Ackerley's awareness of how these shifting queer and animal alignments contribute to a broader critique of identity conceived strictly in psychoanalytic terms emerges, for instance, in a summary of the novel that he included in a letter to his publisher: "Homosexuality and bestiality mixed, and largely recorded in dialogue: the figure of Freud suspended gleefully above."[54] And what would inspire this gleeful Freudian suspense? As this description indicates, the narrative promiscuously knots together hetero with homo and bestial affective ties. And the form of dialogue emphasizes the importance of these mixed and shifting social worlds from the very start.

In his opening conversation with Johnny, Frank immediately confuses Evie with Megan, foreshadowing how the novel aligns Evie and Megan as parallel "breeders" as well as how Frank will be slow to catch on to the implications of this arrangement. Johnny's championing of Megan against Frank's typical hostility leads Frank to the mistaken conclusion that Johnny returned to his wife because he loves her best:

> "I think the world of 'er," muttered Johnny.
>   "Yes," I said acidly. "I noticed you changed your mind."
>   "No, Evie," said he, "Anyway, Megan don't want 'er."
>   "Nor do I, Johnny."
>   He gnawed at his nails.
>   "I don't know what to do for the best." After a moment he added, "She's expectin'."
>   "But I thought she was only a puppy?"
>   "No, Megan."[55]

While the mixed-up pronoun referents work to lighten the ponderous image of Johnny's poverty and imprisonment as it rapidly unfolds, the confusion both relies on and reinforces a direct correspondence between the wife's and dog's similar (and explicitly not mutual) dependence on Johnny through their gendered reproductive capacities. Either one could be the "'er" of whom Johnny thinks the world, and either one could be pregnant. Both will suffer because he is in jail, only in ways that secure the fate of each with a different man.

The emphasis that this conversation puts on their shared potential both to receive Johnny's love and to share responsibility with him in making offspring implicitly positions Frank as their common enemy. But through the course of the narrative, Johnny's bitch and his wife do not work together to block out the men's mutual bond, as Frank fears. Rather, Evie and Megan occupy parallel positions in different, but similarly triangulated, relationships with these men and each other, and thus pivotally build in the difference between the substitutive "rivalry" of dimorphic sexuality and the dynamic triangulations of pack sexualities. Mixing up possible mappings of competing couples, the dog-wife confusion fosters a sense even in this opening conversation that triangulated relations change the stakes of sexual agency.

Bitch and wife may occupy similar social positions, but the novel insists that crossing species lines through dog love structurally confounds what Marjorie Garber (following Yi-Fu Tuan's dominance/affection theory of pet keeping) terms the "erotics of dominance."[56] As Frank falls out of love with Johnny, and the latter proves more loyal to Megan, the dog in turn becomes incorporated in a different position in Frank's life as his own pet, and more. When Evie starts terrorizing another woman because the dog sees her as a rival for Frank's love, retrospectively Frank comes to admire Megan as "a female of heroic stature, as ruthless, uncompromising and incorruptible as Evie" in defense of her beloved.[57]

The actions of wife and bitch both clarify how their own perceived coupling relies on the triangle structure for definition, and this quality becomes in the process more important than stability. In other words, the heroic status of each as defender of the pair bond simultaneously derives from and becomes destabilized by the couple's engagement with a third party. The sense that these erupt within fluidly forming groups or packs proves still more important than Frank's reading of wife and bitch in parallel lines, ultimately enabling the one to encourage Frank's alienation, loneliness, and frustration, and the other to dispel these feelings.

One of the ways in which the bitch alters the terms of coupling is by acting as Megan to Frank's Johnny, putting Frank in the privileged position of the desirable one. Evie not only provides him eventually with constant companionship, but her love also pivotally alters the gay man's sense of himself as the inevitable underdog, so to speak. Frank reflects: "I perceived that the intolerable situation from which I had escaped in Johnny's house was being reproduced in my own, though with a difference. The difference, of course, . . . was that I was now the subject instead of the object of jealousy. Poor Margaret [the kennel-maid] was the latter, and it did not fail to secure for her both my sympathy for her sufferings and my respect for her valour to note that she occupied the odious position I had occupied before" (157). Coming at the end of the novel, this passage marks the tremendous sense of perspective Frank has finally gained on his relationship with Johnny. But it also inscribes Frank's acquisition of the bitch as crucial to the men's breakup, suggesting that Evie helped him not simply out of a bad relationship but also out of an "odious" pattern of self-positioning, in which he used to resign himself to miserable longing for a married man who in turn was using him for money. Seeing Evie treat him as Megan treats Johnny, Frank gains a sense of his isolation as the effect of this sense of self, and not as the inevitable fate of a gay man in 1950s London.

As does the unnamed dog in *My Father and Myself,* Evie enables the narrator to recognize and to appreciate the mongrel for his own critical contributions to pack sexualities. This involves as well his abandoning ideals of polarized solutions (akin to the fantasy of dragging Roger captive into the homosexual fold) and constructing instead an image of sodomite and heteronormative cultures as connected, maybe even co-constituted by rovers like Johnny. Moving between heterosexual-father and homosexual–boy-toy roles, between Welsh and Cockney cultures, and across temporary states of indigence, imprisonment, and employment, Johnny's chief characteristic is to mongrelize. And so he emerges as the novel's seminal figure of instability. More clearly even than Roger, Johnny brings the gay narrator to the canine bitch as an embodied hyphen between their otherwise isolated identities, rather, the one's isolating identity and the other's categorical banishment from the human terms of identity.

This function is at first unclear to Frank, and it dawns on him alongside the impossibility of a more lasting relationship with Johnny through a strikingly reversed use of the animal in metaphor. Also going against the grain of the by-then conventional wildlife photography roles, the dog proves the primary point of connection between people. "I saw that she loved us both and that, whatever image lay uppermost, we were closely connected in her heart as we had lately been connected in her eyes; like a camera . . . she contained us together, clasped in each other's arms; she was a stronger, a living bond between us" (137). Significantly, this observation arises from a rare bedroom scene, one that like Wegman's and Snæbjörnsdóttir/Wilson's images subtly connects a pair to a third entity, whose role is to envision the social complexity of the intimate scene.

In the novel perhaps more clearly than its film version, the image of Evie as an oddly organic "camera," capturing, processing, and ultimately remembering Johnny as coupled with Frank does not mechanize (and therefore downplay) the bitch's participation in constructing this scene so much as, by positioning her as a mediating device, it betrays her special role in altering Frank's views on Johnny. Outlining the group dynamics of pack sexualities, Frank's narration at this moment all the more clearly brings the men together as a couple only through Evie's vision of them as "connected." Again bracketing off questions about the animal's intentions, this image emphasizes how ideas about animal as well as human sexuality as enabled by modernity turn on shifting perceptions of shared human–animal lives.

While Frank and Johnny's sexual relationship resumes under the bitch's gaze, their different understandings of her role in relation to sexuality secure the eventual parting of ways. In this way, the two men and the bitch form the novel's most complex triangle, for the end of the men's affair is signaled by their different attitudes toward the bitch's "failure" to couple in a different sense. Frank seems willing for Evie to have sex as an end in itself, but Johnny's dog love requires breeding in the broadest sense. Unlike Megan, who strikes Frank as perpetually "pupping" new babies, Evie never whelps any pups, let alone the purebreds that Johnny imagines himself selling at a profit. And "the rot set[s] in" the men's relationship when Evie fails Johnny as a "prospective goldmine": Frank observes, "in two successive heats the matings she submitted to did not take and she began to be suspected, in the phrase of a breeder, of being 'a barren bitch'" (120, 145).

With this suggestion that Evie cannot reproduce, Johnny abandons all interest in the bitch. On this point, Frank sees the differences between them as finally insurmountable, and Frank's belief that Evie deserves better motivates him to make Johnny an offer that he cannot refuse. Buying his way out of Johnny's and into Evie's life for good, Frank concludes the narrative with a jarringly negative, stereotypic image of a gay man's future with a canine bitch: "I have lost all of my old friends, they fear [Evie] and look at me with pity or contempt. We live entirely alone. . . . Not that I am complaining, oh no" (158).

Ironically contrasting the "freedom and independence" of his former enslavement to Johnny's whims, Frank describes a peculiar sort of pack membership through a newfound, shared sense of agency through which he and his bitch become at once multiple and singular, and above all happily ever after in each other's company. The film version's framing of these two together in city parks and streets subtly reinforces the broader implications of this partnership. Man and bitch are not a couple in the heteronormative sense, but rather are partners in constructing an intimacy that bolsters a more inclusive social sphere, yet one that still exists within the range of the "pity or contempt" of normative configurations.[58]

As the only nonhuman animal depicted in this narrative, Evie's special positioning raises the question of whether and how effecting this transition from "me" to "we" requires attention to nonhuman social contexts. Although

Publicity still from *We Think the World of You*, featuring Frank (often read as a doppelgänger for Ackerley) alone at the end with Evie.

cross-species intimacy clearly helps the lone gay male character to shed his despair of coupling on the heteronormative model, the novel does not resolve the problem of Evie's failure to couple with another dog. Does the distinction between ideas of sexual success, which leads Frank and Johnny to opposing ideas of Evie's value, lead the one to prevent her from having sex with other dogs just as it leads the other to require that she do so? Ackerley addresses these questions directly in his first (and many say paramount) "dog" book, in which he arrives at this structure of pack sexualities first through canine bodies.

Fuzzy Triangle: My Bitch, Her Mongrel, and Myself

The legal vetting required of *My Dog Tulip* prior to publication—"perhaps the first time that such a step had been taken over an 'animal book'"—provides a glimpse into the imagined synthesis of bestiality and anal sex within the category of "sodomy" in English law, which at that time was still firmly in place.[59] Ostensibly an evaluation of the text's suitability for print (that is, its likelihood for inspiring prosecution for "obscene libel"), the solicitor Thurston Hogarth's formal response to the manuscript also underscores the primary concern with "sodomy" at the core of this text: "I have, of course, not the slightest doubt that there will be large sections of the pekinese owning public who would be shocked to the core by the detailed description of this bitch and her love life, but this can hardly constitute an invitation to sodomy, even for the most depraved."[60] This verdict assumes agreement that the manuscript describes, but it stops short of inviting, bestial sodomy. It also raises questions about the degree to which the text also, if much more subtly, advocates intra-human sodomy as well.

Hogarth's evaluation makes it easier to understand why Ackerley and his publisher were not required, as Ackerley put it, "to cut out *every* dirty joke, every reference to vulvas, vaseline and penises."[61] But it does not anticipate the fact that objections by the printers would lead the publisher ultimately "to geld" the first edition of the text.[62] In spite of these adjustments to its phrasings, the linkage of human–canine bestial and intrahuman anal sex hovers uncertainly over *My Dog Tulip*, and in ways that lead to Ackerley's subsequent adaptation of pack sexualities beyond dog breeding to human sodomite cultures.

In this respect, the memoir's central fiction, namely, the focus on the fictional Tulip and not the historical bitch Queenie, gains significance as a means of frustrating the mechanical reproduction of the live animal. Ackerley's biographer, Peter Parker, speculates that it was at the point of final, mandatory revisions to the manuscript that the photographs with which Ackerley intended to illustrate the text—"snapshots he had taken of Queenie flirting with local mongrels and fouling assorted Putney footpaths"—fell by the wayside.[63] The inclusion of some of these images in Parker's book might be said to rectify this historic occlusion, except that, in bringing these images to light, Parker underscores the fact that Ackerley considered, only to reject, the idea of making images of his own dog part of the memoir.

Thus distinguished from the photographed (and, yes, photogenic) Queenie, whose images, though relinquished to Ackerley's personal papers, might be said to fix a real/live/actual canine identity on the nameless dog of *My Father and Myself* as well as to the fictional Evie (again the canine "camera," whose significance is to deconstruct individuated agency in the pack narrative of human sexuality), the memoir's Tulip belongs to a prior narrative project in which canine contexts dissolve links between sexual acts and identities. Indeed, the importance of her not having a specific identity emerges through Tulip's eventual indication of a distinct preference for sex with a canine mongrel, who, like Roger and Johnny, in the ensuing stories more significantly connects her with the narrator than it distinguishes her sense of self. And her delineation as not one but several bitches ("The Two Tulips" is the title of the first chapter) clarifies further how it takes a narrative pack to resolve the sexual problems of individuals.

My Dog Tulip begins in the situation in which *We Think the World of You* ends: the narrator has acquired an unruly German shepherd bitch who is suspected of being barren. But this suspicion does not diminish his desire to breed her to another dog: "Soon after" Tulip comes into the narrator's sole possession, he "set[s] about finding a husband for her." Contrary to the novel's Johnny, who breeds his bitch in the hopes of producing salable pups, this narrator wishes to breed Tulip in order to amend her "lonely and frustrated life hitherto," to give her instead "a full life," which, he presumes, "naturally include[s] the pleasures of sex and maternity." From the narrator's perspective, puppies are only part of the object of finding a mate for Tulip. With "no profit-making interest in the matter," the narrator sees her puppies instead as posing a "serious problem" to life in his small apartment—as, he cavalierly notes, "a matter to which I would give my attention later."[64] But his plan, like his bitch, demands greater attention. Initially eliding sex and motherhood, he conceives of marrying his bitch as an altruistic act, as a method of putting an end to her loneliness and frustration, and, in a way that echoes the tragic mistake of *Feathers*'s narrator, does not anticipate that the animal will resist absolutely any prospective mates selected for her.

Revealing the pervasive ideology of breed (not to mention its intricate ties to reproductive heteronormativity), Ackerley's disdain for selling pups does not prevent him from requiring that his bitch mate with another purebred. At first, he claims that he thinks it only fair to her pups to share her beauty, which is as "necessary" to mention in this text as it is in *My Father and Myself*.[65] Insisting that "so beautiful a creature as Tulip should certainly have children as pretty as herself," the narrator projects that "desirable suitors" must be other German shepherds—not the neighborhood "stray dogs of other breeds, or of no breed at all," whose attentions she seems to enjoy when she is in heat—without reflecting on whose desires will determine her sexual consummations.[66]

Later in the narrative, these precious distinctions between sold and controlled bodies utterly collapse. Here again, loving pets and exploiting their sexuality entails difficult decisions. In an internal dialogue near the end of *My Dog Tulip*, the narrator interrogates their overlapping frustrations, more specifically how her difficult search for sexual fulfillment intersects with an entirely different set of conflicted desires, namely, his passion for breeding the beautiful Tulip and its consequences:

"But please explain: what has her prettiness to do with it?"

"It will be lost."

"What is that to you? Or to her? Unless, as I suspect, you want one of her babies for yourself to carry on when she is dead?"

"Oh, no! Not all this responsibility again. I don't think I could."

"You don't think. Would it not be true to say that you are woefully lacking in decision?"

"Woefully. It's the frustration really. I hate to see it."

"Then you'll be mating her and destroying her litters every time she's in heat?"

"No, no! Just this once."

"Every time you don't you'll have to see frustration." (143–44)

Invoking only to reject the motivation behind van Vechten's pet-breeding scheme, this imagined discussion arises in a chapter devoted to elaborating how the bitch's three-week heat compounds human responsibilities to canine companions. Notably absent from this weighing of options is the simplest and now most common one, that is, spaying her.

As in Sarton's *Fur Person,* sterilization is addressed in this narrative not in the familiar terms of convenience or moral crusade ("for their own good"), but as a life-altering decision, with consequences for both human and animal. Earlier Ackerley's narrator establishes that not exercising the option to spay his bitch follows from his desire to maintain what makes her so attractive to him. Self-consciously, he owns the contradiction inherent in this position: "[H]ow can I tamper with so beautiful a beast? Yet I *am* tampering with her. I am frustrating her," primarily by not letting her choose her own sex partners (139). Put another way, he claims responsibility for controlling the bitch's frustrating sexual conditions, yet his inability to console her in her heats condemns them together to a seemingly endless struggle. Far from seeing himself or his dog as lone victims amid these conflicts, the narrator eventually sees himself along with his "fellow bitch-owners" as implicated in a confederacy against all dogs. Although they might try to remain responsible while keeping their pets intact within densely populated urban environments, he concludes, they thereby join a "human conspiracy" against canine sexual agency (149).

Blissfully ignorant of such concerns in the beginning of the memoir, "[t]he only question" that the narrator entertains as he sets out to marry Tulip is "the choice of a suitable mate—the question, in fact, that confronts us all, but simplified in the case of bitches by the availability of a stud system of dogs for the hiring" (57). Assumed in this plan is the system of humans who will help him to breed his bitch, and the bulk of the narrative works to unravel its shortcomings and excesses. Simple as dog breeding initially seems, the narrator further complicates the process, "[p]artly out of thrift," by deciding that "hiring a husband" is wasteful "when there were quantities of good-looking Alsatians about who might be borrowed for nothing if one got to know the owners" (ibid.).

Shades of the compulsive cruiser darken this queer plan, which entirely miscalculates the enmeshments of pets in human relationships. And it is hard to miss the critique of human marriage underlying the otherwise contrasting domestic scenes inhabited by the first two candidates: Max, the dog reduced to a butlerlike servility alongside the younger wife of a jealous and domineering husband; and glum Chum, the would-be runaway dog banished to the margins of his formerly doting master's life upon the latter's marriage to an equally controlling neat-freak. Underestimating his own role in bringing Tulip to these canine mates, the narrator fails to anticipate the dampening effects of these cross-species triangulations on canine copulation. And Tulip never fails to demonstrate an Evie-like (and for that matter Megan-like) tenacity in standing by her own man.

Recalling the uneven power dynamics informing the intimacies glimpsed in Snæbjörnsdóttir/Wilson's *(a) fly*, it becomes easier still to see how Ackerley's partial description of the dog here, seen through the doting eyes of her man, inadvertently sets up this breed-dog breeding project for failure long before it gets under way. In deciding to choose a mate for his bitch who shares the looks that he loves, he allows himself to be seduced by the illusion of naturalizing the human aesthetics of breed. A rude awakening to their mixed and multiplying social worlds comes in the form of "quantities of [neighborhood] mongrels," who show up suddenly on the doorstep when Tulip comes into heat. While the narrator feels "extremely sympathetic" toward these canine "courtiers," his commitment to his own breeding choice leads him to act otherwise, enlisting his bitch's help in repelling this "miscellaneous crew" (88, 91).

A parallel and equally strange grouping takes shape through the narrator's odd intimacies with randomly encountered human owners of male German shepherds, who allow their dogs to "service" Tulip. The only common ground of these human interactions is the shared desire for their dogs to have sex, a queerness played up in the narrator's characterization of all these relationships as strictly short-term, embarrassing for all human parties, and futile for sex among the canines. In deciding to avoid the breeders' system, the narrator also fails to reckon with the naïveté of the good-looking intact pets who are not the nymphomaniacs that people imagine. As the property of human owners who severely restrict their canine companionship to these mating moments, these animals are raised within affective relationships almost exclusively with humans. As with Ackerley's other narratives, the relational triangles at the center of these scenes prove highly unstable and instructive. Tulip fights instead of romances all her prospective mates because she is "in love with" the narrator, a condition that Miss Canvey (incidentally, a rare, unequivocally positive representation of a female veterinarian) diagnoses as the root of the bitch's generally unsociable behavior (21).

And this love is unequivocally reciprocated. Like his narrative brethren in Ackerley's oeuvre, this narrator particularly revels in being in his bitch's thrall, most obviously when he describes her in season, a description that again underscores how her beauty resides in an intact body. "My burning bitch, burning in her beauty and her heat," he gushes, "How enchanting she is, the coquettish little bitch, putting forth all her bitchiness" (141). No epithet in this invocation, a range of qualities that distinguish her character are caught up alike in this quality of "bitchiness," rendered all the more pathetic because so woefully frustrated by the man whom she loves most, and who loves her most of all.

Moreover, the early diagnosis of her love for him encourages the narrator mistakenly to think that Tulip's emotional attachment to him precludes her sexual interest in other dogs. Recording her behavior after a typically failed mating attempt, he complains that "as soon as we [returned] home she attempted to bestow upon my leg and overcoat all the love that the pusillanimous Max had been denied" (67). Although the narrator believes, then, that he himself must be the object of all her affections, Tulip desires more options. While he thinks of himself as generously providing more than enough possibilities only to have her perversely reject them all, she perceives only two choices each time: the familiar, loving man or the strange, nervous dog. Tulip growls, barks, bites, and otherwise fends off these other German shepherds as threatening, so that breed-dog mating devolves to a series of stilted rendezvous, stifled at best by ignorance of and at worst insensitivity to cross-species affective ties that squarely center people in what they wish were canine sexual scenes.

As breeding attempts, these arrangements prove disastrous, but as attempts to arrange fulfilling sex for Tulip, they lead eventually to greener pastures. Tulip's attachment to her human companion opens his eyes to his own contributions to her continuing failure to enjoy sex with dogs. While in the broader context, human marriage customs bear part of the brunt of this self-criticism, this elaborately choreographed failure to produce breed dogs inspires no direct comment on the follies of heterosexual marriage from a queer outsider, but secures instead a more significant breach of heteronormative culture in this narrative. The breed-dog "marriage" institution becomes an exceptionally excessive, ritualized violation of sexual desire all the more clearly in opposition to dog love.

As he seeks professional help in his quest to breed his pet, Ackerley's interlocutor repeats the folly of van Vechten's story. He may wish for the unlikely "fate" of "romance" in the form of "an Alsatian dog as handsome as [Tulip], alone and palely loitering in the woods." But he does so only after learning the hard way that it is utterly impossible to realize his initial and fantastic plan: "to organize a large pack of pedigree Alsatians to pursue and fight for" his bitch (87). Along the way he stumbles into the often ugly realities of producing breed dogs: that "breeding was a profitable business, so bitches had to be bred from whether they liked it or not; if they weren't willing they were helped, if they wouldn't be helped they were forced, and many a time . . . muzzled and put into a sling to prevent them from resisting" (83). Such truths are not presented as innocent revelations. Instead, they are offered as evidence of his own complicity with the breed-dog industry. In spite of recognizing that it is not "right," the narrator opts to have his "virgin bitch . . . ravished, . . . without spontaneity, without desire," but with the help of a veterinarian.[67] Because this marriage is not "churched" (that is, it does not fulfill the objective of producing breed pups), Tulip in a sense prevails.

Successful breeding results in this narrative from the canine, not human, selection of mates and inspires the narrator's reevaluation of the aesthetic guiding his rejection of the preferred mongrel suitors.[68] Initiating Ackerley's later narrative uses of mongrels, this turn in *My Dog Tulip* positions pack sexualities as a reaction against the culture of breeders, especially the euphemistic "marriages" through which the gay man finds himself enlisted in the service of coercive heteronormative institutions of sexual coupling. And it also connects the adverse consequences of these institutions to the lives of humans and canines together. For the narrator does not simply acknowledge defeat and grant Tulip the ability to choose her mate: he encourages her choice, observes the results, and shares the consequences.

After the failed efforts to produce breed pups, Tulip proves that she is "not a barren bitch," getting pregnant by "a disreputable, dirty mongrel named Dusty" (107, 104). Underscoring the continuities of mongrels across species lines, this one random sexual act parallels the narrator's description of pursuing working-class men for homosexual relationships in *My Father and Myself.*

In the book, the narrator's elaborate arrangements to stay one step ahead of the law while he selects, solicits, and brings home his own disreputable (to his horror, often dirty) paramours, like the similarly tedious lengths to which the other tries to produce a similarly presentable German shepherd "husband" for Tulip, frustrate rather than kindle sexual desire. In contrast, sexual satisfaction involves spontaneous, self-abandoning intimacies with ill-kempt mongrel bodies.

And just as this sort of desire reveals itself in the presence of a third party in the novel *We Think the World of You,* this moment of sexual coupling involves cross-species triangulation mediated through the eyes of the nonsexual partner in *My Dog Tulip:*

> I returned the stare of the disconcertingly dissimilar eyes, one brown, one pale blue, of this ragamuffin with whom it had always amused Tulip to play, and knew that my intervention was at an end. I smiled at him.
>
> "Well, there you are, old girl," I said. "Take it or leave it. It's up to you."
>
> She went at once to greet him. (104)

Holding the couple together like Evie in the "camera" image of the novel, the narrator's view of the dogs' sex act seems beautiful in the moment, but ultimately it is horrifying because Tulip becomes restless before detumescence occurs. Tulip struggles to break free while still "tied," inadvertently endangering herself (the dog's penis has a bone) and dragging Dusty around in increasingly awkward positions. Half an hour passes before they uncouple and flee from each other.

Relaying these events, the narrator strikes a pose somewhere between witness and feature of the urban landscape, finally abandoning his ideals of absolute human authority and joining with Tulip in dealing with the consequences of the dogs' encounter. Thus disillusioned in his fantasies of canine and maternal sexual fulfillment, the narrator nonetheless opts to shoulder what he can of the burdens brought on by this canine affair. Tulip whelps a litter of nonbreed pups by Dusty, and she quickly proves "bored" in confinement with them in the small apartment (116). Also, the narrator becomes aware that Tulip is not alone in shunning them, subsequently finding it impossible to place them in comparable middle-class homes. Tulip soon outlives her children, most of whom die young as a result of abuse and human ignorance.

Worse, the narrator's observations of their short lives suggest that the pups' miserable stories are typical of urban mongrels, particularly Tulip's daughters, who seem to bear the brunt of unequivocal social prejudice, their individually rotten conditions deriving from a universal identification of their worthlessness with self-selected canine breeding. Only by relating his own experience of their conception through pack sexualities can the sexually active gay man queerly oppose this devaluing of the "dirty bitch" (156). Embracing his active role in the breeding of mutt puppies, the narrator gains an acute awareness of the ways in which the social sanctioning of sex depends on the subordination of sexual acts to a larger cultural project of "breeding." Breed marriages come to stand for the sanctity of pedigree in the individual human self, not so much threatened as complemented by the triangulating circumstances of mongrel sex acts, which again in turn serve as synecdoches for the more fleeting forms of pack sexualities. And the rarity of exercising sexual choices, particularly for breed bitches like Tulip, brings his conclusions closer to home.

Toward the end of the story, Ackerley points to the singularity of the human (if not canine) abdication of the authority of breed: "[I]n all my questionings about the sexual lives of dogs, I have never met anyone else who deliberately threw, as I did, a pedigree bitch to a mongrel—though I have met a few pedigree bitches who managed to throw themselves to mongrels and got families thereby." Serving like Ginger as a coconspirator to the affair, going along with but not otherwise instrumental in this outlaw coupling, he confirms his loyalty by refuting further the common presumption that his breed bitch is in any way "ruined" by her random lover (153).[69] And more than just dog love is at stake.

Especially in relation to the later narratives, Ackerley's sexual politics seem all the more clearly conditioned by these relations of companion species, including but not limited to Foucault's "homosexual." Telling the story of how a pedigreed beauty elects to breed mongrels, Ackerley quietly argues that mongrel outlaws, otherwise incomprehensible in relation to the regulation of sexuality through identity, bring gay men and canine bitches together in a queer counterpublic, the hopeful, productive zone that Berlant and Warner locate at the edges of heteronormative culture. Requiring the assistance of multiple canine and human partners, these outlaw figures define a social space that exposes and resists normative forms of regulation, and more literally in *My Dog Tulip* coincides with rule breaking in public.

Again, the varied "sodomite" implications grow even more apparent in biographical context. Pointing to a 1953 diary entry, Parker surmises that "gradually he began to regard park rules [mandating leashes] as part of a general infringement of liberty, imposed by the same sort of people who declared homosexual acts illegal. . . . Ackerley believed that life should be led off the leash by humans and animals alike" (268–69). Where the London streets that Roger and Ginger traverse between the private spheres of unblended families figure this zone in the later narrative *My Father and Myself,* Ackerley explores this space first in the city's public parks in *My Dog Tulip.*

In a cryptic passage describing a walk with Tulip on Wimbledon Common, the park where he brings Tulip when she comes in heat to roam free from the attentions of their neighborhood's dogs, Ackerley comes to position himself explicitly within the liminal space of the modern gay man.[70] This abruptly integrated, stream-of-consciousness-style interlude connects the pollution of the landscape, Tulip's sexual frustration, news events, and the narrator's memories to give voice to the "inconsiderable, anguished deed[s]" that bear witness to an all-too-familiar potential ending. Coming to the point, he lists in detail the places in the park where gay men have committed suicide, eventually addressing one dead young man directly: "Everyone wished you different from what you were, . . . you perfect but imperfect boy."

At once emotionally charged and trivialized, unthinkable and unmarked, this passage makes of these spaces a place in the narrative for otherwise "lost" figures (147), ones that, as Ackerley described them elsewhere, "made a strong mark upon my young crusading homosexual mind" and were "part of the true furniture of Wimbledon Common" (quoted in Parker, 323). With no attempt to close this gap in the narrative, the narrator drops these musings, leaving it to readers to spell out why the human along with canine sexual frustrations must be played out in such spheres, and to join in these efforts to resist silencing and erasure. Because the narrator of this text says little otherwise of his own sexuality, these stray thoughts do not elicit sympathy for him personally so much as cultivate empathy across the mongrel-breeding bitch's and the homosexual man's reciprocal difficulties, a sensibility that grows more intense across the later narratives *We Think the World of You* and *My Father and Myself.*

As a typical still from Paul and Sandra Fierlinger's animated film version of *My Dog Tulip* (2009) emphasizes, the necessarily public daily rambles of this urban human–dog pair make it so that they are never finally "alone." Man and dog in the city here are surrounded by others, along with the signs of still more lives. In the foreground, the skeletons of animals (stray pets? poisoned rats?) are scattered around the central pair, alongside the ubiquitous litter of city's inhabitants. Complementing the tokens of the built environment's architects surrounding them—the factories, train trestle, warehouses—in the background a child plays while people pass by on foot, on a barge, and on a train. In such scenes, sex in public all the more pointedly concerns how desires are woven into the fabric of daily lives for humans and animals alike, and involve so much more than couplings.

Still from the animated film *My Dog Tulip* (2009), directed by Paul and Sandra Fierlinger, featuring the narrator (voice of Christopher Plummer) with Tulip playing by the river. Far from "alone . . . together" (the odd characterization of this pair at the end of Ackerley's book), man and dog are surrounded by signs of others' lives, including animal skeletons and the child playing ball in the background. Courtesy of Norman Twain Productions.

The role of public space in structuring these open-ended triangulations marks the crucial move of this larger project of mapping pack sexualities across species. Instead of closed, interiorized selves with identities affixed in binary terms, Ackerley's late narratives work together to build alternate models, using the mongrel sex acts of gay men, bitches, and their elusive consorts to recognize and elaborate the role of nonstandard forms of intimacy in public life. From Ackerley's schizophrenic splitting of the narrative bitch from one to two at the start of *My Dog Tulip* to his expressions of deep gratitude to an unnamed bitch for helping him to come to terms with the failure of sexual genealogy at the conclusion of *My Father and Myself,* his narrative transformation of one (biographical) to several (more broadly narrative) dogs proves pivotal to both the critique of the singularity of sodomite identity and the launching of less easily pegged intimacies.

Integral parts of Ackerley's intimate interrogations of the relationships between society and sexuality, these narrative structures of human–canine intimacies also inform the broader potential for the pet memoir to complicate human as well as animal sexuality.

Shagging Sheep and Other Queer Animal Theories

Published in 1956 (the same year as *My Dog Tulip*), *Your Dog's Health Book* includes an article that inadvertently indicates why dogs need such passionate and articulate human sex activists. With little sense of irony, veterinarian A. Barton begins "The Sex Life of a Dog" with the proclamation that "the dog does not have a sex life at all" on the grounds that, even among free-ranging dogs, "there is no conscious anticipation or planning of sexual activity."[71] This is not to say that all canine sex acts are strictly utilitarian, for a more startling difference from Ackerley's narratives emerges in Barton's affirmation that "some homosexual tendencies exist in most normal dogs."[72] A subtle acknowledgment that other scientists at the time were beginning to concede that a rainbow of sexual orientations extends through nonhuman life, this comment also speaks volumes about how breeding intimacies volatilize stories of companion species.

In the same decade that the pet memoir take shape through Ackerley's queer "crusading" with—and never simply on behalf of—animals, scientists systematically began to address nonhuman nonheteronormative behaviors as part of the lives of species, although the discussions that have followed more often than not compound rather than resolve questions of sexual agency.[73] Studies of fish threesomes, bestiality in the cowshed, and dogs' dry-humping boggle ordinary imaginations, and consequently get neglected in favor of animal research that confirms rather than challenges conventional terms of human relating. Especially in the debates surrounding studies of sheep sexuality in the past few years, these patterns have raised broader concerns about collecting thoughts along with data about animals doing it *un*like they do on the Discovery Channel.[74]

Homosexual along with a host of other so-called nonreproductive animal sex behaviors have been documented for thousands of years, as long as people have been writing about members of other species. But their historically fragmentary treatment in laboratory and field studies emerged as a scientific concern only in the second half of the twentieth century. While various approaches to this problem identify prejudices favoring breeders, in the broadest sense, the implications of this work for ideas about sexual and social agency are mixed.

Revered as the goal of all sex acts, reproduction persists as a conceptual focus of biology because it also provides a convenient means of avoiding queries about the evolutionary, social, and other purposes of physical intimacies that do not so clearly result in progeny. Feminist critiques of the sexism and now heterosexism prevalent among scientists show how these prejudices skew results even of studies purportedly debunking norms as myths.[75] The consequent telescoping of sex behaviors in species to normative standards of human cultures severely limits thinking not only about sex and gender but also about their roles in defining species, prompting more comprehensive approaches to the gathering significance of nonhuman nonheteronormativity.

Within the past decade, several scientific compendiums have been published expressly to combat ignorance about the varieties of social and sex lives observed in other animals. These books follow a pattern of gathering together examples as proof that comprehensive reforms regarding sex and gender are in the interest of biological accuracy. Bruce Bagemihl's *Biological Exuberance: Animal Homosexuality and Natural Diversity* (1999) is the first and most ambitious, arguing for a radically different paradigm of science that adds excess and abundance to the list of evolutionary forces (traditionally limited to scarcity and functionality) as factors shaping species life. A trained linguist, Bagemihl concludes that the biology and social behavior of animals "naturally" revolve around procreation only in the homophobic history of science, and recommends that scientists' past mistakes be rectified through cross-disciplinary interrogation that brings careful attention to the historical and cultural contexts of sex categories. Styled as a sort of field guide to animal queerness, the concluding half of this book summarizes scientific documents of nonheteronormative behaviors, a "sketchy and anecdotal" collection of evidence that some argue does not (or not yet) support such a sweeping revision to evolutionary theory.[76]

Not surprisingly, a more precise science of queer animal collecting has followed. Volker Sommer and Paul Vasey, in their introduction to their edited collection *Homosexual Behavior in Animals: An Evolutionary Perspective* (2007), insist that evolutionary thinking already requires attention to animal queerness: "Darwinian theory, unlike anthropocentric philosophies, recognizes the need to identify the unique characteristics of a taxon, while not ignoring the similarities with other organisms that are likely to exist."[77] The pivotal role of perspective in queer pet narratives should give pause to such judgments about differences and similarities: who decides what merits studied avoidance regarding whom, and under whose guidance?[78] Given that, as Harriet Ritvo argues, an ostrich-like or "struthious habit continues to characterize both the scientific community and what is now referred to as the educated general public" concerning sources of influence in phylogeny as much as in the paradigm shifts of science, it seems all the more crucial to address the structuring values of the scientific, social, and sexual senses of agency through and for which this taxonomic research is conducted.[79]

Yet in a way that has become both familiar in animal science and problematized by researchers in animal studies, these questions of agency are precisely avoided. First and foremost, the collectors of queer animal science effectively bracket off questions of agency by equating it with subjectivity or identity as "inappropriate to ascribe to animals," says Bagemihl, and this in turn as distinct from behaviors, which are "discrete acts and interactions," according to Sommer and Vasey.[80] Less obviously, these collections heavily emphasize research on nondomesticates, primarily primates, whose comparatively brief and volatile histories with people alone would seem to render them queer object-choices for comprehensive scientific claims. The longer history of animal sex science reveals instead a more sustained interest in companion species, particularly livestock animals, informing recent debates about studies of sheep sexuality.

Breaking amid the Academy Award season in 2007, public controversies surrounding USDA-funded scientific studies of sexual-partner preference among rams quickly became coupled with the gay-themed Best Picture of that year. "Just up the road from Brokeback Mountain, closeted away in their own private Idaho, the gay sheep were getting it on," begins a *Slate* editorial, accompanied by a photo of one slack-jawed ovine pointed toward another captioned, "I wish I knew how to quit ewe!"[81] Jokes in this vein underscore how now as never before animals serve as sites of slippage between queer acts and gay identities, that is, how nonhuman nonheteronormativity appears to be coming out in the open as a queer subject of inquiry, if not quite a means of accounting for agency beyond identity forms.

For many, the sheep sex-orientation studies become disconcerting not for outing ram-loving rams, but rather for framing animal acts as constitutive of homosexual orientation, and in turn as a scourge for the meat industry targeted for scientific intervention. Their point is to find a means of identifying and culling male sheep who prefer mounting their own kind in order to make insemination more efficient during the limited rutting season, ultimately raising profits for sheep farmers. Off the farm, these attempts to lend scientific precision to animal sexual profiling—or, more precisely, the scientists' equations of sex behaviors with degenerate identities—all too familiarly conjoin genocidal histories of homosexuality with sacrificial philosophies of animality. Even the jokes that symbolically link these rams selected for slaughter ("Brokeback mutton") to the doomed gay human characters of *Brokeback Mountain* register the ongoing dangers involved with being identified as homosexual or animal, and, what is more, the trouble with enlisting science in the service of heteronormativity.

Pursuing the latter point in the queerest of all animal collections, *Evolution's Rainbow: Diversity, Gender, and Sexuality in Nature and People* (2004), herpetologist-turned-transgender advocate Joan Roughgarden says that the funniest thing about these studies is the scientists' conception of ovine heteros as distinct from homos. Rams identified by scientists as "straight" prefer the company of males, self-segregate from females, and regularly engage in anal-penetrative sex with each other except when presented with a ewe in season, and so, concludes Roughgarden, "are actually gay."[82] Or are they all just sheep?

Queer theorists argue against this sort of bed-check approach that equates behaviors with identities among people, in part because it enables the same old identity categories to cover over wildly divergent relations and activities. In spite of the powerful allure of seeing other animals' sex differences, let alone our own, as underwriting the role of the individual or legitimating identity alternatives, calling an animal gay is (as Raymond Williams said of calling literature ideological) "in practice little more than banging one inadequate category against another."[83] Human ways of being may provide useful analogies for beginning to make sense of the strangeness of other animals' lives, but when used in this way as a measure of social agency, they also set precise limits to what can be known about "the" animal, even the autobiographical or anthropomorphizing one.

While Roughgarden pinpoints the grave oversimplification of sheep's sociosexual dynamics as a central problem with such research and the public responses to it, she uses terms like "male-oriented ram" and "gay sheep" interchangeably, and so sets a course for what a few years later becomes the Brokeback mutton confusion rather than clarification of the relations of actions to social agency from farm to plate.[84] As with the emphasis on primates in the other collections, the rush to gather together similarities in human and animal sex lives bypasses more pressing and proliferating conditions of difference. And the more complex imaginative engagements with shared and richly complicated cultural lives of companion species that motivate these studies and are so importantly visualized and narrated through the representations of people and pets mentioned above are all the more easily overlooked. But sheep seem to be emerging as a special case.

Of all mammals, sheep's reproductive systems most closely resemble those of humans, a closeness that informs their positioning as the animals through whom species histories are being most obviously remixed by in-vitro fertilization, cloning, and other innovations in making offspring.[85] Not coincidentally emblematized by Dolly the cloned sheep, these technological repositionings only add to sheep's multifarious roles as pets, as livestock, as eaten animals whose fleeces are harvested to make clothing and other products for people that now potentially include human clones and gene therapies. Part of his ongoing series *The Last Farm in Town* (discussed in chapter 4), photographer Mik Morrisey's image *Wool* (2008) asks: How are we to perceive these conflicting relations when bodies' parts are made to matter more than their living? These increasingly complex integrations of companion species in urban–industrial lives make it crucial not to naturalize so much as to ground traditional relationships and their biotech mutations within a range of agency forms that are conceived apart from degrees of self and otherness.

Looking to the relations of animals with one another in order to gauge what is natural appears to involve a studied avoidance of the basis of these knowledges in negotiations of intimacies shared between agents engaged in mutual observations, whether in labs, across shared months and years of living together in the field, or more ordinarily as domesticates. Speaking from experience, ethologist and former primatologist Thelma Rowell expresses frustration with getting peers to see sheep more generally as complicated animals: "I watched sheep in the same way I have been watching monkeys," only to find rejection from "sheep experts" indicative of more widespread anthropocentric valuations of animals in terms of their imagined degrees of proximity

Mik Morrisey, *Wool*, 2008. Part of his ongoing series *The Last Farm in Town*, the photograph portrays the simultaneous beauty and fragmentation of labor and body parts in the shared human–animal histories bleeding into urban–industrial agriculture. Copyright Mik Morrisey. Courtesy of the artist.

to the human. "We expect social sophistication in our relatives," she concludes, "so we ask more sophisticated questions, and get appropriately sophisticated answers."[86]

Rowell calls for a broader range of comparative scientific studies, in part to combat a "hierarchical scandal" favoring primate studies in ethology. Only through comparisons of multiple species will our evolutionary next-of-kin appear not so singularly cosmopolitan but only seemingly so in what has been up to now strict comparison with the human. But it is in her approach to her research that others are beginning to look for alternatives to the compellation of queer data.

Presenting questions not about but *to* sheep, in other words, framing intellectual engagements with them as open-ended and as bearing on our long-shared histories, Rowell's studies do more than simply contribute new data: they challenge scientific and other assumptions about forms of species and social agency. An ethologist studying ethologists, Vinciane Despret's work with Rowell clarifies the important difference particularly to the social lives of sheep that follows from any researcher who "actively takes into consideration the implications of her presence": "As soon as one focuses on the conditions, the question of knowing 'who' becomes interesting is superfluous. Of interest is he or she who makes someone or something else capable of becoming interesting, . . . who, in turn, make their researchers say more things."[87] As in the queer pet-keeping narratives, the problems of identity become blades of grass scattered across fields of agency, and concern more plainly the structures through which humans engage animals in the politics of collective life. So Despret via Rowell proposes a "sophisticated question" in order to learn from human–ovid companionship: "Do we prefer living with predictable sheep or with sheep that surprise us and add other definitions to what 'being social' means?" (367). This question (or something like it) queers the pet-memoir genre from the outset, and it may prove even more significant for distinguishing scientific from interdisciplinary animal studies.

Foregrounding the broader implications for studying cross-species companionship, Haraway argues further that Rowell's ongoing work with domesticated ovids demonstrates a theoretical reconfiguration of the human and other species with sheep, and so models an approach to collecting experiences that involves constant recalibrations of the delicate balance between owning shared similarities and respecting differences that are inherent in successful companionship. Moreover, this sort of work is required of our investigations of the most obvious points of comparison with social creatures—animals like dogs and sheep, again categorically shaped by and shaping sexual interventions across species and millennia—who therefore also engage humans in a variety of queer relations.

Hardly restricted to questions of sex, these problems of receptivity to the specific and complex social operations embodied in and across agents must be brought to bear on the bewildering intercorporeal intimacies shared across these and many more species that are emerging through genetic and genomic science. The ideals of intersubjective relations, whether the historical Morris Frank's dream of world-forming with the guide dog, or the fictional Velvet's vision of history-making with the Immortal Manifesto, insist with Ackerley that desire runs off-leash. With an eye to choices and responsibilities, examples as varied as Snæbjörnsdóttir/Wilson's art, Rowell's sheep science, and Ackerley's queer dog narratives effectively unsettle habits of mind that otherwise render intimacies within and across other species insignificant, and along the way model approaches to gaining and sustaining more meaningful engagements.

Together they begin to explain why, in lieu of definitively identifying individual agents as subjects, questions about the narrative functions of animals and animality lead directly to concerns about populations, that is, the possibilities for nonsubjective agency forms required of whole ways of life, and so lead to open-ended engagements with the biopolitics of life itself. While more familiar household pets like cats and dogs serve on the front lines of people's everyday attempts to work out these problems, sheep and other traditional (or less controversial) meat animals are complicating them further, in part because they have become vectors of diseases such as scrapie in sheep, which is linked to new-variant Creutzfeldt-Jakob disease (nvCJD) in humans, and its theoretical transmission via bovine spongiform encephalopathy (BSE or mad cow disease) through the movements of subcellular prion proteins. Much more could and should be said about the (non)human intimacies bound up in feminized terms like "mad cow disease," and not just because issues of gender and sex underpin cycles of meat production and livestock reproduction. For these stories of intercorporeal intimacies, the figure of messmates (Haraway's alternate term for companion species, which derives from the root *cum panis*, loosely translated as "those with whom one breaks bread") may be more apt, for it inscribes how eating involves all sorts of messing with others, most immediately the cohabitants that constitute our own bodies.[88]

At the (sub)cellular and other levels below our ordinary organism radars, where imperceptible desires change all the rules from the ground up, meat animal bodies go beyond breeding relations to mediate contests over life itself. Through urban–industrial contexts, meat becomes more than the flesh of one or the food of another. Once the product of time-consuming, local, and often communal activities of hunting or husbanding animals, meat is being transubstantiated into a vector of mutating diseases, even a model of other agency forms. In chapter 4, I will focus on the portrayal of meat animals in narrative, arguing that, even more clearly than these queer pet-keeping tales, such texts locate widespread (if also more precarious) intercorporeal groundings in literary and visual processes even as they push forms of representation to their limits.

Chapter 4   The Fictions and Futures of Farm Animals: Semi-Living to "Animalacra" Pig Tales

"HOW MUCH OF AN ANIMAL has there to be for it to be a dead animal?" asks anthropologist Garry Marvin on the subject of taxidermy, and such a question also applies to the modern experience of meat.[1] Well-meaning people may eschew terms such as "meat animals" and "farm animals" because they reduce forms of life to a use value. But such moves also help to empty out the histories of livestock husbandry conditioning the lives of companion species, and so intensify the evacuation of any sense of agency of all life forms involved in meat production, including that of meat itself.

Transformed from the fly-covered wares of slaughtering butchers to the plastic-wrapped fixture of supermarkets' refrigerated shelves, meat has become far more than a "symbol" of modern societies.[2] For historians, meat-eating patterns provide a "vernacular taxonomy" for the formation and global dissemination of national identity and as well for activists, "an index of racism."[3] Even in traditionally vegetarian cultures, consumer demand for meat is increasing rapidly, reflecting the changing relations of people and animals that propel the meat industry into an unprecedented boom.[4] With world consumption scheduled to double by 2050, meat is now implicated in an array of animal stories, which at once proves an index of global consumerism and a significant contributor to its problems.

The incredible, unprecedented numbers of animals raised to be killed for food threaten the health and environment of nearly every species. While virus outbreaks such as swine and avian flu make headlines, many drug-resistant strains of bacteria quietly grow endemic within industries that significantly contribute as well to climate change. With little hope of solving these problems through business as usual, proponents of the increasingly centralized and globalized meat-making industries focus on mitigating a still-more pervasive sense of discomfort with cross-species intimacies at the site of slaughter. Facing pressure to change, spurred in large part by animal advocates, some have begun to pin their hopes on technologically reconfiguring meat itself as a nonanimal product, and in doing so reveal a deepening sense of confusion about the lives that converge in meat animals and farm stories.

The Web site *New Harvest*, established in 2004, claimed that tissue-cultured meat, or "meat produced in vitro, in a cell culture, rather than from an animal," is the best bet for "advancing meat substitutes."[5] Although packaged as the cutting edge in food science, this technological potential emerges from developments in biomedicine and fine art, which in turn draw from nearly a century of "tissue-culture" (and within the past twenty years, tissue-engineering) research.[6] "Real artificial meat" is another term for its goal, and one that more accurately reflects the contradictions built into this spectral commodity.[7]

New Harvest's claims that laboratory meat-making is "more humane than conventional meat" lead some critics of the industry to the erroneous conclusion that the product is "violence-free meat."[8] So, in 2008, the prominent animal-rights organization PETA announced a controversial million-dollar prize to the first outfit to bring real artificial meat to market. Animal advocacy efforts may be bolstered by the claims of philosophers and policymakers that they are "morally required to support" what appears to be simply an "interesting technological phenomenon."[9] Looking closely at the technical details reveals how such responses portend misunderstandings not only of how animals and animal parts are involved in these processes but also of meat's liminal life among human and animal bodies.

Although the PETA contest aims specifically for real artificial chicken "nuggets," the most successful of the tissue-cultured meat experiments to date have produced a ground- or minced-meat-like substance grown from pigs, muscle-derived stem cells (MDSC) that are cultured on an embryonic cell isolated from piglets. As artificial-meat promoters are quick to note, it is "because of the animal-friendly image cultivated meat must maintain" that they emphasize the potential use of nonanimal polymer scaffolding (required to reproduce the three-dimensional texture of meat) and a cell-growth medium derived from maitake (hen-of-the-woods mushrooms).[10] Genealogically linked back to in vivo farm animals, and closely connected to in vitro meat cultivated from goldfish, sheep, and toad cells kept alive with serum derived from other animal species, real artificial meat promises transcendence from animal life but pursues this dream in ways that further compound the numbers and kinds of bodily intimacies that converge in meat eating.[11]

In the rush to find less controversial means of meeting consumers' meat demands, what remains largely neglected are some serious considerations about what cultured meat is, let alone where it has come from and where it is going in the lives of people and animals (and maybe mushrooms). In this respect, it is curious that, while a Dutch research team holds the patent on the scaffold techniques that seem at this point most likely to produce marketable tissue-cultured meat in the next few years, the viability of these applications was first demonstrated by artists Oron Catts and Ionat Zurr, whose artistic collective, The Tissue Culture & Art Project, designs and stages experiments that link aesthetics to responsibilities in producing and consuming life forms like real artificial meat.

"Scavenging leftovers" from research laboratories as well as food production for this purpose, Catts and Zurr term their results "semi-living sculptures."[12] This ethical approach to the materiality of their art is one of many aspects designed to call attention to the ways in which these creations are not simulations or variations on existing life forms to be commercially exploited but rather "a type of being (semi-being, semi-living) that does not fall under current biological or cultural classifications," one that they argue constitutes "a new class of being," which raises unique concerns about the relations of forms of species and social agency.[13] Against the general trend in biomedicine toward privileging anthropocentric perspectives at the expense of the semi-livings, Catts and Zurr question how the fragile, dependent life forms of cells and tissues made to live outside bodies—"a fragmented out-of-context collection of 'kind-of-alive' beings"—can be seen as exercising "an agency or even a proto-agency," a concern explored in pieces such as *Disembodied Cuisine* (2003).[14]

Part of Catts and Zurr's *Victimless Utopia* series, which examines human ways of relating to semi-living creations, this piece began in a laboratory with a tiny "steak" grown from prenatal sheep cells. In pursuit of the possibility that eating such meat could be victimless, Catts and Zurr created *Disembodied Cuisine*, an installation devised around the proposal to grow two more semi-living steaks from biopsies taken from otherwise healthy frogs, who were housed in an aquarium (later released in a botanical garden) alongside the steaks' bioreactor in a French art gallery. Especially in light of the artists' clarification that the source material for the "frog steaks" actually was a cell line derived from an aquatic toad, what might seem like the central symbolic statements of the piece (about the dubiousness of embracing pure French food in an anti-GMO cultural moment) unfolds in profound tension with an awareness of shifting cross-species involvements in these matters of life and death.[15]

For practical and ethical reasons, the artists choose to end such projects with an elaborate killing ritual involving artists, curators, and even audience

The Tissue Culture & Art Project, *Disembodied Cuisine* installation, Nantes, France, 2003. The dome on the right is the sterile environment required for growing the semi-living "frog steaks." On the left, with the frogs' aquarium in the foreground, the table has been set in anticipation of the exhibition's closing *nouvelle cuisine* dinner, in which the steaks were killed, cooked, and eaten. Courtesy of the artists. Photo by Axel Heise.

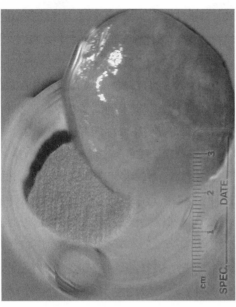

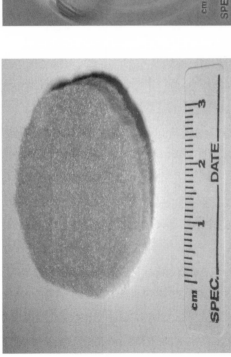

The Tissue Culture & Art Project, *Degradable PGA Polymer Scaffold* and *Tissue Engineered Steak No. 1*, 2000–2001, from a study for *Disembodied Cuisine*. These before-and-after photos illustrate the innovative polymer scaffolding on which prenatal-sheep skeletal muscle was cultured (*left*) and the results (*right*), which demonstrate the viability of producing "frog steaks." Courtesy of the artists.

members. Because the bacteria and fungi in our breath and skin proves deadly to them, ordinarily this just entails casual human contact, like opening up their sterile environments and touching them with bare hands. Connecting such killing to other ordinary practices, *Disembodied Cuisine* was designed more theatrically to end with a *nouvelle cuisine* dinner, in which the steaks were cooked and eaten (two of six participants spat theirs out), while the frogs looked on, not as animal hosts so much as "spectators."[16]

Certain details—like the artists' estimation that serum from a whole calf was needed to grow these two small frog steaks—give the lie to the animal-friendly fantasies of real artificial meat and in addition expose the complex, multispecies agricultural and laboratory systems supporting them. Amid "in-numerable exhibits on the subject of biotechnology" that wildly proliferated at the turn of the twenty-first century, these rare and powerful pieces under-score the unique ethical dilemmas raised by lives that are not (quite) sub-jects.[17] In effect, they address "the lack of current ethical frameworks to deal with the shifts in the continuum of life and the gradient of sentiency" pin-pointed by (in)edible semi-living sculptures, if also widely proliferating through rapid growth in the meat industry.[18] And the wavering status of metaphori-cal forms in particular connects this piece to the conflicts of symbolic and living forms characterizing literary animal agents increasingly through the past century.

To clarify this point, this chapter sketches the modern literary history of meat animals in order to show how narrative emerges as a form through which symbolic connections are not simply contested alongside the rise of real artificial meat but, rather, are broken apart in the process through which meat becomes separated from agency. The science that informs semi-living sculpture demonstrates that, whether tissue-cultured or produced in vivo, meat comprises cells and tissues that survive separately, sometimes for hours, days, or (with laboratory care) forever apart from the life of any organism's body. Yet understanding it as such depends on the efforts of writers and artists who (as Deleuze writes of Francis Bacon) do not say, "'Pity the beasts,' but rather that every man who suffers is a piece of meat," positing meat as the common zone of humans and other animals, "a zone of indiscernibility more profound than any sentimental identification."[19]

This approach to meat as a leveling sphere begins to explain why stories of exploited human workers and meat animals converge in the twentieth cen-tury, and consolidate around what Jonathan Burt characterizes as a fragile "aesthetics of livingness" in part to counter the relentlessly reductive logic of sacrifice.[20] Distinct but never entirely separable from those of animals, including humans, the lives more clearly than the deaths of meat hinge on intercorporeal intimacies perforating species boundaries. Looking at the ways in which the visual narrative practices that are caught up in stories of meat animals exceed the modern forms of cross-species intersubjectivity explored in previous chapters, I want to suggest further that their central aesthetic challenge is not simply to identify or represent life forms but to secure sustainable futures for different models of agency.

Reenvisioning livestock animals as connective nodes in social and techno-scientific networks—for instance, through Donna Haraway's elaboration of the companion-species relations of shepherds, sheep, and herding as well as livestock guarding dogs, or Sarah Franklin's "Dolly mixtures" of in-vitro fertilized (IVF) humans, sheep, and cloned stem-cell lines[21]—some emerging social histories of science offer important correctives to projected severance of "the meat" or embodiment itself from fantasied digital futures that virtually imagine absolute dominion over all sorts of "wetware."[22] Narrative theorists clarify further that such shifts never simply privilege information over bodies, messages over mediums.

Buttressed by increasingly intricate and pervasive coding technologies, the power represented by abstracted information may imply "a systematic devaluation of materiality and embodiment," but, as N. Katherine Hayles insists, the emphasis on pattern is best understood as a complementary aesthetic to (rather than representing an ultimate displacement of) embodied presence.[23] In her argument, David Cronenberg's film *The Fly* (1986) illustrates no cyborg transcendence of species embodiment so much as a posthuman confrontation involving "mutation" of the "human to something radically other than human."[24] But it is also possible to see these complex relations of imaging, technology, and agency as materialized in Nicole Shukin's analysis of the counter/hegemonic potentials of "rendering" as both animal practice and trope, which shows how the making of industrial meat becomes inseparable from the processes of representation following the innovation of photography through animal-derived gelatin emulsions in the 1870s. And it is to elaborate further the "livable alternatives" that can proceed from these connections that I turn to meat animal narratives.[25]

Neither simply sacrificed nor gaining significance as "speaking meat," meat animals emerge as irreducibly social creatures through engagements with the selfsame media that historically accelerated their slaughter. While literary narratives include a broad range of possibilities, including that meat itself can serve as an agent of protest,[26] what follows focuses only on stories that incorporate living meat animals and representational technologies in order to identify the conditions in which agency takes shape beyond rather than between the human and other bodily forms. From the disassembly plants originating in the nineteenth-century Chicago meatpacking industry through the tissue culturing laboratories dissembling carnal pleasures free of animal suffering in the twenty-first century, these narrative patterns lead to the big questions hovering over this book: What are the visual and narrative processes by which animals engage with their own representation? What happens to representation itself when humans imagine animals as having their own stories, even as having history, in the broadest sense? And how do these representational processes relate to ideas about agency in (semi-)living forms?

Through the slippages in representations of farm work—rather, of people enmeshed with "what were once referred to as 'farm' animals" in meat work—these twentieth-century fictions figure meat animals, foremost among them pigs, on the fringes of modern urban industrial centers, entering them as distinctly nonhuman agents.[27] The pig, as the consummate "creature of the threshold," traditionally inhabits an assortment of gray areas, whether between barn and home, pet and pork, or unclean and acceptable meats.[28] The terrific significance of pig parts in modern fiction—whether the chitterlings that "point to the fragility of the boundary that divides food from not-food, self from not-self" in Ralph Ellison's *Invisible Man* (1952), or the pig's bladder, "which turns up everywhere" in Thomas Pynchon's *Gravity's Rainbow* (1973)—indicates a continuing fascination with stories of this animal as an exceptionally versatile symbol, if not messmate.[29] Most important in terms of this discussion, pigs enable the historic transition from rural self-sustaining agriculture to urban industrialized meat production, maintaining a fragile connection across mixed communities of animals and people.

Pigs appeal to country living in many societies for the practical reasons that they fatten so easily on farm waste and that theirs is an efficient, low-tech meat to process and preserve, for instance, as smoked ham, salt pork, and sausage.[30] But these attributes also initially made pigs appealing as industrial resources. While historians debate the exact time and place of the origins of commercial meatpacking, all point to these superior porcine qualities in pairing this species with the human at the center of processes that have radically transformed other industrial operations as well.[31] Amid these changes in which refrigerated beef has become the urban meat of choice, pork and pigs (like the stuttering rube Porky Pig of Warner Brothers cartoon fame) accrue even stronger associations with rural life. But their prominent role in this industrial history begins to explain why pigs also trouble people's involvements in large-scale meat production and its representation.

Along with developing these iconic associations, literary histories in the past century cast pigs as screens for human ego projection, even in some readings of George Orwell's novel *Animal Farm* (1946) for projecting political alter egos, and at the same time chart revolutionary changes to ways of reading animals, if not inhabiting fictions. Especially in recent narratives like director Chris Noonan's film *Babe* (1995) and Margaret Atwood's novel *Oryx and Crake* (2003), the ways in which pigs escape their ordinary fate on the farm flesh out the ambiguities of human–animal relations in postmodern urban–industrial conditions, at present characterized by the tissue-culturing of real artificial meat as well as the genetic modifications embodied in another emergent animal product, Enviropig™.

The first live animal genetically modified in order to solve an environmental problem, Enviropig™ is curious as a rare example not only of how GM technology can be introduced affordably and effectively in animal agriculture but also of how desires of and for the flesh transform material along with social bodies.[32] Enviropig™ eliminates phosphorous pollution from pork production, a problem manifested in runoffs that cause algal blooms and fish kills in waterways and subsequently are addressed with strict regulations enforcing waste management. Like real artificial meat, this animal embodies a tech fix, an industry solution to industrial problems, but for a very different purpose.

Instead of a new world of expanding consumer choices, the point of creating this GM feeder pig is to offer a new lease on the future for independent small-time swineherds at a time when this group is fast becoming economically endangered. More clearly than tissue-engineered meat, the coming into being of transgenic farm animals designed to pass as their predecessors raises grave questions about perceptions of meat animals in urban industrial societies. But only Enviropig™ becomes the latest incarnation of a process whereby, precariously but persistently, pigs at once intensify intimacies central to the cultural and agricultural systems and render these processes imperceptible to the meat-eating urban public.

My point in positioning this GM meat animal alongside Catts and Zurr's very differently designed disembodied steaks is to suggest a way of reading such developments through farm-animal fictions informed by urban–industrial histories of meat work, which in turn are proving deeply ambivalent for people, livestock, and companion species. Fostered by mutual cross-species imprintings across millennia, the agricultural relations of animals and people cut across a wide range of populations: for instance, mutating laterally through prion proteins, the infectious agent of nvCJD in people who eat cattle infected with BSE, which again apparently traveled from sheep infected with scrapie, who in turn were fed to cattle, and theoretically is moving farther afield as CWD (chronic wasting disease) in wild populations of deer, elk, caribou, and moose. In these complexly mixed, if barely intelligible, living conditions, technological changes to industrial meat production involve shifts as well in animal agency and species intimacies that more openly trouble the operations of representation, broadly writ.

Meat at the End of Metaphor

Distinguishing meat itself from the "texts of meat," Carol J. Adams's pioneering study, *The Sexual Politics of Meat* (1991), focuses on "the production of meat's meaning," and like nearly all literary studies of modern animal representations assumes the pivotal role of narrative form to shifting ideas about animals and animality.[33] Reading a broad range of texts—including fictions, advertising images, and industry ephemera—from within a vegetarian–feminist critical tradition, Adams's purpose in linking their stories is not simply to offer "alternative endings" to the literary canon but more comprehensively to "eviscerat[e]" it.[34] But the terms of her project beg further questions about the relations of social and literary forms: How do the human and animal stories of meat become depoliticized through the formal ideal of closure?

One problem with Adams's analysis is that it stops short of addressing representations of meat animals on the hoof. While she implies that novels like *Animal Farm* can enter the canon only on the condition that its animal relations remain metaphors for strictly human conditions, literary history's changing patterns in reading such fictions suggest that a different representational problematic is in play. The centrality of meat-animal fictions in this movement toward reading animals as animals makes sense not so much in terms of a historical progression (or repression) of forms of identity in literature as of chronic ruptures in the ill-formed or incomplete relations of agency and embodiment that move across literary, artistic, filmic, and other narrative forms.

Because the story of modern meat production is often equated with the mechanization of work that has transformed human life, scholars like Adams point to the direct historical role of industrial slaughter facilities—notably Chicago's Union Stock Yards—in developing assembly-line techniques, which later were popularized by Henry Ford.[35] Systematic animal killing in such scenes obviously serves some human interests. And recent scholarship reveals how human as well as animal populations are systematically exploited in these scenes as well.

The ways in which these conflicts reinforce intrahuman divisions of race, class, and sex suggest further that human identity comes apart at the site of animal butchering. Elaborating a historical moment eerily prefigured in Upton Sinclair's 1906 novel *The Jungle,* Jimmy M. Skaggs explains that the 1919 Chicago race riot was fueled by the meatpackers' hiring black people, "who were less likely to be union members," to stem the tide of organized labor in the industry and "set back unity and cooperation in the Yards for at least ten years."[36] Roger Horowitz identifies the pork industry's overtly racist, classist, and nativist strategy for "upscaling" sliced bacon in the early twentieth century as a contributing factor to its abuse of women sausage-makers, which in turn inspired the historic Equal Opportunity Employment Commission's 1969 banning of sex-based discrimination.[37] And Jonathan Burt outlines how, in twentieth-century Britain, the conflation of "orderly and mechanistic" with "unseen and unheard" slaughterhouse regulations in turn became a subtle and effective instrument of racism, providing a rationale of efficiency for attempts to ban *schechita* and *dabh* (respectively, the Jewish and Muslim methods of slaughter). Together these examples bolster Burt's conclusion that industrial slaughter practice therefore operates as "one of the constituting elements of our particular social identity."[38] Yet this emergent picture of industrial meat production as the site of ongoing human social conflicts barely begins to account for the ways in which social agency becomes invested in (as well as divested from) identity forms at such sites. How do people meet more than just their meat through meatwork? And why is it that "the fates of animals of all sorts in the global economy" converge on disassembly lines?[39]

Films and videos deliberately designed to explain where meat comes from to audiences geographically and generationally removed from intensive agricultural operations seem like useful starting points for thinking of animals as "acting beings," especially given the visual gaps central to the rise of industrial slaughterhouses, which along with laboratories require enclosure from public view in order to operate on a massive scale.[40] Yet the revelations of hidden-camera footage are by no means self-evident, and they run the risk of multiplying rather than closing these breaches, making suffering a spectacle or visual abstraction that helps viewers to avoid their own implication in the process. Those who get off on PETA's *Meet Your Meat* as animal snuff may be in the minority, but a similar process of symbolic sacrifice or dis-identification arguably manifests itself in more familiarly defensive responses of viewers who respond with firmer convictions about their own omnivorousness.[41]

Setting aside for a moment their multiple, shifting meanings, it seems perhaps even more startling that meat animals approached as slaughter spectacles remain a consistent characteristic in exposé-style meat narratives, such as Eric Schlosser's best seller, *Fast Food Nation* (2001). This pattern extends at least a century back to Sinclair's *Jungle*. In curious ways, Sinclair's origin-story of mass animal (and its entailment of human) bloodshed for meat also reveals the problems with using dismembered bodies for shock value, seemingly from the start. Six publishers balked at the manuscript's graphic depiction of meatpacking's appalling conditions, which the author "refused to [have] censored."[42]

Told from the perspective of a quickly disillusioned Lithuanian immigrant named Jurgis Rudkus, the novel lays bare the filth and misery of the Chicago meatpacking industry. Consumers' intense and immediate outrage led in the same year as its publication to the passage of food safety laws. Less obviously, the infamous public outcry inspired by *The Jungle* illustrates the difficulty of reading any agents in scenes of industrial slaughter. Although Sinclair wrote with concern for all kinds of lives on the disassembly line, he became embittered by the reforms implemented exclusively for the benefit of consumers. As he reflected in his autobiography, "I aimed for the public's heart, and by accident I hit it in the stomach."[43]

Literary history only provides more justification for Sinclair's lament by pitting human rights against animal rights in interpretations of *The Jungle*, obscuring how, even within the limited perspective of this narration, human and animal lives become entangled through mechanized means of disfiguration and killing. So, for instance, Bertolt Brecht cited *The Jungle* as inspirational to his interest in Marxist philosophy and recycled Sinclair's anecdote of workers falling into lard vats (and consequently leaving the factory in lard cans) in his play *Die heilige Johanna der Schlachthöfe [Saint Joan of the Stockyards]* (1932), part of a series based on the theme of "entry of mankind into the big cities."[44] Although Brecht's play strictly focuses on human tragedies, its framing within human–animal urban–industrial transitions begins to explain why, of all animals, pigs stand out in *The Jungle* as agents of destruction, including their own.

Initially Jurgis, like so many other international tourists, marvels at the "Wheel of Fortune," the massive and efficient mechanism through which pigs are made to power their own demise. Becoming part of the scene as a meatpacker, he later learns to fear becoming collateral damage when pigs break loose on the factory line.[45] Although some still read the "diseased, rotten meat" as the story's focus, and specifically the meat as "a metaphor for the diseased, rotten capitalist system," closer attention to the animals in the text reveals more complicated textual potentials for metaphor and narrative, at least from the perspective of literary animal studies.[46] For these uncertain movements of meat animals make them dangerous to more than just their slaughterers in urban industrial scenes, a concern that links *The Jungle* still more clearly to long-standing problems with animal narrative form, writ large in contemporary meat stories through engagements with visual media.

Although no topic may be more conspicuously absent than animal slaughter in contemporary popular culture, Ruth Ozeki's best-selling novel, *My Year of Meats* (1998) revolves around the factory farm animal, poisoned by antibiotics and hormones and otherwise abused throughout its journey through the food chain. In this story, meat's production becomes a point of contact for the split perspectives of the novel's central pair of characters, a Japanese homemaker who once worked as a *manga* (or graphic-novel) writer and a Japanese American filmmaker who has taken a job in television production, both preoccupied by difficulties with pregnancy. Through *My American Wife!* (the meat-themed television show directed by the one character and unofficially reviewed by the other), food animals become part of a meat text mechanism for the women's networking, inspiring interpretations of the novel as "for those who set the parameters of consumption, not for those consumed in the process."[47] Fans note how the story raises their own awareness of health and eating, an emphasis reflected in one critic's comment that the novel inspires readers to stop eating meat just to avoid ingesting the toxic pharmaceuticals fed to meat animals.[48]

Yet *My Year of Meats*'s emphasis on media-production themes, its juxtapositions of forms within the narrative (including corporate memos and poems), and its central characters' training as skilled visual storytellers also inspire a growing awareness of an "ethical conflict inherent in representation between serving one's agenda and serving the integrity of one's subjects," here people and meats positioned together on television as spectacles of consumption.[49] More explicitly than Sinclair, Ozeki describes a moment of epiphany about the inadequacy of metaphor to represent the relation between the people and animals to whom the carcinogenic, abortifacient, and birth-defect-causing hormone DES has been administered. While researching health risks associated with meat, she discovered that "women weren't just like cows; women and cattle were given the identical drug with equal disregard for safety."[50]

Examples from very different contemporary animal narratives convey a sure sense that meat animals have become a locus of metaphor perceived in crisis. One of Ozeki's sources, Sue Coe's *Dead Meat* (1995), integrates a range of representational forms in order to situate the widespread failure of meta-phor to regulate aesthetic along with political forms of agency. An artist's book—Coe prefers "the self-deprecating term 'gutter journalist'"—on indus-trial slaughter, *Dead Meat* links forms to distinct logics of representation.[51] And it is well worth noting that this project involves considerable risks for the artist/author, who offers rare and sometimes-sympathetic glimpses of a range of intimacies that humans and meat animals share.

The book comprises autobiographical chapters that narrate Coe's brief encounters with meat workers in a range of settings. These stories are inter-spersed with her paintings and drawings, which, although plainly illustrat-ing the scars, missing fingers, and other evidence of injuries to workers, are seen as primarily focusing sentiment on meat animals.[52] Coe explains her for-mal choices as primarily motivated by practicality. In the abattoirs and pack-ing facilities that she insinuates herself into in a variety of ways—including lying about her credentials and motives, dissembling interest in owners and managers, even committing crimes of breaking and entering—her cameras are confiscated upon discovery. Significantly, she does not abandon the use of photography altogether in this project, but rather ranges it alongside other forms as an aesthetic index.

These conditions also prompt Coe to develop in greater detail what Ozeki's fictional filmmaker comes to sense, namely, that any single media form remains all too perfectly manipulative and ultimately is inadequate to the monumen-tal task of moving beyond dis/identifying with the spectacle of lives suspended by meat hooks. In this artist's book, first-person stories and hand-worked images together convey the most egregious sufferings on the floor of nonunion shops, where with increasing frequency humans as well as animals lose life and limb.[53] But other representational forms here, namely, metaphor and photography, call attention to aesthetic disconnections of meat and organis-mal life as informing ethical failures to link identifiable and identified-with bodies in these scenes.

Midway through *Dead Meat*, Coe uses and at once refuses what has be-come among the most offensive metaphorical relationships of humans and animals: "The Holocaust keeps coming to mind, which annoys the hell out of me. I see this reference in so many animal-rights magazines. Is this the com-forting measuring rod by which all horrors are evaluated? In the made-for-TV reality of American culture, the only acceptable genocide is historical. It's comforting—it's over. Twenty million murdered humans deserve to be more than a reference point. I am annoyed that I don't have more power in com-municating what I've seen apart from stuttering: 'It's like the Holocaust.'"[54]

In this passage, Coe acknowledges the grounds for offense in this analogy and more: the inability of metaphor to separate species here is articulated in terms of both an ethical failing (to do justice to "murdered humans") and an aesthetic one ("communicating" reduced to repetitive "stuttering"), and putting it this way emphasizes how these metaphorical inadequacies come together through a concept of history as that which secures or legitimates the human as metaphorical reference points ("historical" as "acceptable genocide"). With such careful treatment, this metaphor—perhaps all metaphor?—appears to be all the more clearly de-formative within the array of visual narrative processes that Coe engages. In other words, it becomes a representational device that is at once devalued by and devaluing the central purpose of the artist "to be a witness to understanding collusion."[55]

It is possible to read this passage as a testament to the incommensurability of human histories and animal lives, to the inevitable failure of writing to bridge the presumed gap between species, or even as a disingenuous counter-offensive. But doing so ignores the complex mixed-media form and deeply mixed-species message of the book and the ways in which these aspects are used to respond to the broader problems with representing meat animals. *Dead Meat*'s success as a fragmentary narrative of the conflicting and converging interests of animals, workers, bosses, activists, and artists meeting at the scene of meat production requires the juxtaposition of this metaphorical technique with other representational tools, especially visual devices, that otherwise make it difficult to close this book—as apparently so many readers of *The Jungle* and *My Year of Meats* manage to do—with only consumer interests in mind.

A similar point about formal choices emerges more starkly in Coetzee's *The Lives of Animals* (1999), when the fictional novelist Elizabeth Costello compares the meat industry and the concentration camps of the Third Reich only to put the comparison under erasure. She invokes the metaphor to illustrate the willed ignorance of collusion in genocides and meat industries, but marks the metaphor immediately as inappropriate, calling attention to how "this kind of talk only polarizes people and cheap point-scoring only makes it worse."[56] This deliberate erasure of metaphor echoes Coe, but in two key ways Coetzee pushes the point further. First, the metaphor erupts this time in the context of an argument that explicitly rejects the logic of analogy (along with all formal methods of human reason) as tautological and therefore inadequate to understanding the lives of animals. Second, this use of metaphor clearly proves not only abstractly offensive of the narrative but actively offending within it when another character, a Jewish poet, expresses outrage at Costello's metaphor.

The poet targets Costello's elaborate disavowal of offending by analogy, and thus holds the speaker to account for her own authorial maneuvering. Delivered indirectly, her provisional response, that "writers teach us more than they are aware of," points to the larger questions of embodiment and engagement looming over the fiction, possibly over all representations of the lives of animals.[57] Structured as a nested narrative—rather, an "experimental metafiction" about a novelist giving a series of lectures that was first delivered by the novelist Coetzee as a series of lectures—*The Lives of Animals* weaves these moments together, and, as Robert McKay argues, in many more ways approaches literary form in a way that "render[s] fictional the reality of the author's beliefs that is supposedly deferred by its writing."[58] In lieu of moving beyond ethical debates of any given animal issue, the novelist's play with narrative form brings the discussion back to consideration of the aesthetic conditions of engagement with nonhuman life.

Coe's and Coetzee's primary concern with animal representation and its failures for humans as well as animals distinguishes them from critics who cite these textual moments from uses of them by others flatly to equate human genocide with animal slaughter.[59] Again, there is much to be concerned about in such positionings, but the most relevant aspect to this discussion is that such criticism sets up humans and animals in a phony competition for social agency, inverting conventional humanist reference points but otherwise not altering the fundamentally anthropocentric logic whereby meat is produced through sacrifice. At once both risking offense and critiquing the grounds of offense, Coetzee's dramatization of the social effects of using this particular failed metaphor might be said to elaborate Coe's position, only at the expense of pursuing these very questions of how authors and artists allow people and animals to enter into a range of agency forms in acts of reading, if not inscription.

From this perspective, it seems even more significant that living animals are absent from *The Lives of Animals,* just as they are in *My Year of Meats.* The overwhelming sense of isolation and helplessness pervading these fictions might be said directly to derive from their deliberate erasure of animals from the lives of humans. Although mentioned at key points, pets of characters in *The Lives of Animals* are kept conspicuously off-stage—shadowy figures like Costello's cats waiting at home, or her son's dog, whose neutering haunts family discussions—so that the traces of dead animals become all the more present, whether as historical figures in the lectures, as the sources of Costello's own leather shoes and purse, and as meat, most uncomfortably the chicken and fish served at mealtimes.

In contrast, *Dead Meat*'s multimedia approach echoes that of other meat narratives by examining how visual technologies invoke a range of potentials for meat animals and social agency, and in ways that undermine the human-animal distinctions crucial to the analogy. Images here often appear to proceed from telling moments, when again Coe is forced to surrender her camera and resorts to witnessing in her "somehow less threatening" sketchbook.[60] More often than not, these instances are marked by people's relationships with one another in the nonunion shops, where the owners' and bosses' clear violations of labor laws, let alone meat-inspection regulations, makes them camera-shy. But they are also made to contrast imaging technologies with very different histories and ideologies.

A few photographs are included in the narrative, and all are reprints of industry-promotional material, like the antique postcard of a beautiful lone sheep, which includes its original caption, "I will feed and clothe you."[61] Against the photorealist documentary tradition, photos here are presented as unreliable evidence, signifiers not of transcendent truth but of artist/ authors' and viewer/readers' responsibilities in sharing texts for the purpose of witnessing collusion. Like metaphor, photography is included not simply as another representational tool but more purposefully as an indicator of another kind of logic, one that links the historical problems of human and animal agency to power vested in representational systems, and one that is deliberately situated as failing amid other options.

Much more can be said about the positioning of people with animals in Coe's work, and at least one painting in *Dead Meat* invites further speculation about why pigs figure so largely in modern and contemporary developments in meat-animal stories, which include the spectacular history just getting under way with Enviropig™. *Union* (in the book titled *The Boss Calls in the Immigration Police*) presents handcuffed, union-labeled men being marched out of a slaughterhouse next to a row of suspended pig carcasses. Pointing to his neck, the central human figure gestures ambivalently; he might be commenting on the dire situation of the arrested men, pointing to (and thereby informing on) the men working behind him, or even just mimicking their work in cleaning carcasses. All of these interpretations draw attention to the ambiguous referent of the book's title, and all resonate with the image's historical message about capital investments in meat as working to deform animals and people on a massive scale. But the image's layout on the same page as reproductions of postcards of Union Stock Yards and its Wheel of Fortune for pigs—again, historic scenes so important to the story of Sinclair's immigrant hero as well as to its critique by writers like Adams—suggests more exacting alignments of people with pigs are incomplete, or (akin to what Baker sees as the hallmark of a postmodern animal aesthetic in art) in need of being deliberately botched in order to tell stories of collective life.

Coe herself makes this point at the end of her discussion of the problems with the Holocaust metaphor. Folding the figure back on itself by musing on "human downers, the winos and junkies" and other "throwaways," who articulate their own situation through this analogy, she concludes that its failure speaks to the ways in which, "[a]s social beings, we desire a shared reality."[62] Who will act to formulate this social sense of reality? In what form do agents effectively confront the distortions or concealments inherent in political as well as aesthetic representation? More to her point, how can a person relate to a meat animal as anything but a "creature without an ego or a sense of self"?[63] Although circumscribed by the human narrative, the multiplicity of porcine and human bodies ranged together here invokes a different set of potentials for meat through mixed populations revolutionizing stories of farm life and industrial death in modern times, possibilities that all the more clearly take shape through the narratives of *Animal Farm* and *Babe*.

Sue Coe, *Union*, 1989, included as an illustration under the title *The Boss Calls in the Immigration Police* in Coe's artist's book *Dead Meat* (1995), mixed media on canvas. Copyright Sue Coe. Courtesy Galerie St. Etienne, New York.

Animal Farms and Films

If it was taught to them in school, some of my undergraduates have read *Animal Farm*. But the uncanny consistency with which they report having seen the film *Babe* surpasses marketing executives' best dreams. Viewing the film as a bastardization of Orwell's story (as so many of its critics do) spells tragedy, but the students refuse to see it that way. "I watched *Babe* every day for one whole summer," one student explained, outlining conditions in which literary traditions instead bleed less legibly into video-on-demand stories of meat animals that even a child can love.

Running through *Babe*'s story about how a pig learns to be a sheepdog (or "sheep-pig") are all sorts of narratives that insist on the precariousness of species, bodies, and other representational forms, some woven in directly through intertextual references and others by implicit contrast. But it is *Babe*'s complex approach to technology, as both an economic factor (as it is represented in the film) and as visual media (as they are represented both in and by the film), that I argue at length elsewhere realizes another potential hanging over meat-animal narratives, namely, that the technological agency of animals extends to visual media literacy.[64] To clarify that these elements are not unique, I will elaborate how they emerge through a longer narrative history encapsulated by changing literary and visual interpretations of *Animal Farm*.

For many critics, Orwell's *Animal Farm* (1946), subtitled *A Fairy Story*, suggests an obvious point of contrast to *Babe*.[65] These fictions are more alike in their differences from the theriophilic fable tradition that imagines animal nature as elevated from the sillier trappings of human culture.[66] Whereas *Babe* takes a decidedly ambivalent position about the role of visual technologies in the construction and regulation of social divisions, including those of labor, gender, sex, and species, *Animal Farm* implicates all technologies as unequivocally serving power.

Written in part as a parable of the 1917 Soviet uprising, *Animal Farm* depicts a violent takeover of a British farm by its animals, a revolution led and later usurped by the farm's pigs.[67] Human attempts to regain control, rebuffed at first, eventually succeed because a few pigs move into the human farmers' roles and exploit the "stupidity" of the other animals, eventually becoming in every respect indistinguishable from their original oppressors "to the creatures outside."[68] Intriguingly, literary interpretations of the novel have reversed this trajectory.

Aided by the emphasis on perception and perspective in the final description of pigs transforming into humans, critical attention moves away from historical metaphor in favor of reading this novel as a straightforward animal narrative. This interpretation is reinforced by the author's autobiographical account of its creation. Evoking the primal scene common to Sigmund Freud's "Little Hans," Friedrich Nietzsche's fateful collapse, and even novels as different as Fyodor Dostoyevsky's *Crime and Punishment* (1866) and Joseph Heller's *Catch-22* (1961), Orwell writes that he witnessed a boy beating a carthorse and then "proceeded to analyze Marx's theory from the animals' point of view. To them it is clear that the concept of a class struggle between humans was pure illusion, since whenever it was necessary to exploit animals, all humans united against them: the true struggle is between animals and humans."[69]

This passage gains renewed significance amid debates about Orwell's difficulties with publishing a "kind of animal story that would never sell."[70] But more often it is being read as proof that the novel is "really" about animals.[71] More than any final agreement about its one, true meaning, the precise struggle through which literary history has arrived at a nonmetaphorical reading, that is, at the interpretation of *Animal Farm* as about animals that now seems so patently obvious, indicates what remains at stake for reading animal stories.

The first to argue for the formal significance of this passage was Raymond Williams, who in a monograph titled *George Orwell* (1971) cites it as evidence against conventional interpretations of the novel as an analogy for the author's final disillusionment with socialist politics. Significantly revising his own argument from over a decade earlier that, if the pigs are "the hypocritical, hating politicians whom Orwell had always attacked" and presented as such in *1984*, then all the other animals must be aligned with the proles as "'monstrous' and not yet 'conscious,'" Williams leads the long, difficult shift away from reading *Animal Farm* strictly in terms of allegory.[72] In Williams's later reflections, the difference of the pigs becomes a difference that matters, one that shows how the metaphor breaks down even within the text, because these animals become both collective exploiters and exploited creatures.

Although Williams does not elaborate this point, it also explains a gaping hole in the plot: why there is never even any pretense of liberating the dogs of Animal Farm. Instead, a litter of orphaned pups at the beginning are seized and secreted away to be raised by one of the pigs, then at a pivotal moment in the story unleashed against the other animals at the pig's command. More than simply contradictory, this aspect of the story builds in limits to both metaphorical and anthropomorphic projection. These nameless, innumerable dogs remain dogs, serving not as extensions of anyone's ego or symbols of any people but rather (in Deleuze and Guattari's terms) as a "demonic" and irreducible figure of animal multiplicity, inaugurating the pigs' campaign of terror against the likewise-transformed meat animals.

So the novel becomes "unique among Orwell's books because it contains no Orwell figure, no isolated man who breaks from conformity but is then defeated and reabsorbed"; instead, it depicts a collectively distributed consciousness-raising that at the end shifts sympathy to the other animals. "What happens is a common, rather than an isolated experience, for all its bitterness; and the whine of ragged nerves, the despair of a lonely trajectory are replaced by an actively communicative tone in the critical narrative."[73] If this emphasis on communication distinguishes *Animal Farm* in the broader context of meat fictions from *The Jungle* and other exposés that emphasize human individual concerns at the expense of a sense of community, then it also situates the novel more firmly within a narrative tradition of barnyard revolts leading up to *Babe*.

The carthorse-whipping scene at this fiction's generative center also connects it to an important (if also importantly unsung) literary predecessor to Orwell's fiction, Gene Stratton-Porter's *The Strike at Shane's: A Prize Story of Indiana* (1893). Stratton-Porter's novel is the earliest that I could find that imagines abused farm animals assembling in opposition to human rule, though to a very different end from Orwell's. Solicited and published by the American Humane Society as (the title page proclaims) "a sequel to *Black Beauty*," this fiction imagines a peacefully resolved collective farm-animal uprising.[74]

Here the whipping occurs at the beginning of the story and prompts the animals to coordinate a temporary work stoppage, which enables the human farmer and son to be persuaded by wife and sister to abandon the cruel ways of man. Fitting Adams's sense of literary fiction as a manifestation of patriarchal meat traditions, father and son do not relinquish manful control of the farm, for Stratton-Porter's point is to demonstrate that human dominion exercised with love and kindness is essential to a profitable and godly farm; animal welfare is the outcome of (not motivation for) commitments to human charity. In pointed contrast, Orwell imagines power as more precariously contested by humans and animals through access to technology, an aspect of this fiction that subsequently becomes reimagined in ways that directly address the implications for technologies of representation.

In *Animal Farm*, the never-completed windmill, the symbol of a technological utopia, fails to deliver the animals from exploitation as workers and instead becomes the means by which the pigs take the human role of working the animals to death. In the end, what makes pigs indistinguishable from humans is their coterminous dependence on and mystification of technology as a means of production, in relation to which the other animals become naturalized neo-Luddites. Orwell imagines that in doing so the pigs collapse any spaces between humans and animals, and so end any possibility of sustaining species distinctions. In the process, visual media become propaganda tools with which pigs, chief among them the boar Napoleon, manifest control over other animals, a trope that is developed more clearly in filmic adaptations.

From the novel's mention of a propagandistic "portrait of Napoleon, in profile, executed by [his henchman] Squealer in white paint," both film versions of *Animal Farm* construct increasingly elaborate animal relationships with visual technologies.[75] Joy Batchelor and John Halas's 1954 adaptation (also the first British feature-length animated film, and the first to use animation as a medium for serious subjects) imagines the animals becoming visually literate as part of their creation of an animal-centered social order.[76] Upon entering the human household, they recoil in terror from a photograph of their former master Jones, unable to distinguish the real from the representation, until the brave but doomed plow-horse Boxer smashes it.

But by the end the pigs have plastered the farm with likenesses they have made of their own leader Napoleon, and through their representations of this pig positioned upright, wearing medals and clothes, begin to enact the anthropomorphic transformation of their kind. This invention of a pig-propaganda machine, together with the altered ending, which proposes a second animal revolution against pigs and people, more clearly than the novel makes the pig Napoleon a stand-in for Joseph Stalin (a point underscored by the recent revelation that the film's production was secretly funded by the CIA).

Although in some ways responding to the success of *Babe*—most obviously by tacking on a frame story of an animatronically "talking" border collie mother and other characters likewise crafted by Jim Henson's Creature Shop—John Stephenson's 1999 film version of *Animal Farm* imagines animal engagements with visual media as actively shaping farm life. At the end, a close-up shot reveals a hoof reaching out to turn on a projector, which then runs a montage in the style of Leni Riefenstahl's *Triumph of the Will*, but here starring the pig Napoleon, who in this scene is also the pig-propaganda film's only viewer. Depicting the pig as clothed and standing upright by this point in the film, this revolutionary image of an animal making, acting in, and watching his own film again is contained by the conflation of literacy with human identification.

Contemporary literary adaptations of the novel often integrate communications technologies to question such conflations. So Jane Doe's *Anarchist Farm* (1996) depicts animals "on a different farm, far across the forest" from Orwell's animals, setting the stage for spontaneous collective actions by printing flyers distributed to all kinds of animals (including human environmentalists) that get sabotaged by rabbits with cell phones spying for "the corporation."[77] And in Doreen Cronin's picture book, *Click, Clack, Moo: Cows That Type* (2000), a discarded typewriter becomes a means by which each species separately and sequentially renegotiates a better lot on the farm. However, in Stephenson's film version, it is strictly visual media literacy that means power; only by making themselves into movie meat do pigs become people.

In spite of this negative valence, these mutations of *Animal Farm* underscore a socially transformative potential for technological integration realized not by Orwell's fiction but by Enviropig™: What if the windmill had worked? What if the animals' technological literacy was cultivated (in today's terms) in order to green farming? Among the more faithful adaptations of *Animal Farm*, it remains uncertain whether they transform only themselves, their kind, or their communities, and to what end, particularly with regard to cross-species intimacies. So the conclusion of this chapter will return to their pivotal positioning of pigs as a point of connection to the realities of farm life but also across fictions that spin out the implications of the modernization of meat animals, including *Babe* and more recently Atwood's *Oryx and Crake*. Getting there involves grappling first with questions of how animals share human technologies, and what happens to them in this process of engagement.

What is important to this discussion is not simply the generic or stylistic difference between these texts and *Animal Farm* but also the veritable sea change they gauge in the role of technology in production and in utopian thinking. *Babe* differs profoundly from all of these texts by assuming pan-species visual media literacy throughout, a fantasy perhaps, but one that disables anthropocentrist views of visual technologies by depicting them as employed to produce the collective fiction of the worker as an individual. Whereas the Orwellian animal narrative reconfigures but does not displace the individual (human, nation, animal) at the center, and therefore contributes to a sense of despair concerning technology and animal agency, *Babe* depicts individuals and centers as "necessary failures" that move toward a productive critique of the past and modeling future engagements.[78]

And it does so by depicting television as the means by which animals escape their doom as essentially meat, using the same visual media technology through which Ozeki's women make connections to avoid a similar fate. Like *Babe*, stories that focus on meat-animal bodies and visual media also provide a means of negotiating a distinctly contemporary collective form of social agency.[79] By invoking the way in which cyborg theory suspends the value of the human in relation to technology, what follows traces a similar displacement enacted along the boundaries of technology and species.

Babes in Arms, Legs, and Wings

A credit to the staying power of Noonan's film, the "Save Babe" campaign launched in 2004 by the advocacy group Animals Australia attempts to raise awareness of how pigs suffer en masse in the meat industry. Unlike the film, the ad campaign includes images of bloodied, muddied adults as points of contrast to those of highly individualized pink piglets (some are stills from the film). As a national campaign, it capitalizes on the Australian location of *Babe*'s shooting, but its impetus—the belief that naming and otherwise individualizing animals changes the story of meat—works at cross-purposes with the film's conclusions about forms of species and social agency.

At the climax of *Babe*, the eponymous pig's performance on television, staged in part for the benefit of the farm's humans and animals, spectacularly secures a shift in the balance of power in favor of the sort of shared,

Flyer for the advocacy group Animals Australia's "Save Babe" campaign, featuring a healthy little pink piglet, like those starring in the film. Courtesy of Animals Australia.

nonanthropocentric model of social agency that emerges (albeit in defeat) at the end of *Animal Farm*. With its special combination of humans, animals, and especially communications technologies, this vision of a networked barnyard might be understood as modeling the ideal that Donna Haraway calls "cyborg community."[80] For the complex circuits through which the film moves displace questions of whether and how humans control machine–organism integration, making room for considerations of under what conditions stories abandon this fantasy to present alternate forms of species and social agency. And it is television that clearly emerges as a crucible for the processes of narrative and characterization that cast the collective and critical consciousness taking shape in *Strike at Shane's* and *Animal Farm*.

Through the film's multiple and fragmentary narratives, anthropocentric systems dissolve again and again into component parts, shattering the illusion of individuated agency whereby an organism becomes a "self" only on the model of a singular human being. Animals are not simply projected through or incorporated into successive visual media forms but are more complexly intermediated here.[81] What these visual narrative conditions enable is the formation of not just animal representations but more purposefully simulated creatures that I term (*pace* Jean Baudrillard's simulacra) "animalacra."[82]

Animalacra emerge not as humans pretending to be animals, machines pretending to be humans (or machines), but as animals pretending to be other animals in such a way that humans and machines are implicated. *Babe's* central concern with simulation erupts in myriad ways within the story, for instance, in the duck Ferdinand's elaborately staged plan to impersonate an alarm clock, which to him is a "mechanical rooster" or a machine that pretends to be an animal. Becoming animalacra, they move beyond these oppositional limits into more purposefully and recognizably violated species forms, acting like Haraway's cyborg as shifters between a complete- or holistic-organism view to a vision of the body as a site of negotiations of "biotic components."[83] In the end, their deliberately botched forms enable animalacra to reformulate narrative agency for everyone.

Babe unsettles the individual pig's *bildungsroman* condensed in slogans around it, like "The talking pig who makes it big" (a phrase appended to publicity materials for *Gordy*, Disney's talking-pig film released the same year as *Babe*), as well as Animals Australia's "Help us Save Babe." The titular animal, Babe the sheep-pig, remains precariously positioned throughout in ways that foreground two huge problems for animal narratives: that we need to learn how to read animals as something besides individuals or objects, and that there are specific formal traits in the film that allow us to do so. A closer look at *Babe's* multiple and conflicting uses of visual technologies suggests how the film relocates animal agency between extreme poles of abjection and subjectivity—significantly, a formal reworking of animal agency—within the narrative.

Perhaps most striking on a first viewing of the film is the way that it overtly involves its audience in the conflicted construction of the animal-individual. Customarily, three film technologies effectively negate each other as ways of representing animals in film: live action, puppetry, and animation. Each of these technologies, when used exclusively to depict an animal in film, bears the burden of masking the labor involved in effecting this kind of performance.

Here the destabilization of the animal subject, so common in film media where actors of similar shapes and colors continue to be used interchangeably, becomes even more apparent because the colors and shapes have not been carefully matched within individuated characters, let alone individuals.[84] The "bad-wig pig" moments (when a shot of the bald puppet-pig cuts inexplicably to a live piglet with long hair and then back again, all together depicting the same character, Babe) are hard to miss, yet the film remains watchable and, according to my students, even enjoyable to watch countless times. Haphazardly combining all these different modes of imaging in its barnyard characters, and with a startling disregard for the conventions of continuity editing at that, *Babe* locates the labor of asserting animal identity as a shared process. At the crossroads of performance and interpretation, these representational forms inscribe as necessary a range of partnerships between humans and animals.

The bared devices of the film might suggest further that visual media-animals primarily work to expose contradictions repressed within the illusion of human subjectivity dominating these environments, extending feminist film theory's exposure of the multiplicity and contradiction that lies within representations of individual characters.[85] By framing them not as animals but as animalacra, I posit a more self-reflexive process that concerns more deeply the mixed relations of species and narrative forms. The illusion of the individual then can be deconstructed in ways that foster a queerer sense of how the experience of individuals is produced.[86] A glance at the genealogy of *Babe*'s animalacra clarifies how this potential for nonindividuated as well as nonanthropocentric social conceptions of agency proceeds across media forms.

The combination of methods used to depict the animal subject affiliates *Babe*'s animalacra with their Muppet kin in Jim Henson's Creature Shop. These hybrid media relations emerged in the mid-twentieth century as a hallmark of this motley crew—consider Kermit the Frog's stick-propelled arms and Big Bird's totally human-inhabited body on the children's television show *Sesame*

Street—and mutate through the live-action and animatronically manipulated characters of Stephenson's *Animal Farm*. These examples alone suggest a sort of technological progression, but the mixture of media in Noonan's film constitutes no simple break with a tradition in which Muppets have been successively "remediated," or reborn in new media that do not simply supersede but more deliberately erase the old.[87] Television remains the constant across this reinvention of characters from their exclusive depiction through puppetry in *The Muppet Show* and Muppet movies to the all-animated 1980s television series *Muppet Babies*. In *Babe*, the botchedness of animalacra narratives indicates a greater significance to their "enframing" within television than a genealogy of media.[88]

The visual narrative conditions of intermediality are announced by the film's giggling mice, who destabilize a linear, chronological development of Babe's place in time by erratically appearing at the edges of scenes as well as in cue-card-like segues. Anonymous and interchangeable like the dogs of Orwell, this murine multiplicity skitters between "real time" events and the retrospective position occupied by the voice of an omniscient narrator; they move from within the scenes to framelike spaces around them and back again into the story in order to read aloud intertitles that, like a DVD or novel's chapter titles, introduce lines from the coming scenes. In some ways punctuating Babe's story, the mice also bring viewers to its fringes, and ultimately to the scaffolding over it.

The laughter of the mice as they repeat lines spoken by others encourages viewers to be critical of whose story this is, all the more so because the mice speak the lines before they erupt in the real time of the story.[89] So, for example, the first two intertitles, "Pigs Are Definitely Stupid" and "The Way Things Are," are uttered by the border collie bitch Fly as aphorisms to Babe the pig, who thereby describes and also enforces the overarching "rule" that the purpose of "stupid" animals on the farm is to eat and then to be eaten. Like Orwell's pigs, whose rhetoric Fly and her partner Rex appear to adopt, the border collie appeals to these truisms in ways that mystify her own position of power. However, as echoes that precede their sounding, copies without originals, the mice's mimicking preemption of the lines ushers in alternatives to this narrative reinforcement of the absolute authority of human subjects.

Babe's transgressions of the laws laid down by the dogs point toward a different sense of agency that shifts the terms of having a place on the farm from biological destiny to social performance. Babe casts doubt on the order of things, and this doubt intensifies through the development of his friendships with members of other species, namely, Ferdinand the duck and Maa the ewe. These creatures, whom the dogs call "stupid," give voice to the oppositional view that humans and dogs are "savages," and Ferdinand speaks for all of these animals at the bottom of the farm's food chain as he declares that the dogs' version of "'the way things are' stinks." Like the rest of the characters openly expressing dissent from the dogs' rule, the duck is portrayed through puppet performances that remain sketchily integrated with animatronic technology in a way that subtly links these botched animal forms to proliferations of narratives and agents.

Thus, the film not only formally denotes animals considered food for the human "bosses" as dissidents but also (and in ways implicitly targeted by Adams's vegetarian–feminist critique) narratively aligns nonanthropomorphic realism with anthropocentric views of reality. Forestalling the formation of a unified oppositional ontology within the narrative, Babe's interactions with Maa and Ferdinand remain abrupt and are fraught with violence. And so they also reinforce an ideological parallel between these foodstuff animals and the exploited animals of *Animal Farm*, doomed alike because they sustain no alternative models of agency to that of the self-centered human.

So how does the film interject an emergent consciousness that, as Haraway initially wrote of the cyborg, "any finally coherent subject is a fantasy, and that personal and collective identity is precariously and constantly socially reconstituted"?[90] Haraway's representational forms prove crucial to her extension of the cyborg model to companion species, in whom "flesh and signifier, bodies and words, stories and worlds" are enlisted in "remodeling and remolding" agents that breach the confines of human individuals. And they begin to explain how *Babe* broadcasts visual images in ways that change everyday stories of cross-species intimacies.[91] Willfully integrated into the farm community, systematically included if not so clearly ideologically converted to the precession of animalacra, humans and animals alike connect by watching Babe on television.

(Tele)Visions of Collective Agency

The final sequence of *Babe* proves the culmination of a pattern in which television provides the means by which the meat animals of *Babe* give new order to their world, and with consequences for others. Direct engagements with this particular visual medium not only signal changes in characters' self-perceptions within the narrative but also demonstrate how it takes a whole farm community to raise a pig above the status of food. Rather than simply overthrowing the human as a symbol of power (that is, revisiting the failed proposition of *Animal Farm*), the animals and humans of *Babe* together become integrated in shared social networks inseparable from this medium, radically altering the representational status of all elements in the new system, while maintaining a precise, or precisely botched, integrity in visual animal forms.

As the story unfolds, human characters are introduced (and the aura of subjectivity consequently eroded) by filtration through conflicting animal perspectives along with a pastiche of visual media.[92] The reticence of the principal human character, Farmer Hoggett (James Cromwell), enables him to elude definitive self-characterization and shifts the burden of elaborating Hoggett's relation to his world onto visual-media animals.[93] Generally referred to as "the Boss" by the animals, Hoggett seems defined by a characteristic silence that aligns him more with stereotypical farm animals than with any of the other characters in the film, encouraging other humans (including viewers) initially to overlook him. Hoggett's silence invites misreading even within the diegesis and also cultivates a point of departure from Orwellian assumptions about the oppressive and self-serving engagements of humans with technology. Particularly through his uses of television, the farmer's actions come to contradict others' views of him.

Hoggett never explains why he begins training Babe as a shepherd, but, given this opportunity, the pig lateralizes, forging a new place for himself on the farm by fostering cooperation among his companions. In addition to new ways of working in the field, Hoggett's intimacy with the animals clearly redefines the rules of the farm when he invites the piglet into his house to watch television. Following the camera angle over his shoulder, television takes center stage in this scene, and the film's viewers are integrated into this animalacral circuit by watching it alongside Hoggett, Babe, and Fly. Although this moment signals how relations of man and pig are permanently altered, this reconstitution of Hoggett is significantly precipitated by his wife's brief departure from the farm with the Country Women's Group, for reasons that I spell out below.

The relationship between farmer and pig proves so successful that Hoggett decides to enter the two of them in a field-trial competition, which (like *International Velvet*) viewers later see through characters watching a live broadcast. For the sheep-pig's courteous use of language (instead of doglike physical aggression) needs to secure more than just a place for himself other than as dinner on the humans' table; he must work to redefine the human as another kind of animal. Cheering on pig, sheep, man, and themselves for their part in a peaceful power transition, humans and animals see themselves and one another as no longer antagonistic and instead are deeply integrated in these new potentials.

There is more to say about how television is introduced in the earlier sequence in *Babe* as a necessary condition for the *erasure* of individuated identity, not only at the human level but also at the animal level. Immediately after the initial television-watching scene, at the moment when the farmer seems to have lifted the pig from the status of meat animal, Duchess, the "bad cat bearing a grudge," shatters this illusion. She tells him that "pigs don't have a purpose except to get eaten by people," a sentiment confirmed later by Fly that reinforces the sacrificial notion of the animal agent as conceived only as a support for the human subject. Perceiving the futility of asserting himself as an individuated subject under these conditions, Babe, Lear-like, wanders off alone, spending a stormy night exposed to the elements, until Hoggett and the dogs find him in the morning shivering in the graveyard. The death of the subject, so to speak, here enables the birth of the farm community, mobilizing even the resistant Rex in the common cause that Babe champions.

But at first, the symbolic death of Babe's isolated "self" leaves him despondent, requiring more than just the attentions of the vet and the sympathy of Rex to get him ready for competition. To get Babe back on his hooves in time to command a broader audience, Hoggett must show his commitment to the dissolution of human dominance, embodied in his song and dance. Placing the animals as viewing subjects and the farmer as performer, Hoggett's routine in the "If I Had Words" song-and-dance sequence functions in the narrative as more than simple role reversal. Risking "a threatening loss of control" and a "radical annihilation of the metaphor of selfhood and of the will," this crucial scene establishes human accountability to the other organisms participating in the farm system, securing the textual deconstruction of anthropocentrism.[94] Hoggett, through self-dissolution more than self-abasement, convinces Babe that the pig's role as shepherd on the farm overrides his efficacy as human food. Serving as a corrective to Ferdinand's attempts to fashion himself as a worker rather than dinner for the humans, this sequence rearticulates a sense of agricultural community explicitly in terms of reciprocity.

With the animals united by their mutual respect for Hoggett and Babe, and with Babe once again ready for competition, the final, unforeseen obstacle—his initial inability to communicate with the strange sheep at the international herding competition—arrives as a test of the integrity of this rearrangement of the farm's component parts. For the narrative to come to fruition, it is not enough for the animal characters to act like other animals: they have to communicate as animalacra. Converted to the new model of interdependence, Rex returns to the sheep at home to ask for assistance. Exacting a promise of civility from him, the Hoggett flock divulges the "paa-aassword," an ovine chant that sounds more appropriate to the rituals of a fraternal order than to a species-specific language, so that Babe can perform on television in order to transform "the way things are." Running back and running out of time, Rex leaps aboard a moving truck—significantly, the electric-company repair truck, which restarts the television in the Hoggett house—and so makes Babe's victory all the more obviously dependent on visual media circuits.

Simultaneously, Hoggett's wife, Esme, in her hotel room and the animals back in the barnyard discover Babe on television and watch together while Hoggett (as the astonished announcers note) "does nothing" before Rex runs on the field to bring the password that will enable Babe to win the championship. Through the dog, the broadcast signal, and the television, at once receiving and conveying it, a synchronization connects various audiences across species and technological forms—the barnyard animals, the showground's spectators, the captivated Country Women's Group overriding Esme's protests, and even the film's audience. Precariously emerging through representational forms, the sheep-pig's story thus ends with a vision of this dependence on visual communication networks. This vision is explicitly drawn from Dick King-Smith's source novel, which also ends with an image of the farmer and pig triumphing on television, a cyborg vision of machine–human–animal integration that defies so much of the history of meat processing.

Although constructed for the viewer as the product of a visual-media integrated, collective process, the film's happy ending, derived from this performance, is diegetically attributed to the emotive nature of the pig, a sentiment that jibes more clearly with the pivotal significance of pigs in modern industrial meat narratives. Although working against the interests of meat industries by depicting animals who proclaim that they do not want to be eaten, *Babe* remains indeterminate on the question of livestock as commodities. Against the film's cues that this conclusion remains "unprecedented," comparison of this circuit with other resistant ones even within the film indicates at what costs animalacra find happiness. Its "subversion" of hierarchies, particularly those of gender, "from within the terms of the law," leads to the reinforcement of others, signaling some more pervasive problems with "pigs" as movie meat.[95]

Barnyard Gender Troubles, or "That'll do, pig"

Babe wields visual technologies in radical ways that challenge the fixity of species identity in meat animals, but it leaves gendered identities unchallenged, which is a huge problem, particularly from vegetarian–feminist perspectives. Although the reinvented barnyard system in the end remains open to all members of the farm community, degrees of equality seem measured in inverse proportion to degrees of gender markings. By implying that gender marks a limit to integration with technology, the film indirectly conveys a more targeted version of *Animal Farm*'s message, namely, that some animalacra "are more equal than others." Because this inequality is conveyed only between the lines, in this respect it also more clearly engages the problems specific to the "post-gender world" that Haraway imagines as encircling the cyborg. More to the point here, gender troubles *Babe*'s vision of collectively and technologically enabled animal agency, revealing how human identity (and possibly any species) forms can neither transcend nor be transcended even by animalacra.

The character Babe poses a singular formal problem in this light. The pig is clearly referred to with male pronouns throughout. But the female human actor, Nancy Cartwright, supplies his voice, just as she does for television cartoon boy Bart Simpson. "And it's not for nothing that Babe's gender remains fluid and ambiguous throughout the film," as one reviewer was quick to note.[96] This primary evasion of stable gender identification, although never explicitly acknowledged in the film, complicates the resolution of Babe's identity crises through domestic attachments. That the border collies' pups are sold off the farm provides Babe with the opportunity to bond with Fly, an adoption by or re-filiation with a gendered maternal body that apparently defies the oedipal trajectory implicit in her claim that "everyone has to leave their mother."

In a strange wish-fulfillment for mother and child, uneasily overseen by a default father whose "law" is based on an apartheid order of species, Babe reinserts himself within the hierarchies of family life on the farm, and from here proceeds to undermine the law of the dog father (which also is invoked in the name of a human one, queer interfaces of species apparently becoming more viable than a queer spectrum of sexualities in this context). In this way the film intimates how, in contrast to suturings of technology with the individual form, its utopian vision of species and collective life could rupture existing social orders of gender, if not sex. But in the end, *Babe*'s domesticated machine–animal interfaces challenge divisive systems that prop up the human forms of subjectivity on the shoulders (and hams) of others—at least, they do so for creatures in the film identified as male.

Fly, as working mother and house pet, born-and-bred sheepdog and elective swineherd, appears most of all caught between systems. This bitch's narrative place is limited to being a mediator of needs and jealousies, and for playing these hybrid roles she is respected, affirmed, and included by Babe only to be rejected, bitten, and perhaps permanently disabled by Rex. From this perspective, it is significant that she can curtail Rex's pattern of abuse only when she asserts herself as an advocate of Babe's way of doing things, and thereby persuades her dog "husband" to complete the circuit of animalacra.

In pointed contrast, Maa, the sheep whose name clearly identifies her with mothering and whose staunchly singular species-identification precludes the possibility of working to change her future as food, is distanced from direct participation in the final collective achievement. At the end, the sheep agree to give Rex the password "for Maa's sake." Because she is dead by this point, there is no way to know whether she would have sanctioned this trust in canine "wolves" (some of whom, after all, kill and eat her). Maa's premature death enables this co-optation by the emergent farm community, but it also begs some questions about how gender and sex factor into the symbolic exchanges

Still image from *Babe*, featuring the gallant (and here a "bad-wig" or live) pig himself alongside the wounded border collie bitch Fly.

and deaths beginning with agriculture and extending through all commodity systems. Why, in addition to being the most puppetlike characters, are the film's only corpses also female? How does the mobilization of animalacra involve the destruction of gendered bodies? Why are females, especially mothers, the only casualties of this postgender utopia?

Babe does clarify that these are problems for the human no less than the meat animal. Mrs. Hoggett, the fat woman whose multifarious claim to mothering is constantly reinforced in her constant expressions of concern with feeding her daughter, grandchildren, husband, and cat, exemplifies how, at every level, meat concerns the domestication of gendered bodies. In Adams's terms, she appears interpellated by the pornographic ideology of meat, constantly talking of Babe in terms of "big, juicy hams" and other body parts, possibly to be prized on display at the county fair before being more literally consumed, but always as absent referents to his eventual slaughter and butchering. Throughout the film, Mrs. Hoggett is always eating or discussing how to prepare food for or from others, so it is not surprising that, of all the inhabitants of the farm, Mrs. Hoggett becomes the most tenuously transformed component of the animalacral circuit.

In the final sequence, Mrs. Hoggett physically obscures, adamantly denies, and eventually bursts into cathartic tears at the sight of Babe and her husband on television. While her choking on a cookie and fainting with her teacup in hand seems calculated to provide comic relief, these actions also align her autocratic authority, large woman's body, and limitless oral appetite within to the tradition of the female grotesque. This sequence, placing her in a hotel room with a group of other women, is the apex of a specifically oral and de-eroticizing (but no less feminizing) portrait of the farmer's wife. Ham-handed, to say the least, this dramatization of resistance to animalacra hinges on the redemptive qualities of the farm animals' winning performance as much as on her being immediately surrounded by another agricultural collective, the Country Women's Group, who force her to join them in watching the revolution that will have to be televised.

These menacing images of the female therefore do not emerge against a utopian picture of the animal as (post)gendered so much as they propel criticism of prescriptive identity forms derived from function, whether in relation to the individual human center or the noncentered barnyard community. So, for instance, Mrs. Hoggett's relationship with her feminized feline involves another engagement of cross-species relations with visual-media histories, only to different ends. The housecat Duchess's identification with the woman of the farm inspires a different sort of oppositional rhetoric from those of Babe and the dogs. Whereas the rest of the animals refer to Farmer Hoggett as "the boss," and his spouse as "the boss's wife," the cat inverts these terms, referring when she speaks to "the boss" (meaning Mrs. Hoggett) and "the boss's husband." Appealing to the symbolic feline/feminine identification that marks a long tradition of cinematic *femmes fatales*, the animal–human relation in this instance clarifies that the authority of the subject is always questionable, a matter of perspective.

On close inspection, it appears that *Babe* pairs woman and cat in a quiet struggle with the pig and man for barnyard power. While the film sharply limits this contest by stacking the deck against the feline/female duo, it imagines the greatest challenge to animalacra as coming not from an Orwellian singular male farmer shadowed by the pig and dogs but rather from the woman and cat, and the terms of this struggle in turn trouble biological hierarchies and Derridean "carnophallogocentric" progressions alike. Taking into account how Fly's mediating role as working mother partially counteracts this double-edged demonization/victimization of female characters, it seems all the more important that the emphasis in the final sequence is placed on Mrs. Hoggett's reconciliation with other women as well as to the farm's new order, productively aligning the visual performance of gender and species in the service of something other than human identity.[97]

Situated amid these conflicting models, the last line of the film—"That'll do, pig," spoken by Hoggett to Babe—resounds with threats and promises. However gently or affectionately Hoggett delivers the line, it is an order; and "pig," although zoologically correct as a generic term of address for this particular animal, also bears pejorative and female-sex-specific connotations, suggesting that Babe's feminine coding legitimates a possible restoration of the human order of dominance.[98] Reinvoking identity, the human's line might be read as signaling a foreclosure of the film's potential to situate individuating culture (what others might call "nature") as a production indebted to institutional culture (what others might call "culture"). And it begins to explain why some see *Babe* as moving far away from *Animal Farm* toward a "post-benefits world," in which the privileged individual takes the credit for collective labor and only condescendingly throws this last bone to the pig.[99]

However, to dismiss *Babe* in this way is to disclaim as well the power of the animalacral elements that I have been at pains to draw out, and that work against such totalizing visions. And it is in this respect that animal multiplicity proves most significant. Watching Babe and Hoggett on television with the other animals at the end, the mice never directly interact with the film's characters in any other way. Together they skitter through stories and animalacral circuits, staking out in this final appearance a sense of unity as necessarily fleeting, as amplifying even as it transmits changes across film and viewing communities.

In other words, their incomplete yet coherent figuration of multiplicity— what otherwise might be construed as the failure of the film to cultivate a unified heroic agent through a bafflingly schizophrenic approach to agency— indicates how visual media become infused with animals, and in ways that suggest how the psychic subject of postmodernity might be construed in (Haraway's) terms of coalitional networks, or how the collaborative agents of posthumanism might be conceived through (Deleuze's) coordinations of "singularities."[100] Certainly the primary link between meat-animal narratives and shared futures, including those of the genetically modified organisms bookending this chapter, becomes apparent here through Babe's many shifting porcine forms.

Agri/cultural Constituents

Strangely unnoted by commentators are *Babe*'s many resemblances to *To and Again* (later published under the title *Freddy Goes to Florida*), the 1928 opening installment of Walter R. Brooks's popular twenty-six-volume children's novel series featuring Freddy the Pig. Most obviously, Ferdinand's ongoing battle with the alarm clock inverts the premise of Brooks's fiction, in which the rooster Charles laments his position on a farm too poor to have an alarm clock, for his own oversleeping puts him in constant danger of "being fricasseed." The rooster's desire for a respite from these and other drudgeries of rural farm life inspires him to propose that the farm animals "migrate" like birds, an argument that is so persuasive that they are quickly joined by spiders and mice. Introducing the question of who must stay behind to fulfill the animals' "duty" to the farmer, a dog again enforces a human sense of order at a meeting of the animals that elaborates the revolutionary barnyard assembly scene in *The Strike at Shane's*, which is retooled in subsequent fictions like *Animal Farm* and *Babe*.[101]

Largely read as celebrating the agrarian values for which pigs stand, *To and Again* introduces the "clever" pig trope elaborated in more famous children's fictions such as E. B. White's *Charlotte's Web* (1952), where, too, the meat animal's lot improves when he works with others to manipulate media, and, more explicitly, to garner good press.[102] Appearing to contrast *Animal Farm* and *Babe*, these early twentieth-century fictions posit communications media together with other technological means of modern living as unequivocally advantageous for all of the farm's constituents. Upon his animals' return, for instance, the temporarily abandoned farmer of *To and Again* draws up a labor contract for a six-hour farm-animal workday with overtime benefits and promises to invest their money in new barns "with all the modern conveniences."[103]

Even within an early and relatively mild farmyard-revolt story, one that envisions a happy ending in the modernized farm, in which some animals lead others, including humans, to a technological escape from the inconveniences of endemic rural poverty, forms of species and social agency remain troubled. The adventures of Brooks's animals bring them to the capitol and a visit with the president, "who shook them each by a claw or a paw or a hoof," a meeting expedited by a senator who recognizes their growing fame:

> "By George! I have heard about these animals! They belong to one of my constituents. They're going to Florida for the winter, and I believe they're the first animals that ever migrated. This, gentlemen, is one of the most important occurrences in the annals of this august assemblage. I'm going to order a band, and take them round and show them the city." . . .
>
> "What's a constituent?" asked [the cow,] Mrs. Wiggins.[104]

Not even the clever pig can say, but amid this image of electively free-range meat animals, celebrated on a national scale for their decision to walk off the farm, this question flashes with all the potential for animal agency to change the modern industrial conditions of meat, resonating in a precise way with the more recent mutations of pig stories in the context of mass slaughter.

The specter of death haunts all farm-animal fictions, and, clever pigs notwithstanding, the slaughter of an individual hog conventionally marks a narrative moment as pivotal in human character development, often providing an opportunity for protagonists to dis-identify with rough living. So, for instance, the title character of Thomas Hardy's *Jude the Obscure* (1895) introduces himself to the misery of a bad marriage in rural poverty by following his big, bossy wife Arabella's orders to kill their pig. Revolting Jude, Arabella's thirst for the animal's blood is as sure a sign of debasement here as it is among the pack of castaway boys in William Golding's *Lord of the Flies* (1962), who signal their turn to savagery by first hunting wild pigs, and along the way develop the skills that enable them to hunt down one of their own, the fat boy auspiciously nicknamed Piggy. Rapacious appetites and corpulence again link *Babe*'s Esme Hoggett to a narrative role defined in conjunction with the transformation of pigs to pork. In addition, concurrent developments in fiction position pig killing and eating as sites of more profound changes in the character of agricultural communities.

Exemplifying this complementary development, *Little House in the Big Woods* (1932), Laura Ingalls Wilder's first installment of her popular, nostalgic, and loosely autobiographical children's book series, includes a detailed description of her father killing and butchering the family pig before the onset of winter. The casualness with which children get into this process seems as startling to today's readers as other scenes in which children are beaten by their parents and teachers. Yet the girlish fascination with the food that follows the pig-killing scene also begins to explain why backyard "pork slaughtering and curing," which provided both trade items and means of sustenance for people with little access to cash, became so "widespread in rural America."[105] As human populations grow, and grow more urban, such scenes clarify further how human and animal populations remain connected by the fragile, rusty chains of mutual dependence that define rural subsistence living.

Similar scenes included in more recent documentary films like *Brother's Keeper* (1992) and *Dead River* (2002), the latter touted on its DVD cover as "the most popular film requested in the Maine State Penitentiary," instead flesh out more adult themes, illustrating what land-poor people do to get by. Earlier I suggested this shift in ideas of animal farming as a condition from which one might be saved through modern living—the theme developed in *To and Again*, where modern conveniences deliver animals and people from drudgery—to a more ambivalent state a generation later in Orwell's novel, where again modernity fails to deliver salvation through the windmill. In these and other recent narratives, pig butchering at home on the farm comes to stand not so much for old, rural folkways as for an idea of farm community as itself in need of saving.

These conditions begin to explain why the prospect of the farm's foreclosure begins the film sequel *Babe: Pig in the City* (1999), and more broadly why later twentieth-century fictions use human–porcine relations to narrate a significant change in the operations of agriculture, which many see as beginning with the farm crisis in the United States in the 1980s. A credit crunch in banking, accelerated by natural disasters, put small-scale, family-owned farms in jeopardy. They quickly became heavily mortgaged, then sold (often at foreclosure auctions) and reorganized as large-scale, absentee-owned businesses. Some former owners have been recruited as lower-level managers or workers for these corporations. But many more lost the only livelihood they knew, and rural communities consequently have been decimated. Moreover, the operations that replaced them—the kind of densely populated confinement facilities that minimize human–animal contact from which Babe is fortuitously plucked at the beginning of the first film—facilitate the transformation (more precisely, the real subsumption) of agricultural labor to factory farming for animals and humans alike.[106]

These stories emphasize how hard financial times especially threatened independent pig farmers, who by the end of the 1970s were already struggling to stay in business due to the widespread closure of pork slaughterhouses following declining consumer demands. Like any industry, centralization poses problems for workers and consumers. In this case, it also affects whether and how people and animals live together, a concern central to artist Mik Morrisey's ongoing series *The Last Farm in Town*. A view in part of the pig farm on which Morrisey grew up, *Country Funk* (2008) at once frames the everyday intimacies of feeding animals swill made from a community's waste and confronts the nostalgic, sanitizing views of farm life inspiring the community to shut down its last outpost against suburban sprawl, its last open views of where their food comes from. The emphasis here on intercorporeal relations echoes a turn in recent meat-animal fictions toward acknowledging how these increasingly difficult circumstances surrounding farm life did not lead to the death of the meat industry but rather to its transformation into a technological dystopia for humans and animals alike.[107]

Mik Morrisey, *Country Funk*, 2008. From the series *Last Farm in Town*, this photograph of a farmer feeding his pigs homemade swill explores the fragility of human–animal intimacies in modern American food production. Copyright Mik Morrisey. Courtesy of the artist.

Most often lauded for its clever retelling of *King Lear* from Goneril's perspective, Jane Smiley's novel *A Thousand Acres* (1991) also significantly resets Shakespeare's tragedy as that of an Iowan family's struggle over land ownership in the 1980s. For the tragic ambition here is to rule not over a kingdom but over the lean hog market, and its doom is sealed when the bank refuses to extend credit to complete the rebuilding of the pig yard into the kind of vertically coordinated feedlot that would have allowed the family business to join the ranks of the few viable owner-operated agricultural operations left in the United States. Although never as a character, the ubiquitous Iowan pig centrally figures as a source of income, indeed as all upon which the future of the farm family's ownership depends. But in myriad other ways throughout this novel, from the fateful pig roast at the beginning to the poisoned pickled sausages destroyed at the end, pigs also suggest more direct threats to people's lives that inhere in these reinventions of farm communities.

The changing potentials for pigs as icons and actors in these circumstances emerge in Bharati Mukherjee's *Jasmine* (1989), a novel that follows an immigrant's journey from India to Iowa in the 1980s. Toward the end, as the title character comes to the realization that there is no future for her in farm country, the sound of hungry hogs leads her to discover that a sympathetic farmer has hung himself over the sty that he had been building with an unsecured loan, no longer able to handle the stress of awaiting the bank's unlikely decision to finance it. Jasmine flees the scene, haunted by the spectacle of pigs who "leap and chew" at the dead man's "bloodied boots," and immediately after leaves Iowa for good.[108] While these fictional animals could be read as metaphors for the independent farmer's way of life consumed by debt, the horror witnessed in scene after scene of farm failure also concerns a world turned upside down, in which meat animals turn people into food.

Frightening en masse, bodying forth exceptionally menacing figures of animal multiplicity, herds of swine fed human flesh also haunt *Hannibal* (2001), the sequel to the 1991 blockbuster *The Silence of the Lambs*, upping the ante on the original cannibal theme with pigs raised to kill and eat people. These stories and images reflect no simple inversion of hierarchies, say, of a person's life threatened instead of a pig's, but rather the agribusiness (or "farmageddon") threat to whole ways of life shared across species. This point is forcefully made with the deliberate deferral of this very spectacle of pigs eating humans alive in Atwood's *Oryx and Crake*, a speculative fiction that pursues yet another mutation in the narrative developments of meat-animal agency.

Suturing the eyewitness narrative with the other tradition outlined above that concerns the modern conditions (and limits) of human–animal community, this novel is structured around the perspective of an industry initiate through whom audiences encounter intensively farmed meat animals as commodities and agents alike. Further, these potentials emerge here through a story that ranges pigs along at least two other meat-animal genealogies that return to the concerns about real artificial meat with which I began this chapter. Contrasting pigs' representational histories with those of chickens, and both to less formally coherent genetic hybrids, the novel introduces a variety of meat animals as agents only to conclude that their intercorporeal forms, rapidly proliferating in modern-industrial animal husbandry, threaten sustainability on a global scale.

Questions about whether and how tissue-cultured meat remains animal—and consequently what it means to read such creations as agents or things—emerge in *Oryx and Crake* through the spectacle of ChickieNob, a biotech creature designed as a renewable meat source. Arguably, through animal-husbandry techniques, all domesticated animals become renewable meat sources, and with increasing technical sophistication comes the increased threats of breeding zoonoses. This complex mutation of animal agency is apparent even in a U.S. government poster that attempts to raise awareness of avian flu and other viruses with the image of a comic chicken using optical devices, a sort of monstrous realization of the hopes floated by *Babe*.

Atwood's choice of source species historically ties ChickieNobs to Nobel laureate Alexis Carrel's success with keeping an embryonic chicken muscle growing in a bowl fed with nutrients for thirty-two years, an experiment that as some commentators on real artificial meat note inspired Winston Churchill in a 1932 essay titled "Fifty Years Hence" to observe wryly, "We shall escape the absurdity of growing a whole chicken in order to eat the breast or wing, by growing these parts separately under a suitable medium."[109] Meeting these desires and more, the fictional ChickieNob regenerates its own flesh and has no face, and therefore seems to anticipate as well PETA's desire for chicken rendered incomprehensible as such. Incapable of expressing any suffering, the utilitarian's dream creature in Atwood's novel lends itself to seemingly endless harvesting for fast-food-chain products designed specially around it, like the ChickieNob Bucket'o'Nubbins.

It is intriguing to think of this animal as a techno-fantasy inspired in part by ancient Nordic mythology, specifically Særimner the pig, who every day gets cooked, its meat eaten by the inhabitants of Valhalla, then every night grows its own flesh back for more of the same. Atwood's ChickieNob directly

Logo for "Biosecurity for Birds," an outreach initiative launched in 2004 by the United States Department of Agriculture's Animal and Plant Health Inspection Service to help prevent the spread of Avian Influenza, Exotic Newcastle Disease, and other outbreaks.

reflects a literary predecessor, the amorphous Chicken Little of Frederick Pohl and C. M. Kornbluth's novel *The Space Merchants* (1954).[110] Both fictions present these meat animals as examples of a larger problem—corporate greed run amok—and introduce them through narrators who are both admen, content with eating the chickenlike meat yet expressing horror when confronted with its biotech source. The admen's mixed responses to meat and meatmaker might be read as adumbrating the ambivalence with which they eventually turn against their bosses as part of global capitalist implosions (these are, after all, speculative fictions). But only *Oryx and Crake* imagines the real artificial meat creature as an animal with no agency.

Unlike ChickieNobs, the amorphous Chicken Little plays an active role in the story, sheltering members of the resistance movement working to bring down the system that exploits her (and she is distinctly gendered in this novel as well). Chicken Little's capacity to react, even think, however, becomes figured in *Oryx and Crake* by very different animals, the bioengineered pigs nicknamed "pigoons," who, more like real artificial meat, enter human food chains through medical biology, not food science. In the longer history of meat narratives outlined above, this development intertwines clever and threatening qualities, emphasizing how form matters to perceptions of encounters between meat-producing and consuming creatures. And with their movement out of the secure, confined spaces of intensive bioengineering production, the pigoons underscore how animal as much as posthuman futures hang in the balance.[111]

In Atwood's novel, the genetically modified pigoons are created initially to customize and thereby render more efficient the process of xenotransplantation. Like real artificial meat, this fantasy extends current medical practice, where pigs are already in use (for instance, as sources of valve replacements for human hearts). But *Oryx and Crake*'s protagonist's first encounter imagines people with pigs taking this technology into more dangerous territory: "When [as a child he] went in to visit the pigoons [in his father's lab,] he had to put on a biosuit that was too big for him, and wear a face mask. . . . He especially liked the small pigoons. . . . They were cute. But the adults were slightly frightening, with their runny noses and tiny, white-lashed pink eyes. They glanced up at him as if they saw him, really saw him, and might have plans for him later."[112]

Artist Jason Courtney's illustration of the glances exchanged between boy and pigoon emphasizes how humans make themselves more machinic amid conditions in which pigs are being made to be more human. Infused with human genetic material, eventually hosting "genuine human neocortex

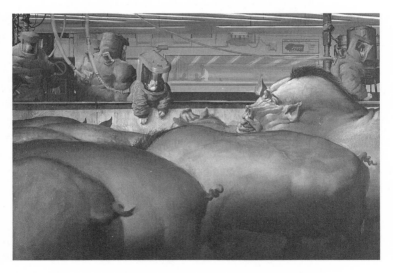

Jason Courtney, *Jimmy Went in to See the Pigoons*, oil on canvas, 2004, part of a series titled *Oryx and Crake*, described by the artist as "illustrations to Margaret Atwood's dystopian novel, taken on as a personal project." Copyright Jason Courtney. Courtesy of the artist.

tissue," pigoons puncture genomic boundaries between species with this penetrating gaze, and more.[113]

The impending future scarcity driving the production of real artificial meat becomes compounded in Atwood's speculative fiction by bioengineered diseases that are deliberately spread as a form of corporate sabotage (hence the biosuits). Consequently, the novel's pigoons, like cloned animals in the United States, quietly get added to the human food chain as a by-product of research and development for the biomedical industry. But the cleverness of these pig-shaped genetic hybrids proves another unintended consequence of developing this animal as a biotech fix to human medical problems, only far more deadly. After humans unleash a plague on themselves of one last exceptionally virulent GM pathogen, the pigoons roam free, becoming a sort of piggy goon squad. Given this advantage, these newly feral animals apparently use their human brain matter to plan and coordinate the hunting of humans. In this way, the novel twists together the demonic pig images characterizing the more realistic contemporary fictions of farm life in collapse and the clever pig narrative trope to envision how, along with the physical and social spaces that might sustain it, farm life has already become a thing of the past.

Atwood's speculations about industrial meat-animal production not only concludes with ecocide on a global scale but also insists that these conditions are fostered by the corporate creation of masses of impoverished, displaced humans. Even before the apocalyptic plague strikes, these folks are restricted to urban-as-ghetto environs called "pleeblands" by the biotech industry elite, who live safely gated inside palatial corporate suburban-style compounds, at least before the apocalypse comes. Along with the physical and social spaces that might sustain it, farm life has already become a thing of the past by the time the novel begins; this is why the only meat depicted is produced in laboratories. While the pigoon "pork" and ChickieNobs Bucket'o'Nubbins vividly illustrate the costs to consumers of real artificial meat, *Oryx and Crake* introduces one more kind of meat that illustrates how more than just humans and meat animals are affected by these developments.

Ranged alongside the more familiar chicken and pork derivatives, the novel mentions a hybrid meat animal bioengineered for a different reason. The "kanga-lamb, a new Australian splice that combined the placid character and high-protein yield of sheep with the kangaroo's resistance to disease and absence of methane-producing, ozone-depleting flatulence," points to a new potential for meat animals as environmental agents.[114] Mentioned only once as high-end restaurant fare, the kanga-lamb inscribes the frontline challenges of biotech implementations of GM meat animals as actors, in this case working to reduce pollution (though not very well, if not also reducing meat animals' much more eco-threatening belching). In curious ways, this fictional meat animal also extends the sense of independent farm life as inextricable from rural community relations and so begins to figure how this kind of meat animal extends the sense of barnyard as ongoing community relations, all the more so because its counterparts are coming to market in the form of pigs.

Perhaps because tissue-cultured meat has moved from fiction to fact, *Oryx and Crake* inspires critical discussions "focused on [the] agency of animals" that exceed bioengineering designs for meat.[115] But it seems all too often that they do so to the exclusion of broader labor and environmental issues, introduced at the beginning of the novel by "burning piles of animals"—an all-too-real media spectacle today following foot-and-mouth and avian-flu scares—in fiction "intentionally infected, very possibly to drive up meat prices."[116] This extends the problematic pattern of response to novels like *The Jungle* and *Animal Farm* in the critical tradition, that is, the interests of animals are pitted against those of people more clearly in interpretations than in the texts themselves. Again, critical questions hinge on perceptions of whether meat is the message or the medium: Is the point to expose meat-as-laboratory animal exploitation? Or is it to educate readers about the privileges and risks for human society of implementing genetic technologies to "culture the pleebland"?[117] Reading the pigoons as extensions of this changing twentieth-century literary and cultural history of representing pigs, I suggest yet another option: that it is becoming increasingly necessary to see pigs as involved and involving people in creating and sustaining shared lives in open country.

More so than in the responses to earlier meat narratives, the simultaneous development of these parallel critical trajectories indicates how anthropocentric concepts of agency founder amid the transformation of traditional breeding, farming, and slaughtering practices within the enclosures of confined animal feedlot operations (CAFOs). In other words, industrial meat fictions of the past century do not indicate a progress narrative, say, of the human-interest story giving way to concerns about animal lives. Especially in contrast to the polarizing patterns of interpretation, these fictions beg questions about how the interests of all life forms—human, animal, plant, tissue, cellular—converge in the multiform intimacies on which meat industries depend and the viability of narratively and visually representing intercorporeal life. And with the arrival of Enviropig™, new developments in the genetic science of pig breeding make these concerns appear not to be matters of idle speculation but arguably the most pressing issues of our time.

Developers of this creature position Enviropig™ conceptually as a meeting

ground for agri-food flows. But when introducing live Enviropigs™ to the public, scientists take care to normalize these GM creatures as ordinary meat animals. As with the exchange of gazes connecting Atwood's narrator to pigoons,
perceptions are a big part of what will determine whether this kind of creature will consequently prove, as does the piglet in *Babe: Pig in the City*, the
actor who can save the family farm. Pending approval for commercial implementation, Enviropig™ seems also to await a narrative potential for animal
agency, even for meat's semi-living agency, that would allow for envisioning
such creatures as more than simply commodities.

Regardless of whether this creature follows cloned cattle quietly into the
all-important U.S. market, or consumers suddenly balk at the prospect of eating "Frankenfood" with a face, those who stand to gain or lose the most from
their commercialization will be the swineherds and animals who now occupy
the indeterminate openings between the government- and corporate-owned
lands. Their only future is one in which together pigs and people flag the last
outposts of what has come to be defined as rural sustainable life, an option
that is foregone in Atwood's vision of our near future and that the fallout of
the global credit crisis of 2008 seems to be making all the more ephemeral.
Therefore it seems all the more crucial to ask: How do those involved in meat-
making, from livestock to (un)dead meat, shape histories and futures, whether
as commodities (ChickieNobs), as afterthoughts in the processes of commodi-
fication (kanga-lambs), or as mutations of such creatures into feral and other
agency forms (Chicken Little and pigoons)?

Escape from contact with rendered animal products, distributed in such
rarified forms as asphalt and machine lubricants, is not an option for those who
live in industrial societies. Rather than ethical solutions, dreams of animal-
free real artificial meat present at best a convoluted solution to meat's image
problems, a plan that involves not stopping the rendering of animals as food
products but rarifying it, not removing animals from meat-making but deeply
altering the roles of humans along with various species, including potential
new life forms. From *Animal Farm* to *Disembodied Cuisine*, formal problems
with perspective and perception suggest that productive interventions in the
relations of meat animals, along with the living fragments of their bodies
incorporated by others, start from the deeply embedded conditions of intercorporeality. Taken together, these texts suggest that meat animals share in
deeply ambivalent cultural histories that predict how real artificial meat (coming soon in minced porklike products) remains rooted in agents that, even as
people mess with them, cannot help but mess with people, too.

Rising today to unprecedented levels, global meat consumption rightly becomes cause for environmental concern, but these stories clarify that much more is at stake than minimizing ecological footprints with Enviropigs™ or alleviating animal suffering in a future in which meat derives from tissue culturing. Reflectively and speculatively, meat-animal narratives show how technological engagements extend beyond the human, offering ways of beginning to rethink not simply how meat histories are shared but, more complexly, how they are involved in co-constructed futures that exceed the reference points once stabilizing and now dissolving species divisions. As vital for critical thinking as they are for sustainable living, the incomplete, ill-formed stories of meat on the borders and hemlines of posthumanist thinking prompt the difficult and necessary work of framing ever more possible answers to Mrs. Wiggins's query as it grows all the more pressing for meat animals and people permanently displaced from farm communities: "What's a constituent?"

Conclusion   **Toward a Narrative Ethology**

At the beginning of the video documentary (a companion to her 1999 memoir of the same title) *Reason for Hope*, primatology superstar Jane Goodall pokes fun at how a particular set of novels influenced her. Recalling how she loved reading Edgar Rice Burroughs's Tarzan novels as a child, she opines that she "hated" his Jane, then says what her fans have always known: "I'd have been a better mate for him." One of her signature moves, appealing to a stereotype at the same time that she successfully manipulates it, Goodall's story here is as much about the work of storytelling as it is of science.[1] It reflects a strange pattern not only within narrative history but also across literary studies and ethology, the study of animals in their ordinary habitats, which has provided the basis of scientific ecology.

Of course, it would be a stretch to claim that the Tarzan novels and films do much more than project fantasies of companionship onto species that overwhelmingly elect to live apart. Rather, it seems that Goodall appeals to a sense of animal narrative forms as proving useful for interrogating key elements of identity and society, inspiring as well as confronting the limitations of knowledges. In part to draw out the implications in the last two chapters of the connections between literary and scientific animal stories, this book concludes with a brief exploration of why this understanding arises when it does, and how.

Many note that, by the mid-twentieth century, the institutionalization of academic disciplines might be said to reinforce a "two-culture" split, novelist and scientist C. P. Snow's famous metaphor that is often mistaken for his ideal, rather than his horrified vision of the future of academics. These conditions favor formalist arguments that it has become the exclusive work of literature to serve and protect our humanity (if not *the* humanities) from the sins of scientific hubris. Yet they also make it difficult to reconcile literary criticism with accounts of preeminent, popular ethologists as disparate as Goodall and Konrad Lorenz, who point to animal fictions as models enabling significant epistemological shifts within animal science.

While groundbreaking ethological studies provide the basis for policy and other changes in the ways in which people live with animals in industrialized societies, best-selling ethological narratives of life in the field influence broader imaginative engagements with elusive species like the great apes that are otherwise largely mediated through film, video, and digital media. Obscuring the more mundane realities of data-driven science, such stories promote instead popular ethologists themselves as skillful storytellers. But in so doing, they also forge links in chains of literary influence, raising questions about how this pioneering scientific field traces its roots back to fiction, and continues to send out shoots through visual narrative forms.[2]

Generations earlier, this cross-disciplinary development seemed possible only in spite of (rather than because of) the rising popularity of companion animal fictions at the turn of the twentieth century. Styled frequently as first-hand accounts of the everyday horrors of maltreated working animals and pets, Sewell's *Black Beauty* inspired a number of imitations, such as Stratton-Porter's *Strike at Shane's* and the more successful *Beautiful Joe* (1894) by [Margaret] Marshall Saunders, which was Canada's first best seller. Such fictions were solicited and promoted by animal advocacy organizations that proved influential in enacting public policy changes concerning the rights and welfare of companion animals. Although their didactic purposes and younger target audiences harken back to animal fable traditions, again wherein animals are inserted as metaphors or humans-in-animal-suits, these fictional animal biographies proved so successful in inspiring interest in the lives of animals that they immediately raised concerns about the social effects of anthropomorphism, and especially anthropocentrism, on impressionable readers.

In hindsight, it seems obvious that the focus of these fictions on animals (especially as narrators) contributed to a post-Darwinian awareness of the broader consequences of cross-species interrelations, if not the moral imperatives of animal advocacy. At the turn of the twentieth century, however, the relationship of animal agency to subjectivity in fiction was hotly debated, particularly as interest in popular companion-animal stories fueled the development of a new sort of wild-animal narrative that expanded the welfare concerns of these domesticated-animal fictions along with the realistic details typical of the wildlife essay form.[3] Voicing a growing anxiety about the irreducibly literary and scientific credibility at stake in these kinds of animal narratives, novelist Charles G. D. Roberts in 1902 proclaimed that the "best" animal stories must eschew sentimentality and melodrama, and instead delineate "a psychological romance constructed on a framework of natural science."[4]

Roberts's judgment, frequently cited in the debates that swarmed around these issues at the time, reflects broader social desires for animal stories not simply to convey the truth of humans or of animals, but also to value non-utilitarian human–animal relationships. Such notions were central to what were at that time innovative (if also contested) developments of wildlife conservation policies. The sense that this potential was compromised by popular animal fictions fueled a controversy centered on writers who came to be known as "nature fakers."[5] These writers purportedly espoused a benevolent view of animal life that was anchored by strictly anthropomorphic story-telling techniques, and for this they were loved as well as reviled.

Part of the reason that the nature fakers were assailed in public discussion was that they almost immediately proved so successful. Animal narratives dominated the literary marketplace at the turn of the twentieth century, a trend that began with the unprecedented success of the domesticated animal activist fictions of Anna Sewall and Saunders, and became more controversial with the rapidly growing popularity of such naturalist story collections as Ernest Thompson Seton's *Wild Animals I Have Known* (1898) and William J. Long's *School of the Woods: Some Life Studies of Animal Instincts and Animal Training* (1902). Although relatively obscure today, the nature fakers in their day notoriously gauged how politically volatile readers' perceptions of animal stories could become, all the more clearly when their collections began to be marketed as children's textbooks.

Premier American naturalist John Burroughs thought these texts so dangerous to education about wildlife, especially regarding legislation of the land, that in 1903 he publicly denounced their authors for promoting distorted views of animal happiness, the supposed outcome of natural benevolence, at the expense of the harsh realities of survival, or the inevitable misery involved in the contests that supposedly prove Darwinian fitness. His argument indicates the complex genealogy informing the animal-homosexuality debates today that recycle less often than they contest these morally infused rhetorics. More immediately, it sparked a war of words waged via newspaper editorials among virtually all authors at the time with any stake in animal stories.

The deciding vote was symbolically cast by big-game hunter and then president Theodore Roosevelt (who coined the term "nature fakers"), but the political and institutional repercussions for animal stories were far from over.[6] As ecocritics note, narratives of animal life remain at the center of conflicts surrounding preservationist and sustainable land-use approaches to conservation today.[7] And, in the history of animal narrative, these debates also indicate how a more pervasive struggle with animal agency continues to move across literary, scientific, and popular imaginaries.

More specifically in the development of the discipline of ethology through the past century, animal stories seem to trouble the aspirations of those who lambasted "nature fakers" for conflating science and sentiment in guiding public understanding of the lives of animals. Even within the field, storytelling troubles such clean-cut distinctions, for instance, in the history of ethology that emerges through Frans de Waal's memoir *The Ape and the Sushi Master: Cultural Reflections of a Primatologist* (2001). Striking in this context is de Waal's insistence that narrative has been an integral part of the structures and methods through which ethologists gain credit for breaking up the human monopoly on culture by the end of the twentieth century; in other words, that story becomes a means of negotiating alternatives to nature/culture, animal/human, and related hierarchic dualisms in thought itself.

These complex relations of the forms of species and narrative come most clearly through his argument about the importance of storytelling in the field's formative years. Contrasted with Niko Tinbergen, the first and foremost exemplar of the ethological scientist, his contemporary Konrad Lorenz emerges in this account as securing the future of this field by drumming up public support through his skills as a storyteller. In popular books and to packed crowds, Lorenz offered timely, well-crafted fictions of his own attempts to study mostly domesticated animals' interactions with their worlds, stories that at once argued for the practical relevance of this innovative approach to animal science and extended its allure to nonprofessionals. While de Waal's point is to recover a sense of uncertainty characterizing the early days of ethological research, if not to redeem Lorenz himself,[8] he nonetheless argues that form is pivotal: it is on narrative that the popular triumph of field over laboratory animal science hinges, and not the other way around. Thus, the nature fakers are redeemed, and not just by de Waal.

Lorenz himself invites this idea that animal science follows literary developments, only much earlier in his best-selling memoir *King Solomon's Ring* (1952). His praises for the singular "truth" of Jack London's novels—in particular, the "obviously true-to-life descriptions" of "sledge-dog life"—are hard not to read as evidence that this kind of realist fiction emerging by the turn of the twentieth century served as a direct influence on this kind of animal science.[9] For depicting dogs as out-maneuvering wolf–dog hybrids in fights, for instance, London was branded a nature faker (a label that he contested), so half a century later Lorenz's accolades in part reflect a growing acceptance of the scientific validity of representing animals as reasoning beings, rather than strictly as creatures of instinct.[10] Further, Lorenz treats novels like *Call of the Wild* (1903) not simply as points of contrast to unscientific literary representation but as early documents and models of ethological notation.

Although Lorenz's literary references sometimes highlight egregious affective fallacies through dramatic and poetic representations, such as Oscar Wilde's female singing nightingale—to the student of ethology, "as comically incongruous [as] it would be to the student of literature had Tennyson invested Guinevere with a beard"—more often fiction provides the substance of human behavioral evidence.[11] Overwhelmingly, for Lorenz literature provides the corresponding "truth" of human relations that serves as a point of comparison for ethological claims, yet his treatment of London's fictions reveals a deeply seated assumption that interactions with animals inform a different potential for literary representation.[12] While sociobiologists today debate the veracity of such claims about literature, a subtler point about representational forms appears to have more lasting significance to the lives of all species situated between and beyond disciplinary ways of knowing.

Like Goodall's Tarzan joke, Lorenz's praise of London's novels looks forward to the ways in which ethological studies are popularized today through narrative and visual media, expanding perceptions precisely by appealing to what readers know through living with animals. And it also echoes the terms by which, a generation earlier, George Moore (the novelist–critic with whom I began this discussion) attempted to recover in fiction a sense that companion-species relations are central to formal innovation. Again and again praising the author of *Oliver Twist* for sparking the rise of the English novel, Moore likewise points to "Dickens's description of Bill Sikes' dog," the complex creature named Bull's-eye, who both brings his murderous man to justice and commits suicide rather than live without him, and therefore "shows that the writer had observed dogs and was in sympathy with their instincts."[13] Visualizing this canine character's dramatic behavior, Dickens's contemporary George Cruikshank pairs illustrations that set the cringing Bull's-eye as at first ineffectually rebuffed for following Sikes, and later precariously perched on the ridge-line of the roof from which they are about to drop to their deaths. Far from resolving questions of influence, let alone those of any definitive truths about animals or animality, these slippages of knowledges and feelings position animal narrative form as an indicator of the changing historical conditions of species and agency and, more important, as a site of literary and visual integration, of what aesthetic explorations now uniquely offer to the lives of species and vice versa.

After all, the twentieth century marks major turning points not only for scientific ethology but also for literary narrative and visual media forms. Again, it is important to note that the assumption that animal metaphors contain a higher understanding only about human life begins to give way with the mid-twentieth-century development of structuralist aesthetics. Tellingly, literary theorist Terry Eagleton's argument about the disciplinary rise of English, although explicitly not about animals in literature, uses a strikingly modern urban representation of companion-species relations—a sign that reads "Dogs must be carried on the escalator"—to illustrate the various possibilities that open up with structuralist attention to semantic ambiguity, particularly the theoretical implications of conceptualizing reading in terms not just of passive reception but complementary and creative interpretive-writing processes.[14] In lieu of struggling over a single or true human meaning, the consequent focus on the proliferations of meanings (not to mention purposes and forms) of stories and their relation to historical and cultural contexts in poststructuralist theory helps to explain the animal "turn" in literature, art, and other traditionally humanistic fields of study.

And I think there is something more specifically in the development of animal narratives across formal divisions that accounts as well for the conceptual separation of agency from the human across the disciplines. Attempting to move the animal-homosexuality debates into less readily identifiable forms and rhetorics, Joan Roughgarden elaborates the reluctance of biologists to see threesomes and other complex manifestations of animal gender and sex diversity as analogous to their resistance to biologist Lynn Margulis's symbiosis theory that all eukaryotic organisms survive only through cooperation at the cellular level. Symbiosis emphasizes that cells are constituted by partnerships of formerly independent bacteria, blasting away the hierarchic model of human evolutionary descent from bacteria with the more likely notion that "we still *are* bacteria, a deeply humbling thought," particularly for a former scientist like Roughgarden.[15]

But a more pressing implication of this theory, particularly in light of the commercialization of gene-altered organisms, is that genetic mutation does not occur randomly or blindly, but rather is negotiated purposefully and by many partners at (or below) the cellular level. Genomes change across species lines even within our bodies, and with motives and purposes attributable to forces of agency that we have only just begun to conceptualize, including Margulis's theory of symbiogenesis, the biological forces of cross-species genetic manipulation through which any given species evolves only ever with the help of others queering reproduction. So symbiogenesis is embraced alternately as validating the evolutionary and other significances of what happens when species meet, prompting investigators across the arts and sciences to widen the focus beyond the conventional terms of selfsame reproduction.

From this perspective, Margulis's theories become problematic not for having been avoided by scientists (as Roughgarden claims) so much as for the ways in which they appear to have been retooled in order to affirm the terms by which science remains a humanist project. Capitulating to the dictates of an older biological paradigm, in which cells, selfish genes, and all other significant relations are read exclusively in terms of little individuals, or microcosmic metaphors for the human subject, Margulis's more recent collaborations with her son Dorion Sagan reframe cellular partnerships in terms of autopoeisis, a holistic systems theory that Donna Haraway rejects as incompatible with symbiogeneis because it obscures the imbrication of cross-species partnerships in self-making.[16] Recursivity and relentless differentiation prove the far more significant outcomes of companionable transactions across species, agential relations only ever partially realized by autobiographical animals.

Focusing on more visible and local—as against universal—patterns of relating, the narratives that I have assembled in the foregoing chapters bring to the fore the kinds of relationships among cross-species companions that lurk largely in the background of even popular evolutionary accounts. In arranging and elaborating my own story about them around the concepts of intersubjectivity, then intercorporeality, it seems that I also started in the urban environments where people might most readily be expected to be seen, and ended on the rural frontlines, where animals, people, and their ancient ways of living together are disappearing.

My contention is not that these fictions support any given political platform, or that they can be used just to recalibrate the baselines of philosophical and scientific models. Instead, I propose a simpler formula, namely, that commitments to living with and learning from animals ethically—in Rosi Braidotti's reading of Deleuze and Guattari, "cultivating the kind of relations that compose and empower positive passions and avoid negative ones"—can proceed from creative engagements with narrative forms.[17] Getting out from under the master narratives of evolution, ecology, and more pervasively of disciplines requires this understanding that stories can (and indeed always) do more than represent selves at the expense of others.

And it requires dramatic reconceptions not only of species and their stories but also of the formal interplay between the two, what I want to call a "narrative ethology" that emphasizes embodied relations of agency and form as distinct from, say, the content through which ethological, fictional, and all other narratives get sorted and shelved as the political problems of representation. This formulation affirms the ways in which ethology and fiction alike proceed from the complicated operations of affect, and leads to an ethics premised on feelings honored as concrete, intense, and shared.[18] Narrative in this way provides a means of visualizing how this concern with life itself—what Éric Alliez terms "onto-ethology"—follows from Deleuze's model of the system as heterogenesis, which proceeds through the critique of philosophy and representation that is again implied, yet pointedly avoided, in Margulis's elaboration of symbiogenesis.[19]

Clarifying the more pervasive and deliberate construction of obstacles to just this sort of perspective, Deleuze uncovers a counter-history of "Bergsonism," mobilized through Bergson's responses (via Spinoza) to the biological theories of Jakob von Uexküll. Others claim a divided legacy in von Uexküll's distinction of species members through their *Umwelt* or perceptual worlds as providing, on the one hand, the theoretical foundation of scientific ecology (the emphasis on perception as defining species), and, on the other, the key to Western humanism's ruination (the acknowledgment that the human animal cannot transcend these processes). For Deleuze (and later Agamben), however, this deferral of the possibility of any absolute distinction between man and animal also activates an intellectual tradition that short-circuits dualistic and hierarchic structures with highly charged—multiple, intense, and lateral—points of connectivity to thinking through life itself.

What the stories gathered together in this book indicate further is that forms of representation matter to the development of theories of species life, and, moreover, that these forms do not illustrate or define so much as they promise to deconstruct disciplinary habits of mind via their "metonymic, not metaphoric" strategies.[20] For this reason, Erica Fudge insists that the poetics of narrative float the hope that "if we acknowledge some of the—frequently cruel—contradictions in the ways in which we live and think about animals we might be on the road to creating a new language," and that the way to get there is through recognizing the importance of this particular representational form: the "stories that we tell ourselves to make" the ways in which we currently live with animals "acceptable" are not only historically constructed by and for humans but also "just that: stories."[21] The trick, as narratologists are quick to note, is not to escape the stories so much as to reckon with the ways in which life continues only ever within them.

Taken together, the patterns outlined throughout *Animal Stories* present admittedly partial views of far more complex, messier operations of agency. While their focus on human–animal stories in many ways underscores the limitations of disciplinary perspectives, they also model ways forward through looming epistemological crises. Particularly in the past century, literary studies of species have clearly enriched as much as been enriched by the methods of life sciences, and in these conditions animal narratives demonstrate the emergence of posthumanistic and other extradisciplinary perspectives that are relevant to far more than just forms of species and social agency. In this way, such stories offer hope for more sustainable or equitable patterns of engagement between species. And, more important, they clear the field for cultivating a politics based not on the rights of homogenous, atomized individuals so much as the affects that have always held together the heterogeneous, molecular groupings made so apparent in cross-species companionship.

Notes

Introduction

1. George Moore, *Avowals* (New York: Boni and Liveright, 1919), 8.

2. Ibid., 83.

3. A generation after Moore, Ian Watt makes this argument in *The Rise of the Novel: Studies in Defoe, Richardson, and Fielding* (Berkeley: University of California Press, 1957).

4. In *The History of Sexuality*, Michel Foucault posits that the (human) subject is produced as social agent through "anatamo-politics" (or disciplinary regimes trained on bodies), and distinguishes these formations of individuals from the social bodies of human and other species relations that take shape through the "bio-politics" of irreducible populations. Michel Foucault, *The History of Sexuality: An Introduction*, trans. Robert Hurley, 3 vols. (New York: Random House, 1978), 1:147.

5. On the notion of intersubjectivity that emerges in the work of cultural anthropologists Barbara Noske, Myrdene Anderson, and Elizabeth Atwood Lawrence, see Annabelle Sabloff, *Reordering the Natural World: Humans and Animals in the City* (Toronto: University of Toronto Press, 2001), 35–38.

6. Sarah Whatmore, in *Hybrid Geographies: Natures, Cultures, Spaces* (London: Sage, 2002), outlines a sense of "intercorporeal" as a leveraging concept to reposition "'our' being-in-the-world" as connected to "the metabolic frailties and corporeal compulsions of multifarious 'others' that share the precarious register of life and redistribute its energies through all manner of intermediaries and configurations," that is, a concept of "relationality . . . that necessarily extends the social beyond the human or, more properly, through which the human and other kinds are con-figured in particular and provisional ways" (118).

7. Mary Midgley introduces the concept of the human as a condition of species mixture or "mixed community" dependent on animals who "com[e] to understand the social signals addressed to them." Mary Midgley, *Animals and Why They Matter* (Athens: University of Georgia Press, 1983), 112. Here I propose pluralizing it to "mixed communities" in order to emphasize how immediate, intersubjective human–animal affective ties concern long-standing intercorporeal relationships of species and social life.

221

8. The earliest literary critic to argue for eighteenth-century children's literature as the origin of something akin to a sense of animal agency is Victor Link, "On the Development of the Modern Animal Story," *Dalhousie Review* (1956): 56, which inspired William H. Magee, "The Animal Story: A Challenge in Technique," *Dalhousie Review* (1964): 44, to make the case instead for the nineteenth-century animal stories (especially those of Charles G. D. Roberts) as the source.

9. Samuel Beckett, *Texts for Nothing: Stories and Texts for Nothing* (New York: Grove Press, 1967), and Foucault, "What Is an Author?" in *Language, Counter-Memory, Practice: Selected Essays and Interviews,* ed. Donald F. Bouchard (Ithaca: Cornell University Press, 1977).

10. I borrow these terms from Jacques Derrida's theory "of the trace, of iterability, of *différence*," the "possibilities or necessities, without which there would be no language," and that *"are themselves not only human,"* in "Eating Well, or The Calculation of the Subject: An Interview with Jacques Derrida," *Who Comes after the Subject?* ed. Eduardo Cadava, Peter Connor, and Jean-Luc Nancy; trans. Peter Connor and Avital Ronell (New York: Routledge, 1991), 116.

11. Nigel Rothfels makes the early and helpful distinction between natural and "unnatural" history in *Savages and Beasts: The Birth of the Modern Zoo* (Baltimore: Johns Hopkins University Press, 2002), 6. On the current problems of naming (or subspeciating) the field through proposals for human–animal studies, animality studies, critical animal studies, even anymal (Lisa Kemmerer's all-encompassing term for any animal, including human) studies, see Kenneth J. Shapiro, *Human–Animal Studies: Growing the Field, Applying the Field* (Ann Arbor: Animals and Society Institute, 2008), 7–8; and Marianne DeKoven, "Why Animals Now?" *PMLA* 124 (2009): 368 n. 3.

12. Although "discursive formation" is Foucault's term, here I borrow more directly Stuart Hall's argument (via Raymond Williams) about the formation of cultural studies to elaborate what I have witnessed in the rise of animal studies, namely, that its conflicted origins, histories, materializations, and discourses converge decisively, if unstably, in what Williams called "a common disposition of energy and direction," which for Hall stays relevant only through a productive tension between "simply pluralist" (anything-goes) and singular (dogmatic) politics. Stuart Hall, "Cultural Studies and Its Theoretical Legacies," in *The Norton Anthology of Theory and Criticism,* ed. Vincent B. Leitch et al. (New York: W. W. Norton, 2001), 1899.

13. In the earliest book-length study of literary animals, *Animals in American Literature* (Urbana: University of Illinois Press, 1983), Mary Allen observes that "the metaphorical far outnumber the literal animals in literature" (6).

14. Percy Bysshe Shelley, "A Defence of Poetry, or Remarks Suggested by an Essay Entitled 'The Four Ages of Poetry,'" in *The Norton Anthology of Theory and Criticism,* 699. It is curious that the wild-animal figure exemplifies a poet's isolation to Shelley, a powerful advocate for what Raymond Williams terms romantic literature's "emphasis on love and relationship" as "necessary not only within the immediate suffering but against the aggressive individualism and the primarily economic relationships [that

his] new[ly industrialized] society embodied." Raymond Williams, *Culture and Society, 1780–1950* (London: Chatto and Windus, 1958), 42.

15. See Christine Kenyon-Jones, *Kindred Brutes: Animals in Romantic-Period Writing* (Burlington, Vt.: Ashgate, 2001), and Erica Fudge, *Perceiving Animals: Humans and Beasts in Early Modern English Culture* (New York: St. Martin's Press, 2000). More recently, Fudge's *Brutal Reasoning: Animals, Rationality, and Humanity in Early Modern England* (Ithaca: Cornell University Press, 2006) contextualizes humanist ideologies arising in this period to demonstrate the ways in which critics today risk oversimplification "by ignoring the presence of animals or by ceasing to interpret the animals as animals" (176).

16. So, for instance, Ivan Kreilkamp characterizes animals in Victorian fiction "as semi-humans in the realm of culture and as semi-characters in the realm of literature." Ivan Kreilkamp, "Dying Like a Dog in *Great Expectations,*" in *Victorian Animal Dreams: Representations of Animals in Victorian Literature and Culture,* ed. Deborah Denenholz Morse and Martin A. Danahay (Burlington, Vt.: Ashgate, 2007), 82.

17. John Berger, *About Looking* (London: Writers and Readers, 1980), 14.

18. Giorgio Agamben, *The Open: Man and Animal,* trans. Kevin Attell (Stanford: Stanford University Press, 2004), 22.

19. Jacques Derrida, *The Post Card: From Socrates to Freud and Beyond,* trans. Alan Bass (Chicago: University of Chicago Press, 1987), 474n.

20. Jacques Derrida, *The Animal That Therefore I Am,* ed. Marie-Louise Mallet; trans. David Wills (New York: Fordham University Press, 2008), 11.

21. Again, Derrida proposes a route around this problem through a more expansive notion "of the mark in general, of the trace, of iterability, of *différence*" that "should allow us to take into account scientific knowledge about the complexity of 'animal languages,' genetic coding, all forms of marking within which so-called human language, as original as it might be, does not allow us to 'cut' once and for all where we would in general like to cut" ("Eating Well," 116). Akira Mizuta Lippit notes how in this formulation "the sacrificial cut that implements subjectivity" positions animality as the cutting tool inevitably "lacerat[ing]" and not neatly edging "the discourse of the subject." Akira Mizuta Lippit, *Electric Animal: Toward a Rhetoric of Wildlife* (Minneapolis: University of Minnesota Press, 2000), 16.

22. Cary Wolfe proposes that, only by starting with the assumption that "the other-than-human"—or, more accurately, "the infra-human"—does not languish outside so much as it "resides at the very core of the human itself," can literary criticism begin to trace the discourse of species outside a speciesist framework. Cary Wolfe, *Animal Rites: American Culture, the Discourse of Species, and Posthumanist Theory* (Chicago: University of Chicago Press, 2003), 17. Following this line of thinking of the central modernist conundrum as "humanism's response to a threat that issues from beyond the human but also, oddly, from within it," Carrie Rohman intimates further that a deep suspicion of human–animal relations aligns key literary modernists with their contemporary critics.

Carrie Rohman, *Stalking the Subject: Modernism and the Animal* (New York: Columbia University Press, 2009), 16.

23. Margot Norris, *Beasts of the Modern Imagination: Darwin, Kafka, Nietzsche, Ernst, and Lawrence* (Baltimore: Johns Hopkins University Press, 1985), 65.

24. Ibid., 131–32.

25. Jonathan Burt, "Morbidity and Vitalism: Derrida, Bergson, Deleuze, and Animal Film Imagery," in *Thinking with Animals,* ed. Richard Nash and Ron Broglio, special issue of *Configurations* 14 (2006): 161–62.

26. Donna Haraway, *Primate Visions: Gender, Race, and Nature in the World of Modern Science* (New York: Routledge, 1989), 310. As she elaborates, this understanding proceeds from the slippage between "the apparatus of bodily [and] . . . literary production" (418 n. 8).

27. Glen Elder, Jennifer Wolch, and Jody Emel, "*Le Pratique Sauvage*: Race, Place, and the Human–Animal Divide," in *Animal Geographies: Place, Politics, and Identity in the Nature-Culture Borderlands,* ed. Wolch and Emel (New York: Verso Books, 1998), 73. For a cross-cultural comparison of how companion animals are systematically subjected to this treatment along (even to the point of being equated) with such people, see Kirsten McKenzie, "Dogs and the Public Sphere: The Ordering of Social Space in Early Nineteenth-Century Cape Town," in *Canis Africanis: A Dog History of Southern Africa,* ed. Lance von Sittert and Sandra Swart (Leiden: E. J. Brill, 2008), 93–95.

28. George Bensoussan clarifies that, around 1903, the "murder of an indigenous [in this case African] person was called *animalicide.*" George Bensoussan, *Europe. Une Passion Génocidaire: Essai d'histoire culturelle* (Paris: Mille et une nuits, 2006), 112.

29. Wendy Woodward situates the contemporary concern with kinship between humans and animals to "some traditional African relationships with animals and African knowledges such as shamanism, which implicitly interrogates mainstream Western philosophy just as it endorses recent animal philosophies." Wendy Woodward, *The Animal Gaze: Animal Subjectivities in Southern African Narratives* (Johannesburg: Wits University Press, 2008), 4. Introducing the "Real Toads in Imaginary Gardens: Animals in Literature and History" section of *What Are the Animals to Us? Approaches from Science, Religion, Folklore, Literature, and Art,* ed. Dave Aftandilian (Knoxville: University of Tennessee Press, 2007), Marion Copeland contends that the disparagement of such traditions informs a trend in which "literary critics and historians"—in pointed opposition to "poets/shamans"—require each representation of an animal to remain just an "image or symbol" (89).

30. Harriet Ritvo elaborates: "If keeping a well-bred dog metonymically allied its owner with the upper ranges of society, then the elaborate structure of pedigree registration and show judging metaphorically equated owner with elite pet." Harriet Ritvo, *The Animal Estate: The English and Other Creatures in the Victorian Age* (Cambridge, Mass.: Harvard University Press, 1987), 93.

31. Steve Baker elaborates this aesthetic in terms of "botched taxidermy," in which the "botchedness or gone-wrongedness" in contemporary fine-art images of animals

does not signal artistic failure so much as a more complicated set of engagements with animal form, each of which is "deliberate, and has its own integrity." Steve Baker, *The Postmodern Animal* (London: Reaktion Books, 2000), 156.

32. In "BSE, Hysteria, and the Representation of Animal Death: Deborah Levy's *Diary of a Steak*," included in the collection *Killing Animals* by the Animal Studies Group (Urbana: University of Illinois Press, 2006), Robert McKay explores how the expectation that these representations bear meaning becomes problematized in a contemporary experimental literary intertext, one in which a simultaneously abject, animal, and "protesting agency" puts authority under erasure and makes way for "new corrupted meanings" (158, 167).

33. Philip Armstrong, in *What Animals Mean in the Fiction of Modernity* (New York: Routledge, 2008), clarifies the latter in terms of authors' attempts "to find ways of describing agency at work through the interactions of a complex and widely-dispersed network of actants, both human and other-than-human" (196).

34. Thus "the practices that are folded into the making of representations" inscribe more options for nonhuman participation in representational processes than just serving as empty vessels to fill with human meanings, including the possibilities that animals actively "destabilize, transgress or even resist our human orderings," according to Chris Philo and Chris Wilbert, "Animal Places, Beastly Places: An Introduction," in *Animal Places, Beastly Places: New Geographies of Human–Animal Relations*, ed. Philo and Wilbert (New York: Routledge, 2000), 5.

35. Jonathan Burt, *Animals in Film* (London: Reaktion Books, 2002), 31.

36. As Midgley puts it, animals became tame "not only because the people taming them were social beings, but because they themselves were so as well" (*Animals and Why They Matter*, 112).

37. Vicki Hearne, *Animal Happiness: A Moving Exploration of Animals and Their Emotions* (New York: HarperCollins, 1994), 71.

38. Noting that human–animal contacts even today overwhelmingly involve farmed animals, Una Chaudhuri qualifies this "self-identification as animal lovers that we perform every day" as "part of a paper-thin but rock-hard veneer on an animalculture [a neologism derived from Haraway's natureculture, in turn a derivation of technoculture] of staggering violence and exploitation." Una Chaudhuri, "(De)Facing the Animal: Zoöesis and Performance," in *Animals and Performance*, ed. Chaudhuri, special issue of *TDR* 51 (2007): 10.

39. Gilles Deleuze and Félix Guattari, *A Thousand Plateaus: Capitalism and Schizophrenia*, trans. Brian Massumi (Minneapolis: University of Minnesota Press, 1987), 240, 241.

40. Ibid., 241.

41. On this critique of Deleuze and Guattari, see especially Haraway, *When Species Meet* (Minneapolis: University of Minnesota Press, 2007), 30; and Alice Kuzniar, *Melancholia's Dog: Reflections on Our Animal Kinship* (Chicago: University of Chicago Press, 2006), 4. I elaborate the cross-cultural disparagement of relations between women

and little dogs from antiquity to the present in *Dog* (London: Reaktion Books, 2004), 79–89.

42. Tom Conley, "Pantagruel-Animal," in *Animal Acts: Configuring the Human in Western History*, ed. Jennifer Ham and Matthew Senior (New York: Routledge, 1997), 45. Conley cautions that their concept of *"devenir-animal"* or becoming-animal, formulated as part of a "political ethnography," is "not easily extrapolated from its source or applied to other works to any efficacious degree" (45). But Conley's analysis clarifies further how becoming-animal works as a human form that promotes "affective agency" or "benevolent empathy" with "things and bodies that are other" (49). Rosi Braidotti more recently explains how these aspects provide the basis for a relational ethics for the "subject-in-becoming," in "Animals, Anomalies, and Inorganic Others," *PMLA* 124 (2009): 531.

43. As Lippit argues, Deleuze and Guattari take "the logic of becoming from Darwinian and Bergsonian evolution as a complementary (and to them superior) force to being" (*Electric Animal*, 131).

44. Deleuze and Guattari, *A Thousand Plateaus*, 241. Like Norris, they point to Kafka as exemplary: "Josephine, the mouse singer, sometimes holds a privileged position in the pack, sometimes a position outside the pack, and sometimes slips into and is lost in the anonymity of the collective statements of the pack" (243).

45. Just as Kathleen Kete understands the significance of the displacement of the pet with domestic machinery in bourgeois Parisian life as largely "symbolic," in *The Beast in the Boudoir* (Berkeley: University of California Press, 1994), Cecilia Tichi outlines a similar case with the displacement of cowboys-and-horses imagery with that of engineers and motorized vehicles in American material culture at the turn of the century (117). Cecilia Tichi, *Shifting Gears: Technology, Literature, Culture in Modernist America* (Chapel Hill: University of North Carolina Press, 1987), 98.

46. Virginia Woolf, "Character in Fiction," in *The Essays of Virginia Woolf*, ed. Andrew McNeillie, 3 vols. (San Diego: Harcourt Brace Jovanovich, 1986), 1:334.

47. Marianne DeKoven elaborates how "the defining literary form(s) of modernism," which contain a notoriously "ill-defined and massive corpus," proceed from "the *sous-rature* [or impossible dialectic] developed in early modernist narrative." Her linkage of revolutionary story and social forms helps to explain why "modernist formal practice emerged unevenly within a general period," and how story and species forms enter into an ongoing procession or rather spiraling outward of this connection. Marianne DeKoven, *Rich and Strange: Gender, History, Modernism* (Princeton: Princeton University Press, 1991), 179, 5.

48. Erica Fudge, "A Left-Handed Blow: Writing the History of Animals," in *Representing Animals*, ed. Nigel Rothfels (Bloomington: Indiana University Press, 2002), 9.

49. Donna Haraway puts it more bluntly: "Stories are much bigger than ideologies. In that is our hope," in *The Companion Species Manifesto: Dogs, People, and Significant Otherness* (Chicago: Prickly Paradigm Press, 2003), 17.

50. Isabelle Stengers, "The Cosmopolitical Proposal," in *Making Things Public:*

Atmospheres of Democracy, ed. Bruno Latour and Peter Weibel (Cambridge, Mass.: MIT Press, 2005), 994–1003.

51. Haraway, *The Companion Species Manifesto,* 50. John Simons argues instead that poststructuralist literary theory demonstrates "the totalizing effect of theoretical discourse *per se*" and "has the effect of closing off thinking rather than liberating it" (66). Although eschewing it himself in favor of a return to sentiment, Simons concedes that such work can "invoke the model of narrative as a way of understanding how power operates and how we might strive against its pressures." John Simons, *Animal Rights and the Politics of Literary Representation* (New York: Palgrave, 2002), 66, 193. Michael Hardt and Antonio Negri identify the biopolitical potential for love that enables "the encounter of singularities, which compose new assemblages and constitute new forms of the common," in *Commonwealth* (Cambridge, Mass.: Belknap Press of Harvard University Press, 2009), 186.

52. Lisa Uddin, "A Gorilla Lover's Discourse," in *Animal Being,* ed. Tom Tyler, special issue of *Parallax* 12, no. 1 (2006): 118.

53. For an elaboration of Williams's "structures of feeling," a concept that concerns "neither the character nor the experience but as it were the actual experiences through which these were lived" as against "the culture of the selective tradition" (figured by the literary canon) and the (secondhand) narratives of experience, see Raymond Williams, *The Long Revolution* (New York: Columbia University Press, 1961), 47. A marxist humanist who emphasizes at every turn that "all our experience is a human version of the world we inhabit," Williams nonetheless raises concerns about how the human subject form draws attention away from the social complexities informing its isolation and elevation as a figure of thought: while "the individuals who bear . . . particular cultural rules are capable of altering and extending them, bringing in new or modified rules by which an extended or different reality can be experienced," he explains, "these need not be limited to any one individual, but can, in certain interesting ways, be communicated, thus adding to the set of rules carried by the particular culture" (18). Elspeth Probyn explicitly extends Williams's model in order "to elaborate a theory and practice of signification which could entertain the centrality of experiences of and in the material world," outlining an approach to collective life that I consider the only one that makes sense of and for animal studies. Elspeth Probyn, *Sexing the Self: Gendered Positions in Cultural Studies* (New York: Routledge, 1993), 21.

1. Seeing Eyes/Private Eyes

1. Representing a family pet as a "guide dog," two actual American would-be-runaway girls were not denied access to ride on a city bus, but attracted the attention of police on it by sickening the dog with treats meant to keep him quiet, a story that garnered the attention of syndicated feature writer Chuck Shepherd, "News of the Weird: Man's Best Friend (Except Sometimes)," *Austin Chronicle,* April 21, 2006, 74.

2. Clinton R. Sanders elaborates, "All states have exceptions to the public health regulations that ban dogs from certain public settings in order to accommodate guide

dog users," but general ignorance of these laws means that the "most irritating public experience guide dog users routinely encounter is being excluded from stores, restaurants, and other commercial establishments because they are with a dog." Clinton R.
Sanders, *Understanding Dogs: Living and Working with Canine Companions* (Philadelphia:
Temple University Press, 1999), 52. Here I follow his example in adopting the more
colloquial "guide dogs" as my default term in lieu of "dog guides," which is the generic
term "approved" by the main North American training schools (150 n. 3). Seeing Eye
dog owner and historian Peter Brock Putnam likens the latter to "dog police or dog
shepherd" as "unnatural," in *Love in the Lead: The Fifty-Year Miracle of the Seeing Eye
Dog* (New York: Dutton, 1979), ix.

3. Vicki Hearne initially framed this suggestive question to address the incompati-
bility of training realities and rights sensibilities, and it has been more recently revis-
ited by Donna Haraway in *The Companion Species Manifesto*, 53.

4. As I discuss below, this development of the blind detectives thus reverses the
implied progress narrative that Rosemarie Garland-Thomson illustrates through a
growing sense of disabled artists, for instance, as now becoming successful "not in spite
of disability but because of disability," in "Disability and Representation: Papers from
the Conference on Disability Studies and the University," *PMLA* 120 (2005): 524.

5. The following claim precedes the title page of the first edition of Kendrick's first
Maclain novel, *The Last Express* (Garden City, N.Y.: Doubleday, 1937): "It is believed
that this is the first fictional use of a Seeing Eye dog, though the dogs themselves have
achieved an international reputation."

6. Putnam cites *The Demand for Guide Dogs* (the findings of the first large-scale
scientific survey of guide-dog use, commissioned by The Seeing Eye) as clarifying that,
by 1960, "only about 1 percent of the legally blind population . . . combined sufficient
motivation with the mental and physical capacity to learn to use guide dogs successfully" (*Love in the Lead*, 203). Drawing together the conclusions of other studies, Sanders
notes that by "the mid-1980s, only from 1 to 3 percent of visually handicapped people owned or had interest in using guide dogs" (*Understanding Dogs*, 89).

7. Morris Frank, as quoted by Dickson Hartwell in *Dogs Against Darkness: The Story
of The Seeing Eye* (New York: Dodd Mead, 1960), 233, 227.

8. Reinforcing how it is not just able-bodied-ness but species-being that is at stake,
Garland-Thomson conceptualizes the "normate" or social figure through which people can represent themselves as "definitive human beings," in *Extraordinary Bodies:
Figuring Physical Disability in American Culture and Literature* (New York: Columbia University Press, 1997), 8.

9. Frans de Waal, *The Ape and the Sushi Master: Cultural Reflections by a Primatologist* (New York: Basic Books, 2001), 76. More precisely, in *Corporal Compassion: Animal
Ethics and Philosophy of Body* (Pittsburgh: University of Pittsburgh Press, 2006), Ralph
Acampora characterizes Nagel's as a philosophical attempt to "demonstrate[e] that it is
impossible for reductively materialistic theory to provide a phenomenology of conscious
subjectivity" (25). Offering instead a theory of "transpecific conviviality," Acampora

exposes via Heidegger an underlying miscalculation regarding forms of life: "Being in the world with others is one of the major ways in which our experience is structured" (27).

10. Lennard J. Davis, *Bending over Backwards: Disability, Dismodernism, and Other Difficult Positions* (New York: New York University Press, 2002), 4. Although these animal aspects are clearly not central to Davis's discussion, the blind detectives' dramatic distancing from the "autonomy and independence" characteristic of "the dominant, . . . white, male, 'normal' subject" of power that they used to embody can be understood in terms of enacting a transition to what Davis calls "a dismodernist mode," but I would add only when their relationships with their dogs anchor a more complex sense of "dependency and interdependence" (30).

11. Putnam makes this connection to the initial resistance of a prominent contemporary of Frank's, "Edward Allen, head of the prestigious Perkins School for the Blind, [once] characterized [guide-dog use] . . . as 'a dirty little cur dragging a blind man along at the end of a string, the very index of incompetence and beggary'" (*Love in the Lead*, 15).

12. Christopher Danielson, "Does *Blind Justice* Do Justice to the Blind?" *Voice of the Nation's Blind* (March 1, 2005), http://www.voiceofthenationsblind.org.

13. Davis notes that disability is often represented as a source of "personal tragedy" rather than a "social and political problem" (*Bending over Backwards*, 139). Moreover, the latter distinction itself is paradigmatic, defining the British and social constructionist models of disability in contrast to the earlier civil rights model of autonomy and independence, which was "based on the struggles of African Americans in the US" (12).

14. Irving Kenneth Zola, "Depictions of Disability—Metaphor, Message, and Medium in the Media: A Research and Political Agenda," *Social Science Journal* 22, no. 4 (1985): 9.

15. Harlan Hahn, "Advertising the Acceptably Employable Image: Disability and Capitalism," in *The Disability Studies Reader*, ed. Lennard J. Davis (London: Routledge, 1997), notes that "estimates indicate that approximately two-thirds of disabled persons in most industrialized nations are unemployed, a level that exceeds the unemployment rate among other deprived and disadvantaged groups" (172).

16. Davis, *Bending over Backwards*, 2.

17. Sally Robinson's analysis of later twentieth-century fiction clarifies how white masculinity becomes "visible not as a secure and self-evidently normative standard of American identity" but rather as one produced through unequal relations with others. Sally Robinson, "'Unyoung, Unpoor, Unblack': John Updike and the Construction of Middle American Masculinity," *Modern Fiction Studies* 44 (1998): 333.

18. While Danielson's review of the show overall is favorable, he notes that Dunbar's relationship with Hank, along with "the whole issue of travel," remains underdeveloped. In lieu of dramatizing mobility problems, this presentation of the dog ultimately reinforces an untenable ideal, what Sanders terms "the popular image of the guide dog as *the* answer to a blind person's problems with mobility" (*Understanding Dogs*, 165 n. 2).

19. Garland-Thomson, "Disability and Representation," 526.

20. Cary Wolfe, *What Is Posthumanism?* (Minneapolis: University of Minnesota Press, 2010), 140–41.

21. Martha Nussbaum, *Frontiers of Justice: Disability, Nationality, Species Membership* (Cambridge. Mass.: Harvard University Press, 2006), 366.

22. Ibid., 376.

23. Georg Frei and Neil Printz, *Warhol: The Andy Warhol Catalogue Raisonné*, vol. 1, *Paintings and Sculpture, 1961–1963*, ed. Frei and Printz (New York: Phaidon Press, 2004).

24. Ronald Paulson, *Detective Fiction and the Rise of Forensic Science* (New York: Cambridge University Press, 1999), 10.

25. Baynard Kendrick, "Autobiographical Memoirs," *Blindness: American Association of Workers for the Blind Annual* (1970): 82.

26. Ibid., 87.

27. Ibid., 88, 89.

28. Dickson Hartwell emphasizes this notion of the dog as a modern technology: "Today the capable Seeing Eye Dog is accepted as a commonplace along with the airplane and the radio" (*Dogs against Darkness*, 65).

29. Putnam, *Love in the Lead*, 73–74.

30. Baynard Kendrick, *Blind Allies* (New York: William Morrow, 1954), 95.

31. Baynard Kendrick, *The Whistling Hangman* (Garden City, N.Y.: Doubleday, 1937), 43.

32. Kendrick, *The Last Express*, 64.

33. Kendrick, *The Whistling Hangman*, 106.

34. Kendrick, *The Last Express*, 63.

35. Kendrick, *The Whistling Hangman*, 106.

36. Sanders, *Understanding Dogs*, 12–13.

37. Ibid., 53.

38. Ibid., 58.

39. Ibid., 40.

40. Sanders, *Understanding Dogs*, 56.

41. In the first chapter of the first novel, *The Last Express*, Maclain informs a new client, skeptical of his dog, that "both of us were trained at the Seeing Eye" (6), and Spud Savage later reflects that "Morris Frank and his dog Buddy" have unequivocally demonstrated the "feasibility and safety" of The Seeing Eye's methods (64).

42. Aaron Skabelund notes that many credit the society's founder, retired Prussian cavalry captain Max von Stephanitz and his wildly popular 1901 book *Der deutsche Schäferhunde in Wort und Bild* (translated into English 1923 as *The German Shepherd in Word and Picture*) with the making of this breed, in *Empire of Dogs: Canines in the Making of the Modern Imperial World* (Ithaca: Cornell University Press, forthcoming).

43. Featured in David Wroblewski's novel *The Story of Edgar Sawtelle* (New York: Ecco Press, 2008), Eustis's Fortunate Fields kennel was conceived as an adjunct project to The Seeing Eye. Putnam notes that it differed from earlier dog-breeding projects for

its focus on performance instead of conformation, its guidance by scientific method, and its lack of any profit motive, the last "made possible by Eustis's wealth" (*Love in the Lead*, 7).

44. Putnam, *Love in the Lead*, 109, 86. The accusation that guide-dog work constitutes "abuse" continues to be leveled against guide-dog users in the United States, according to Sanders's informants in *Understanding Dogs* (52).

45. Hahn, "Advertising the Acceptably Employable Image," 173.

46. Kendrick, "Autobiographical Memoirs," 95.

47. Baynard Kendrick, *Lights Out* (New York: William Morrow, 1945), 139.

48. Martin F. Norden, *The Cinema of Isolation: A History of Physical Disability in the Movies* (New Brunswick: Rutgers University Press, 1994), 182. Writing long after the film was released and deep in the civil rights era, native southerner Kendrick echoes this shifting emphasis in his claim that he was attempting to represent "the fact that blinded veterans as a group, through the years, had influenced each other positively and constructively on the subject" of race prejudice ("Autobiographical Memoirs," 96).

49. Kendrick, *The Last Express*, 189.

50. In Kendrick's *You Die(t) Today!* (New York: William Morrow, 1952), Maclain explains that the original and legendary Seeing Eye trainer Jack Humphrey persuaded him "to use two dogs instead of one" because the combination of guide and police dog "might be a risky one" (47). Kendrick clarifies that, in his research before starting the series, discussions with Humphrey and other staff members at the Seeing Eye convinced him to abandon his initial plan of creating an all-purpose dog for Maclain ("Autobiographical Memoirs," 91). Incidentally, the original typescript of the title *You Die(t) Today!*—a murder mystery set on a "fat farm"—includes a cross-out mark over the "t" in "Diet." Because this symbol proved difficult to reproduce here, the erasure instead is indicated throughout within parentheses.

51. Clinton R. Sanders, "'The Dog You Deserve': Ambivalence in the K-9 Officer/ Patrol Dog Relationship," *Journal of Contemporary Ethnography* 35 (2006), 149. Nigel Rothfels kindly explained the adjectival qualities of these names in German: "Schnuck" means "cute," and it is often used with animals, such as the sloth character with this name in the PBS series *It's a Big World*. "Dreist" translates as "audacious, brazen, impudent," though more in a cheeky than outright nasty sense, such as a *"drieste luege,"* which means "a brazen lie." Kendrick clarifies that the Seeing Eye staff members chose these names ("Autobiographical Memoirs," 91).

52. These phrases are repeated in Kendrick, *The Last Express*, 109, and *The Whistling Hangman*, 218.

53. Kendrick, "Autobiographical Memoirs," 91. In *Death Knell* (New York: William Morrow, 1945), the one instance in the series in which the guide dog acts out of character is clearly flagged as such: "It was then [Maclain] learned that even a man who has owned one for years can't always tell what a dog will do. For the only time in her gentle life, Schnuke," faced with an unknown assailant in his office," barked a bark of real defiance, which ended in a terrifying growl" (200).

54. Baynard Kendrick, *Reservations for Death* (New York: William Morrow, 1957), 47.

55. Sanders, in "The Dog You Deserve," notes that German shepherd dogs "unsuitable for assisting people with visual disabilities had the characteristics that made them ideal candidates for K-9 [or police service] work" (153). And the inverse would also appear to inform the fact that the "Army K-9 corps supplied dogs to The Seeing Eye," according to Guide Dogs for the Blind (*Looking Ahead* [San Rafael, Calif.: Guide Dogs for the Blind, 1990]), 10, a similar organization that was founded in 1942 in Los Gatos, California, in part to serve the needs of veterans of World War II blinded in the Pacific.

56. Maclain handles both dogs at once only at two moments in the series, and in novels published after the one featuring this startling cover image. See Baynard Kendrick, *Blind Man's Bluff* (Boston: Little, Brown, 1943), 223; and *Clear and Present Danger* (Garden City, N.Y.: Doubleday, 1958), 183. Describing how this highly unlikely configuration might work, *You Die(t) Today!* describes the "guide dog [as] trained to work on his left and [the] . . . protective police dog [as] trained to work on his right" (47). Later, in *Clear and Present Danger*, Maclain more plausibly explains, "[Dreist] only worked on [the right] when I had Schnuke along" (183).

57. This phrasing is repeated in Kendrick, *Blind Man's Bluff*, 131, and *Death Knell*, 133.

58. Kendrick, *Blind Allies*. 12. In Kendrick, *The Spear Gun Murders* (London: Robert Hale, 1961)—a reprint of *The Aluminum Turtle* (1960)—they tacitly agree that this "scarcely human" condition serves a purpose in stressful times, for instance, when Spud is nearly killed: "For the moment, [Sybella had] lost the man she loved, and she couldn't regain him until justice was done, and murders paid for. . . . Duncan Maclain, with his partner close to dying, had become a human juggernaut, an inflexible, inexorable, blind machine" (160).

59. Kendrick, *The Spear Gun Murders*, 137.

60. Hartwell, *Dogs against Darkness*, 191.

61. Far from dismissing similar sentiments among pet owners, the plot of *Frankincense and Murder* (New York: Dodd, Mead, 1961) pivots on the cyanide poisoning of canine character Mr. Kilty, whose plausibly bereaved owner, Ben Ferguson (also appearing to be a would-be victim, but eventually outed as the murderer), is persuaded immediately to seek Maclain's (in lieu of the police's) help to find justice (172–73).

62. Kendrick, *Blind Allies*, 92.

63. Kendrick, *You Die(t) Today!* 47, and "Autobiographical Memoirs," 91.

64. Vicki Hearne, *Adam's Task: Calling Animals by Name* (New York: Alfred A. Knopf, 1986), 93–94.

65. Sanders, "The Dog You Deserve," 165.

66. Kendrick, *Blind Allies*, 100.

67. Ibid., 103.

68. Kendrick, *Reservations for Death*, 52.

69. Kendrick, "Autobiographical Memoirs," 91.

70. Ibid.

71. Norden, *The Cinema of Isolation*, 149.

72. Ernest Lewis [Ernest Blakeman Vesey], *Beowulf: Guide Dog to the Blind* (New York: E. P. Dutton, 1936), 13.

73. Ibid., 206.

74. Susan McHugh, *Dog* (London: Reaktion Books, 2004), 124.

75. Sanders, *Understanding Dogs*, 51.

76. In this respect, the films are in keeping with the limiting tradition of what Norden terms "the Cinema of Isolation," typified by the Dr. Kildare series, in which exceptional individual disabled characters win their battles only to lose the war against ableist prejudice (149).

77. McHugh, *Dog*, 118–19.

78. Kendrick, *The Odor of Violets*, 294.

79. Nicholas Mirzoeff, in "Blindness and Art," in The *Disability Studies Reader* (ed. Davis), notes that this notion "has long outlasted the medical theory . . . from which it was devised," which posited "a finite number of spirits to enable the senses," so that losing "one sense leaves more spirits available for the others and they are thus enhanced" (384–85). The superhero Daredevil of Marvel Comics (1964–present) and film (2003) fame, whose blinding radioactive accident raises his remaining senses to superhuman capacities, illustrates how this myth continues to shape popular representations of blindness.

80. Paul de Man, *Blindness and Insight: Essays in the Rhetoric of Contemporary Criticism* (Minneapolis: University of Minnesota Press, 1983), ix. This is predicated on de Man's idea of "reading as disfiguration," which Vincent B. Leitch glosses as "activity that accepts randomness," in *Deconstructive Criticism: An Advanced Introduction* (New York: Columbia University Press, 1983), 189.

81. Lennard J. Davis, "Constructing Normalcy: The Bell Curve, the Novel, and the Invention of the Disabled Body in the Nineteenth Century," in *The Disability Studies Reader,* 20, 26.

82. In *Allegories of Reading: Figural Language in Rousseau, Nietzsche, Rilke, and Proust* (New Haven: Yale University Press, 1979), de Man elaborates that such literary disfigurings might be understood rhetorically, not as "the instrument of the subject, of the object, or of the relationship between them" but rather as "categories . . . standing in the service of the language that has produced them" (37).

83. Kenneth J. Shapiro notes the "interesting, relatively recent social construction of a 'dog' as an extension of human eyes or hands." Shapiro, "Understanding Dogs through Kinesthetic Empathy, Social Construction, and History," in *Social Creatures: A Human and Animal Studies Reader,* ed. Clifton P. Flynn (New York: Lantern Books, 2008), 46.

84. One viewer complaint about this aspect on the *Internet Movie Database* Web site also invokes the specter of rivalry between service dog and spouse without the humor (and perhaps knowledge) of Maclain's Sybella: "Jim's guide dog Hank deserves to be recognized as an official cast member in the show's credits. Hank is loyal and faithful

to Jim no matter what in their relationship. Jim's relationship with Hank is closer than Jim is with his wife who feels out of place in their relationship."

85. Only the Japanese film *Quill* (2004), told from a guide dog for a blind man's perspective, explicitly develops the potential for failure in this kind of relationship; it follows the training, initially unsuccessful placement, and rehab of the dog. *Quill*, like *Sue Thomas*, is based on a true story.

86. Hartwell, *Dogs against Darkness*, 120.

2. Velvet Revolutions

1. Lida Fleitmann Bloodgood, *The Saddle of Queens: The Story of the Side-Saddle* (London: J. A. Allen, 1959), 46.

2. Gilles Deleuze and Félix Guattari clarify the stakes of embodiment in forging political alternatives to hierarchical dualisms: "The question is not, or not only, that of the organism, history, and the subject of enunciation that oppose masculine to feminine in the great dualism machines. The question is fundamentally that of the body— the body they steal from us in order to fabricate opposable organisms." Exemplifying the limitations of the psychoanalytic Oedipal model of identity, they say enigmatically, "The girl is the first victim, but she must also serve as an example and a trap," a problem writ large by the girl–horse narrative tradition (*A Thousand Plateaus*, 276).

3. John E. Schowalter, "Horses and Horsewomen," in *Mental Zoo: Animals in the Human Mind and Its Pathology*, ed. Salman Akhtar and Vamik Volkan (New York: International Universities Press, 2005), 81.

4. Jennifer Mason, *Civilized Creatures: Urban Animals, Sentimental Culture, and American Literature, 1850–1900* (Baltimore: Johns Hopkins University Press, 2005), 32. By the late twentieth century, competitive riding becomes a "highly unusual activity" in the sporting world, "open to women and men equally," and, as Gail Cunningham argues, a "main outlet for women's physical power." "Seizing the Reins: Women, Girls, and Horses," in *Image and Power: Women in Fiction in the Twentieth Century*, ed. Sarah Sceats and Gail Cunningham (New York: Longman, 1996), 67, 68.

5. Midas Dekkers, *Dearest Pet: On Bestiality*, trans. Paul Vincent (London: Verso Books, 1994), 63. Peter Singer explicitly characterizes girls riding horses as a form of substitution for "sexual contact" with men in a review of Dekkers's book titled "Heavy Petting," *Nerve*, March 1, 2001, http://www.nerve.com.

6. For an example of a woman on horseback responding to a flasher with humor ("I don't think you want to be doing that around a barn—we see bigger and better every day"), see Susan F. Boucher, "Partnering Pegasus," in *Intimate Nature: The Bond Between Women and Animals*, ed. Linda Hogan, Deena Metzer, and Brenda Peterson (New York: Ballantine Books, 1998), 229.

7. Lynda Birke and Keri Brandt, "Mutual Corporeality: Gender and Human/Horse Relationships," *Women's Studies International Forum* 32 (2009): 196.

8. Hearne, *Adam's Task*, 263.

9. Ibid., 113.

10. Audrey Wipper, "The Partnership: The Horse-Rider Relationship in Eventing," *Symbolic Interaction* 23 (2000): 48.

11. Natalie Hansen, "Queering the Horse-Crazy Girl: Part 2," *Thinking Gender Papers* (Los Angeles: University of California Los Angeles Center for the Study of Women, 2008), 8.

12. Peter Winants, *Steeplechasing: A Complete History of the Sport in North America* (New York: Derrydale, 2000), 65. Winants clarifies that Kusner not only won many races but also a landmark 1968 legal battle with the Maryland Racing Commission, which subsequently issued her a jockey's license. Due to a combination of injury and a conflicting appointment to the U.S. Equestrian Team, she was not, however, the first female jockey that it licensed, exercising her hard-won right to join men in the higher-stakes races only years later.

13. Deleuze and Guattari, *A Thousand Plateaus*, 257.

14. David Hoadley Munting, *Hedges and Hurdles: A Social and Economic History of National Hunt Racing* (London: J. A. Allen, 1987), 51.

15. Williams, *The Long Revolution*, 23.

16. Giorgio Agamben theorizes a relational understanding of existence "without being tied by any common property, by any identity" that, when filtered through language, "exemplars of the coming community" become transformed into "members of a class," reduced to "examples," and perceived as "individuals." Giorgio Agamben, *The Coming Community*, trans. Michael Hardt (Minneapolis: University of Minnesota Press, 1993), 10.1.

17. Fredric Jameson, *Marxism and Form: Twentieth-Century Dialectical Theories of Literature* (Princeton: Princeton University Press, 1971), 123. This point is informed by Jameson's marxist hermeneutic of utopian visioning in Ernst Bloch, whose "experience of astonishment" caps a narrative process centered on "implicit or explicit perception of the future concealed within that which already exists[,] . . . carr[ying] within itself a story line, the trajectory of the not-yet-finished, the struggle of the incomplete to free itself from the as-yet-formlessness of the present" (123–24).

18. Lynda Birke, "'Learning to Speak Horse': The Culture of 'Natural Horsemanship,'" *Society & Animals* 15 (2007): 237 n. 1.

19. Anne Alcock, *"They're Off!" The Story of the First Girl Jump Jockeys* (New York: J. A. Allen, 1978), 17. See also anthropologist Rebecca Cassidy's narrative of working as a "lad" in the British racing industry in *The Sport of Kings: Kinship, Class, and Thoroughbred Breeding in Newmarket* (New York: Cambridge University Press, 2002).

20. Enid Bagnold, quoted in Anne Sebba, *Enid Bagnold: The Authorized Biography* (New York: Taplinger, 1986), 124.

21. Steven D. Price, in the introduction to *Riding's a Joy* (New York: Doubleday, 1982), credits Jacqueline Kennedy Onassis (then a celebrity horsewoman and Doubleday consulting editor) with dubbing the book "the American National Velvet story" (14).

22. Frei and Printz, *Warhol: The Andy Warhol Catalogue Raisonné.*

23. Lenemaja Friedman, in *Enid Bagnold* (Boston: Twayne, 1986), 46. Likewise, Ellen

D. Kolba describes how rereading the novel as an adult "revealed a Velvet struggling not only to take a horse over the obstacles of the Grand National but to define herself. . . . Gone were my memories of Elizabeth Taylor rapturously hugging a horse," in "Recommended: Enid Bagnold," *English Journal* 72 (1983): 50–51.

24. Frei and Printz, *Warhol: The Andy Warhol Catalogue Raisonné.*

25. Enid Bagnold, *National Velvet* (New York: Avon, 1991), 67.

26. Peter Stoneley, "Feminism, Fascism, and the Racialized Body: *National Velvet,*" *Women* 9 (1998): 260.

27. Bagnold, *National Velvet,* 19.

28. Katherine Grier contextualizes this sort of shift from urban transport fixture to family pet in *Pets in America: A History* (Chapel Hill: University of North Carolina Press, 2006), clarifying that in U.S. cities equine populations "steadily increased until the 1910s, the first decade that automobiles were widely available, and horses remained the source of motive power for a declining number of small businesses and some urban services into the 1930s" (188).

29. Sebba, *Enid Bagnold,* 124. The author's account of its production in *Enid Bagnold's Autobiography* (Boston: Little, Brown, 1969) reinforces this sense that mixed communities are central to the story: "I started National Velvet as a study in a girl's relationship with her pony. But it turned immediately and by itself into a story. All our gay life and its details, dogs, canaries, emotions of children, everything jumped into my hands. I had only to snatch and type on and all our full life was on the page" (223).

30. Sebba, *Enid Bagnold,* 126.

31. Ibid., 124, 123.

32. Bagnold, *National Velvet,* 1, 2, 5, 2, 7, 5.

33. Ibid. 13.

34. Ibid. Three years before the novel's publication, Diana Shedden and Lady Apsley's handbook *"To Whom the Goddess": Hunting and Riding for Women* (London: Hutchinson, 1932) warns readers to be selective in choosing clothes for riding astride in order to "avoid the appearance of looking like a hermaphrodite or someone's groom!" (140).

35. Bagnold, *National Velvet,* 58, 88, 189, 238, 159, 241.

36. Ibid., 70, 2, 93, 141.

37. Ibid., 27.

38. Ibid., 49, 56.

39. Ibid., 60.

40. Ibid., 4.

41. Gilles Deleuze and Clare Parnet, *Dialogues,* trans. Hugh Tomlinson and Barbara Habberjam (New York: Columbia University Press, 1987), 110. Deleuze and Parnet counter the pathologizing of the anorexic with the argument that refusing to eat can flag a story of resistance from within capitalist societies, an attempt "to escape from the norms of consumption in order not to be an object of consumption" (110). For an interpretation of Velvet as anorexic due to parental pressure ("It is through her

difficulty with eating that Velvet fulfills her mother's wishes for her"), see Lisa Tyler, "Food, Femininity, and Achievement: The Mother-Daughter Relationship in *National Velvet*," *Children's Literature Association Quarterly* 18 (1993–94): 154.

42. Bagnold, *National Velvet*, 120, 122.

43. Ibid., 105.

44. Mason, *Civilized Creatures*, 33.

45. Grier argues further that manuals and memoirs concerning this equine ideal "represented a relatively new way of thinking about the most important source of transport power in American cities prior to the 1920s" (*Pets in America*, 193).

46. See http://www.horseland.com.

47. Writing of the effects of the 1976 anti-sex-discrimination act in the UK for female riders, up to then barred by the Jockey Club's licensing rules, Alcock uses Bagnold's fiction as a touchstone: "Within days, the first National Velvet–type dream was coming true, swiftly followed by others. By the end of that season, 145 horses had been ridden by women, and ten had won" (*"They're Off!"* 16).

48. Janet Phillips and Peter Phillips, "History from Below: Women's Underwear and the Rise of Sport," *Journal of Popular Culture* 27 (1993): 133. They add that although yeast can infect many body parts (including horses' frogs), it thrives in moist, warm areas like the vagina, and can lead to "ulcers, bleeding, and septicemia," and presumably contributed to the high morbidity rates of women in childbirth (133).

49. Meriel Buxton, *Ladies of the Chase* (London: Sportsman's Press, 1987), 66.

50. Fleitmann Bloodgood, *The Saddle of Queens*, 36.

51. Among the earliest of these, John Allen's *Principles of Modern Riding for Ladies* (London: Thomas Tegg, 1825) suggests that "pouches in the skirts of the habit, with leads in them, are very convenient" to minimize potential embarrassment (31).

52. Mrs. Stirling Clarke, *The Ladies' Equestrian Guide; or, The Habit & Horse; A Treatise on Female Education* (London: Day and Son, 1857), 22. Against associations with "coarse and vulgar," even "bold and masculine" behavior, she argues that "riding is both feminine and graceful, when so cultivated," and credits Queen Victoria for bringing riding into fashion for girls (6).

53. Mason, *Civilized Creatures*, 36.

54. Robert Smith Surtees, *Mr. Sponge's Sporting Tour* (London: Folio Society, 1950), 473. Although everything else seems fair game for his satires, Frederick Watson notes in *Robert Smith Surtees: A Critical Study* (London: George G. Harrap, 1933) that "Surtees never ridiculed good horsewomen," and instead "gave them full marks for nerves, skill, and hands" (211).

55. Surtees, *Mr. Sponge's Sporting Tour*, 506.

56. Robert Smith Surtees, *Mr. Facey Romford's Hounds* (Westminster: Folio Society, 1952), 92.

57. Ibid., 72.

58. Ibid., 85.

59. Cunningham, "Seizing the Reins," 69.

60. Fleitmann Bloodgood, *The Saddle of Queens*, 50, 51. See also Kari Weil, who argues that Loyo was "the first of successive generations of [women riders] who would dominate the circus" as part of a broader democratization and Anglicization of riding in mid-nineteenth-century France. Kari Weil, "Purebreds and Amazones: Saying Things with Horses in Nineteenth-century France," *Differences* 11 (1999): 5.

61. Moira Ferguson, *Animal Advocacy and Englishwomen, 1780–1900: Patriots, Nation, and Empire* (Ann Arbor: University of Michigan Press, 1998), 76, 85.

62. Elsie B. Michie, "Horses and Sexual/Social Dominance," in *Victorian Animal Dreams: Representations of Animals in Victorian Literature and Culture*, ed. Deborah Denenholz Morse and Martin A. Danahay (Burlington, Vt.: Ashgate, 2007), 164.

63. Following a pattern that was to become ordinary by the mid-twentieth century, in 1903 Somerville took over the West Carbery Hounds of County Cork, Ireland, from her brother (it had once been their grandfather's hunt). Later she reflected that "at that time there was but one other Lady Master of Foxhounds [Mrs. T. H. R. Hughes of the Newadd Fawr in Wales, who had taken over the pack from her husband] . . . in the preceding year" and so she "sprang at a bound into the limelight" (*Wheel-Tracks*, 131). Buxton notes that Hughes switched from side to astride in 1910 (*Ladies of the Chase*, 103).

64. E. Œ. [Edith Œnone] Somerville, "Prefatory," *Notes of the Horn: Hunting Verse, Old and New*, ed. Somerville (London: Peter Davies, 1934), ix–x.

65. E. Œ. [Edith Œnone] Somerville, *Stray-Aways* (London: Longmans, Green, 1920), 233.

66. Ibid., 231. Generations earlier, Fleitmann Bloodgood, in *Comments on Hacks and Hunters* (New York: Scribner's, 1921), anticipates only to warn women against the fleeting source of Dekkers's fantasies: "The young slips of girls, who appear so attractive in their trim little breeches and boots, are no standard to go by; wait until they are fair, fat, and forty and watch how many of them will have given up riding because they look so queer" (83).

67. Mrs. [Nannie] Power O'Donoghue, *Riding for Ladies with Hints on the Stable* (London: W. Thacker, 1887), 7.

68. Betsy Skelton, *Side Saddle Riding: Notes for Teachers and Pupils* (London: Sportsman's Press, 1988), 53.

69. Hawley Smart, *Cleverly Won: A Romance of the Grand National* (New York: George Munro's Sons, 1902), 22.

70. Vladimir S. Littauer, *The Development of Modern Riding* (New York: Howell, 1991), 221.

71. Ibid., 216.

72. Otherwise opposing Fleitmann Bloodgood's arguments point for point, M. F. McTaggert, in *Mount and Man: A Key to a Better Horsemanship* (London: Country Life, 1925), concedes that "there is no sound reason why ladies cannot ride perfectly well astride, as long as we do not expect them to ride steeplechases and other dangerous and strenuous exercises" (66).

73. Enid Bagnold, *National Velvet*, 72. Phillips and Phillips note that cheap cotton

and new synthetics like rayon and nylon "put light, often drip-dry articles of underwear" with closed gussets "into the shops and women's wardrobes," but for athletic females "the big star was elastic," which was reliable, durable, and stretchy enough for comfort in clothing and quickly adopted in the manufacture of "an efficient, comfortable, and more or less trouble-free belt to secure disposable sanitary pads" ("History from Below," 137, 138). As women did a century before, competitive riders today often opt to wear no underwear, only (like their counterparts in track sports) to avoid chafing injuries, enabled by the development of Lycra and other materials woven through with elastic fibers.

74. James Agee, quoted in Jerry Vermilye and Mark Ricci, *The Films of Elizabeth Taylor* (Secaucus: Citadel Press, 1976), 51.

75. Alexander Walker, *Elizabeth: The Life of Elizabeth Taylor* (New York: Grove Weidenfeld, 1990), 41.

76. Bagnold, *National Velvet*, 231.

77. Deborah Bright, "Being and Riding," *GLQ* 6 (2003): 479.

78. Deborah Bright, "Horse Crazy," in *Horsetales: American Images and Icons, 1800–2000*, ed. Ezra Shales and Susan H. Edwards (Katonah, N.Y.: Katonah Museum of Art, 2001), 22.

79. Elspeth Probyn, *Outside Belongings* (New York: Routledge, 1996), 54.

80. Elucidating Deleuze and Guattari's notion of becoming-animal, Probyn cautions that the movement she traces "should not be misunderstood as a simple projection onto horse of being a horse but rather entails a certain dissolution of the body-image as known, as my body, in favor of another image, that of becoming-horse" (*Outside Belongings*, 51).

81. More precisely, Deleuze and Guattari's reading of Little Hans's interest in a fallen and beaten horse—"an ordinary sight in those days (Nietzsche, Dostoyevsky, Nijinsky lamented it)"—illustrates how the same animal can be oedipalized by humans and also can thwart attempts at oedipalization of the human and the animal alike. Animals "with which one can . . . play family," as Freud does by interpreting the horse as Hans's father, can also "draw us into an irresistible becoming," an "irresistible deterritorialization that forestalls attempts at professional, conjugal, or Oedipal reterritorialization" as they are drawn through the connections of Hans to so many other different stories and histories (*A Thousand Plateaus*, 257, 233).

82. Elaborating this in terms of a process that begins with a girl's "becoming-woman"—which they cavalierly gloss as "the key to all other becomings"—and leads directly to "becoming-animal," they suggest precise limitations for their applicability in other contexts, not the least because of the implicit (male, adult, human) points of reference in such terms (*A Thousand Plateaus*, 277). Extending this analysis through the Deleuzian framework, Probyn argues that the boy's description can be construed as challenging the logic of identity: "Although it could suggest a certain romanticism of becoming one with the animal, it is, in Deleuze's [later elaborations, explicitly] a rudely impersonal state" (*Outside Belongings*, 52).

83. Probyn, *Outside Belongings*, 55.

84. W. J. T. Mitchell, *The Last Dinosaur Book: The Life and Times of a Cultural Icon* (Chicago: University of Chicago Press, 1998), 257. In his discussion of dinosaurs as cultural icons, Mitchell moves away from the limited notion of animals as psychological constructs, producing "a general, ahistorical account of the individual as producer of culture," and toward a notion of them rather as tools for culturally historicizing this very imperative, instruments with which to "study . . . the ways in which societies produce—and sometimes do not produce—a thing called 'the individual'" (257).

85. Shapiro, "Understanding Dogs," 192. Elizabeth Atwood Lawrence argues further that the horse may be peculiarly poised to "merge action and awareness," for among companion species, "it is the horse . . . [who] partakes of the human kinetic and spatial rhythm, sharing those qualities that make us dance." *Hoofbeats and Society: Studies of Human–Horse Interactions* (Bloomington: Indiana University Press, 1985), 187.

86. Elspeth Probyn, "'Girls and Girls and Girls and Horses'": Queer Images of Singularity and Desire," *Tessera* 15 (1993): 23; Probyn, *Outside Belongings*, 54.

87. Bagnold, *National Velvet*, 162.

88. Ibid., 134–35.

89. See especially Lauren Hillenbrand, *Seabiscuit: An American Legend* (New York: Random House, 2001), which argues that horse-racing simulcasts foster a particular, interwar sense of U.S. national identity that becomes first mediated through (and ultimately secures the place of) radio.

90. Paul Brown, *Aintree: Grand Nationals—Past and Present* (New York: Derrydale, 1930), 93; David Hoadley Munroe, *The Grand National, 1839–1930* (New York: Huntington Press, 1931), 127.

91. T. H. Bird, *A Hundred Grand Nationals* (New York: Scribner's, 1937), 185, 186.

92. Brown, *Aintree*, 93. "Tubed" (also known as "cannoned") forelegs are considered a conformation fault because the horse's tendons grow too close to the cannon bone, thus giving them a rounded appearance and greater potential for injury.

93. Bird, *A Hundred Grand Nationals*, 188.

94. Bagnold, "Author's Note," *National Velvet, or The Slaughterer's Daughter* (New York: William Morrow, 1935).

95. Bagnold, *National Velvet*, 219.

96. Ibid., 229.

97. Alcock notes that Charlotte Brew, the first woman to ride in this race in 1977, "was mobbed like a pop star," and found this "more frightening than the National itself" (*"They're Off!"* 114).

98. Bagnold, *National Velvet*, 225

99. Ibid., 224. In Deleuze and Parnet's terms, Velvet's unusual "stammer," that is, "a vocal or written line [that] . . . make[s] language flow between . . . dualisms," indicates the complexity of the position she is trying to articulate, the impossible position of speaking at once "on behalf of" and "as part of" a community (*Dialogues*, 34).

100. Bagnold, *National Velvet*, 169.

101. Probyn, *Outside Belongings*, 54.

102. Pat Smythe, foreword to Hylton Cleaver, *They've Won Their Spurs* (London: Robert Hale, 1956), 9.

103. Barbara Jones, "Just Crazy about Horses: The Fact behind the Fiction," in *New Perspectives on Our Lives with Companion Animals*, ed. Aaron Katcher and Alan Beck (Philadelphia: University of Pennsylvania Press, 1983), reports from interviews with child riders that nonriding peers criticize especially boys for engaging in "a sissy, easy activity, a girl's sport. There was no appreciation of the hard work and skill involved" (98).

104. Sarah Wintle, "Horses, Bikes, and Automobiles: New Woman on the Move," in *The New Woman in Fiction and in Fact: Fin-de-Siècle Feminisms*, ed. Angelique Richardson and Chris Willis (London: Palgrave, 2001), 71.

105. Raymond Williams, *The Country and the City* (London: Chatto and Windus, 1973), 282.

106. Jackie C. Burke, *Equal to the Challenge: Pioneering Women of Horse Sports* (New York: Howell, 1997), 60.

107. Ibid., 74.

108. Alice O'Connell, *The Blue Mare in the Olympic Trials* (Boston: Little, Brown, 1955), 213.

109. Sam Savitt, *Vicki and the Brown Mare* (New York: Dodd, Mead, 1976), 152.

110. Burke, *Equal to the Challenge*, 103.

111. In an interview with William Wheeler Dixon, director Bryan Forbes describes the film's initial reception: "It was as if I'd introduced a new strain of cancer to the United States; the notices were really, really bad in America, although in the rest of the world it did very, very well" (*Classic Images* 270 [1997]: 39).

112. Jane Spence Southron, review of *National Velvet, New York Times*, May 5, 1935, 6. Locating its emergence in eighteenth-century travel narratives, Donna Landry notes "an often unthinking reliance upon Englishness as a guarantee of cultural superiority—and horsewomanship as a guarantee of that Englishness," in "Horsy and Persistently Queer: Imperialism, Feminism, and Bestiality," *Textual Practice* 15, no. 3 (2001): 469. But Elspeth Probyn more precisely sees this female form of "British horsiness" operating as a mechanism for "British colonization (of lands and girls)" in the twentieth century, exemplified by her Canadian mother's dreaming of "the upper class hunts of the south of England" even as they rode bareback through their Welsh town (*Outside Belongings*, 55, 39), which, I would add, echoes the evident colonizer–colonized pattern mapped onto mother–daughter differences in these narratives.

113. Bryan Forbes, *International Velvet* (New York: Bantam Books, 1978), 55. Deleuze and Parnet, *Dialogues*, 35.

114. Forbes, *International Velvet* 74.

115. Wipper, "The Partnership," 62.

116. Jonathan Burt notes that, in the film's conclusion, "trauma is overcome even if we cannot assume that" the perspectives of girl and horse "are necessarily united" (*Animals in Film*, 56).

117. Keri Brandt, "A Language of Their Own: An Interactionist Approach to Human–Horse Communication," *Society & Animals* 12 (2004): 304.

118. Baker, *The Postmodern Animal*, 140.

119. The film is included as part of the discussion thread titled "Race Horse as Rock Star: Fandom and Zenyatta" initiated by curator Holly Cruise as part of the *in media res* project, http://www.mediacommons.futureofthebook.org.

120. Haraway, *When Species Meet*, 223.

121. Joanna Swabe, *Animals, Disease, and Human Society: Human–Animal Relations and the Rise of Veterinary Medicine* (New York: Routledge, 1999), 153.

122. James Herriot [James Alfred Wight], *The Lord God Made Them All* (New York: St. Martin's Press, 1981), 210.

3. Breeding Narratives of Intimacy

1. Aaron Honori Katcher and Alan M. Beck, *Between Pets and People: The Importance of Animal Companionship* (New York: Putnam's, 1983), 238.

2. J. V. Lacroix, *Animal Castration* (Chicago: American Journal of Veterinary Medicine, 1915), 12.

3. Hal Herzog, *Some We Love, Some We Hate, Some We Eat: Why It's So Hard to Think Straight about Animals* (New York: HarperCollins, 2010), 125–27.

4. Yi-Fu Tuan, *Dominance and Affection: The Making of Pets* (New Haven: Yale University Press, 1984), 89.

5. Clare Palmer argues that the ethical dilemmas of "humane" animal killing common to modern abattoirs and shelters are troubled further by our own implication in having created "unwanted but dependent animals." Clare Palmer, "Killing Animals in Animal Shelters," in *Killing Animals*, ed. The Animal Studies Group (Urbana: University of Illinois Press, 2006), 374.

6. For a comparative analysis, see, for instance, C. Victor Spain, Janet Scarlett, and Katherine Houpt, "Long-Term Risks and Benefits of Early-Age Gonadectomy in Dogs," *Journal of the American Veterinary Medical Association* 224 (2004): 380–87. Whereas studies in the 1960s and '70s unequivocally claim health benefits of gonadectomies, studies published from the 1980s into the 2000s increasingly call such claims into question, particularly in the case of young animals, and often intriguingly on the basis of the same sort of hormonal research fueling the gay-sheep debates.

7. Marie Fox outlines this position in "Taking Dogs Seriously?" *Law, Culture, and the Humanities* 6 (2010): 53.

8. For a good overview of the latter, see Julie Urbanik, "Hooters for Neuters: Sexist or Transgressive Animal Advocacy Campaign?" *Humanimalia* 1, no. 1 (2009): 40–62.

9. Elizabeth Grosz makes the broader claim that such shows, along with the sort of scientific studies analyzed in this chapter's final section and even "books on various animals species . . . all testify to a pervasive fascination with the question of animal sex: how do animals *do it?*" (188). Elizabeth Grosz, *Space, Time, and Perversion: Essays on the Politics of Bodies* (New York: Routledge, 1995), 188.

10. Jens Rydström argues further that urban-based initiatives to enclose animal copulation—"the very basis for a cattle-herding economy"—away from public view, especially from children, indicate how even sex among animals increasingly is perceived as threatening the transition to a modern society and its very different orientation toward an incipient model of citizenship. Jens Rydström, *Sinners and Citizens: Bestiality and Homosexuality in Sweden, 1889–1950* (Chicago: University of Chicago Press, 2003), 72.

11. Derrida notes that the animal is "more other than any other" when seen "on the threshold of sexual difference. More precisely, of sexual differences" (*The Animal*, 36). What my questions tease out are the plural potentials for sexual agency that Derrida implies are threatening to collapse the absolute self/other binary.

12. See especially Alice Kuzniar's chapter on mourning in *Melancholia's Dog: Reflections on Our Animal Kinship* (Chicago: University of Chicago Press, 2006).

13. Susan McHugh, "Video Dog Star: William Wegman, Aesthetic Agency, and the Animal in Art," in *The Representation of Animals*, ed. Steve Baker, special issue of *Society & Animals* 9 (2001): 229–51.

14. Karl Benediktsson, "Rekyavík—Animal City," in Snæbjörnsdóttir/Wilson, *(a)fly (between nature and culture)* (Reykjavik: National Museum of Iceland, 2006), 16–17.

15. On human animality, see Snæbjörnsdóttir/Wilson, *(a)fly*, 6–8; and Ron Broglio, "Making Space for Animal Dwelling," in Snæbjörnsdóttir/Wilson, *(a)fly*, 25.

16. W. J. T. Mitchell, *Picture Theory: Essays on Verbal and Visual Representation* (Chicago: University of Chicago Press, 1994), 362.

17. Wendy Doniger, "The Mythology of Masquerading Animals, or, Bestiality," in *Humans and Other Animals*, ed. Arien Mack (Columbus: Ohio State University Press, 1999), 358.

18. Although primarily drawing from legal and medical documents, Rydström also cites popular novelist Ivar Lo-Johansson's naturalized and autobiographical account of perpetrating bestiality as a lonely boy with a "frisky and agile heifer" (*Sinners and Citizens*, 65). More to the point of this chapter, he shows how "The Bull of Nybacken," a farmhand known for engaging in bestiality in Vilhelm Moberg's novel *The Emigrants* (1949), illustrates how the "heterospecial" ideas of this practice "did not threaten the masculinity of the perpetrators but rather enhanced it and made it grotesque" (18).

19. Soseki Natsume [Kinnosuke Natsume], *Wagahai wa Neko de Aru [I am a cat]*, trans. Aiko Ito and Graeme Wilson (Rutland, Vt.: Tuttle, 2002), 153.

20. Ibid.

21. Biographer Bruce Kellner notes that "a Philadelphia bookseller" voiced the "single dissenting opinion" not about the content but the box-cover illustration of "a cat performing his daily ablutions in a perfectly natural but not altogether delicate position." Bruce Kellner, *Carl van Vechten and the Irreverent Decades* (Norman: University of Oklahoma Press, 1968), 121.

22. Carl van Vechten, *Feathers* (New York: Random, 1930), 20.

23. May Sarton, *The Fur Person* (New York: W. W. Norton, 1983), 66.

24. Ibid.

25. Vladimir Nabokov, *Lolita* (New York: Vintage Books, 1989), 15.

26. Joseph Bristow, *Effeminate England: Homoerotic Writing after 1885* (Buckingham: Open University Press, 1995), 2.

27. J. R. Ackerley, *My Dog Tulip* (New York: Poseidon Press, 1987), 158.

28. Foucault, *The History of Sexuality*, 1:43.

29. Ackerley, *My Dog Tulip*, 149.

30. Ibid., 154.

31. Ackerley quoted in Peter Parker, *Ackerley: The Life of J. R. Ackerley* (New York: Farrar, Straus and Giroux, 1989), 261.

32. Jonathan Goldberg in *Sodometries: Renaissance Texts, Modern Sexualities* (Stanford: Stanford University Press, 1992) develops the "categorical confusion" by which "sodomy [as buggery] is equated with bestiality" in English law (3). See also Jonathan Ned Katz on the historical conflation of "human–animal sexual contacts and male–male sexual relations," in *Gay/Lesbian Almanac: A New Documentary In which is contained, in Chronological Order, Evidence of the True and Fantastical HISTORY of those Persons now called LESBIANS and GAY MEN, and of the Changing Social Forms of and Responses to those Acts, Feelings, and Relationships now called Homosexual, in the Early American Colonies, 1607 to 1740, and in the Modern United States, 1880 to 1950* (New York: Harper and Row, 1983), 668 n. 3.

33. Bristow, *Effeminate England*, 150.

34. See Michael Warner, introduction to *Fear of a Queer Planet: Queer Politics and Social Theory*, ed. Warner (Minneapolis: University of Minnesota Press, 1993).

35. Warner and Berlant, "Sex in Public," in *Intimacy*, ed. Berlant, special issue of *Critical Inquiry* 24 (1998): 558–64.

36. See Deleuze and Guattari, *A Thousand Plateaus*, 26–38, 232–309.

37. Judith Roof, *Reproductions of Reproduction: Imaging Symbolic Change* (New York: Routledge, 1996), 26. The mongrel's involvement complicates a simple substitution of metaphoric for metonymic reproduction, however, operating instead as what Roof later calls a "transitive term" ("We Want Viagra," *Post Identity* 2 [1999]: 5–23).

38. Probyn, *Outside Belongings*, 54.

39. On the pivotal role of dogs in formulating her concept of situated knowledges, see Haraway, *Simians, Cyborgs, and Women: The Reinvention of Nature* (New York: Routledge, 1991), 190.

40. Ackerley, *My Father and Myself* (New York: Poseidon Press, 1968), 110.

41. W. H. Auden, "Papa Was a Wise Old Sly-Boots," *Forewords and Afterwords*, ed. Edward Mendelson (London: Faber and Faber, 1973), 450. *My Father and Myself* is cryptically inscribed, "To Tulip."

42. Bristow, *Effeminate England*, 149.

43. Ackerley, *My Father and Myself*, 28–29.

44. Ibid., 199.

45. Auden, "Papa Was a Wise Old Sly-Boots," 452.

46. Ackerley, *My Father and Myself*, 201.

47. Lauren Berlant, writing with Elizabeth Freeman, conceptualizes "negative identity" as the position inscribed in the space "between persons and collective identities, . . . a space where suddenly the various logics of identity . . . come into contradiction and not simple analogy." Lauren Berlant, *The Queen of America Goes to Washington City: Essays on Sex and Citizenship* (Durham: Duke University Press, 1997), 169.

48. Ackerley, *My Father and Myself*, 217.

49. Bristow's reading is in this respect typical: "In the . . . novel, it is only too clear that the beloved dog becomes a figuration for an idealized sexual partner that Ackerley [never] found" (149). In her book *Dog Love* (New York: Simon and Schuster, 1996), Marjorie Garber critiques the "'substitution' theory" implicit in such readings of human–canine relationships, noting how this mode of critique directs the sort of "pity and contempt . . . , more often than not, toward women and gay men" (135), which James Serpell documented earlier as a sociological phenomenon.

50. John M. Clum notes that, in this respect, the novel "gives the lie to the working-class fantasy celebrated by many British gay writers," in "Myself of Course: J. R. Ackerley and Self-Dramatization," *Theater* 24 (1993): 85. On Ackerley's broader concerns with class, space, and sexuality, see Clum, 86; and Bristow, *Effeminate England*, 149–50.

51. Ackerley, *We Think the World of You* (New York: Poseidon Press, 1988), 8, 11, 157.

52. David Bergman, "J. R. Ackerley and the Ideal Friend," *Fictions of Masculinity: Crossing Cultures, Crossing Sexuality*, ed. Peter F. Murphy (New York: New York University Press, 1994), 263.

53. Bristow, *Effeminate England*, 136.

54. Ackerley quoted in Parker, *Ackerley*, 315.

55. Ackerley, *We Think the World of You*, 11.

56. Garber, *Dog Love*, 125. Rejecting Garber's "unconditional love" thesis about canine affect, Haraway sees significance instead in the auto/biographical record of intense engagement between species: "His unswerving dedication to his dog's significant otherness," or "permanent search for knowledge of the intimate other, and the inevitable comic and tragic mistakes in that quest" are what "command . . . respect" in Ackerley's narratives (*The Companion Species Manifesto*, 34, 35).

57. Ackerley, *We Think the World of You*, 157.

58. Garber, *Dog Love*, 135.

59. Parker, *Ackerley*, 320.

60. Ibid.

61. Ibid., 319.

62. Walter Kendrick, "Heavy Petting: J. R. Ackerley Goes to the Dogs," *Village Voice Literary Supplement*, October 1990, 14.

63. Parker, *Ackerley*, 322.

64. Ackerley, *My Dog Tulip*, 56–57.

65. Ackerley, *My Dog Tulip*, 11; *My Father and Myself*, 216.

66. Ackerley, *My Dog Tulip,* 57.

67. More recently, veterinary researchers D. Edward Jones and Joan O. Joshua inadvertently underscore the continuing problems of conceptualizing canine sexual agency as they use negative constructions and passive voice to elaborate: "While some bitches and most dogs are promiscuous, in many instances the selected pair are not mutually attracted and mating does not occur unassisted." D. Edward Jones and Joan O. Joshua, *Reproductive Clinical Problems in the Dog* (Boston: Wright, 1982), 49.

68. Ibid., 86. Offering a conventionally autobiographical interpretation of this aspect, Parker speculates that "like her master, [the bitch] preferred the local strays" (*Ackerley,* 281).

69. Such prejudices, Ritvo clarifies, were lent authority by Victorian scientific theories of telegony, "or . . . the influence of the previous sire" on the issue of subsequent matings with any others, that contributed to both breeders' fixation of "disciplinary energies on female animals," as well as a broader symbolic linkage of breed status, pedigree, and "prepotency" (or the "heightened power to shape progeny"), imagined as a controllable, "concentrated reproductive force." Harriet Ritvo, *The Platypus and the Mermaid and Other Figments of the Classifying Imagination* (Cambridge, Mass.: Harvard University Press, 1997), 103, 106, 115.

70. Parker suggests that the regular sight of "men bathing naked" also identified this particular park as a gay zone (*Ackerley,* 274). A generation after Ackerley, in his contemporary American gay-man-and-his-bitch narrative, Lars Eighner documents the safe-sex campaigning advantages to the park as "a traditional place that men met to have sex" in *Travels with Lizbeth: On the Road and on the Streets* (New York: St. Martin's Press, 1993]), 138. As Vicki Hearne notes, the "shabbier parts of parks and racetracks" likewise persist as preservation zones for knowledges of animals. Vicki Hearne, "Can an Ape Tell a Joke? Learning from a Las Vegas Orangutan Act," *Harper's,* November 1993, 58. Such moves distinguish "re-appropriation" of a space that in modern park-design history is "geared towards the conspicuous display of androcentric heterosexual desire, courtship and conquest," according to Lisa Uddin, "Panda Gardens and Public Sex at the National Zoological Park," *PUBLIC: Art/ Culture/ Ideas* 41 (2010): 6.

71. A. Barton, "The Sex Life of a Dog," in *Your Dog's Health Book,* ed. Jack Denton Scott (New York: Macmillan, 1956), 160.

72. Ibid., 164.

73. Volker Sommer and Paul Vasey credit Wolfgang Wickler with introducing in a 1967 paper the theory of "socio-sexual" behaviors, or sexual gestures that create social meanings, through which homosexual acts might be seen as adaptive and not (as was previously assumed) automatically disadvantageous from an evolutionary perspective. Volker Sommer and Paul Vasey, "Homosexual Behavior in Animals: Topics, Hypotheses, and Research Trajectories," in *Homosexual Behavior in Animals: An Evolutionary Perspective,* ed. Sommer and Vasey (Cambridge: Cambridge University Press, 2006), 6.

74. Cynthia Chris elaborates this reference explicitly in relation to its heterosexual human cultural enframing: "In 1999 a band called Bloodhound Gang released 'The

Bad Touch,' a song that contained the lyrical refrain, 'You and me baby ain't nothing but mammals / So let's do it like they do on the Discovery Channel.' The Geffen Records CD single's cover pictured copulating zebras. In the music video that aired on MTV, members of the group, costumed as monkeys and armed with blow darts, chase miniskirted women through the streets of Paris." Cynthia Chris, *Watching Wildlife* (Minneapolis: University of Minnesota Press, 2006), xv.

75. See Lynda Birke, "Is Homosexuality Hormonally Determined?" *Journal of Homosexuality* 6 (1982): 34–49; and Jennifer Terry, "'Unnatural Acts' in Nature: The Scientific Fascination with Queer Animals," *GLQ* 6, no. 2 (2000): 151–93.

76. Sommer and Vasey, "Homosexual Behavior in Animals," 7.

77. Ibid., 9.

78. Or, as Sommer and Vasey put it, "Which of these same-sex activities and their formations into patterns count as homosexual? And who gets to decide?" ("Homosexual Behavior in Animals," 12).

79. Ritvo, *The Platypus and the Mermaid*, xii.

80. Bruce Bagemihl, *Biological Exuberance: Animal Homosexuality and Natural Diversity* (New York: St. Martin's Press, 1999), 12; Sommer and Vasey, "Homosexual Behavior in Animals," 10.

81. William Saletan, "Brokeback Mutton: Gay Sheep and Human Destiny," *Slate*, February 2, 2007, http://www.slate.com. The jokes, repeated in all sorts of media, were inspired by Charles E. Roselli, Kay Larkin, Jessica M. Schrunk, and Fredrick Stormshak's "Sexual Partner Preference, Hypothalmic Morphology, and Aromatase in Rams," *Physiology & Behavior* 83 (2004), which (perhaps too predictably) identifies the important brain bits and hormone levels that distinguish "straight" rams as respectively bigger and higher than in male-oriented rams and ewes (233).

82. Joan Roughgarden, *Evolution's Rainbow: Diversity, Gender, and Sexuality in Nature and People* (Berkeley: University of California Press, 2004), 139.

83. Raymond Williams, *Marxism and Literature* (Oxford: Oxford University Press, 1977), 52.

84. Cultural critics do this in pointed contrast to researchers themselves. Note the discomfort with this kind of linguistic slippage in Roselli et al.'s conclusion: "Although there is no direct correspondence between same-sex sexual behavior in animal and human homosexuality, identifying hormonal and neurological correlates of the expression of same-sex behavior may provide clues to factors (genetic, hormonal, environmental) involved with or influencing its occurrence in humans" ("Sexual Partner Preference," 233).

85. Sarah Franklin, *Dolly Mixtures: The Remaking of Genealogy* (Durham: Duke University Press, 2007), 77.

86. Thelma Rowell, "A Few Peculiar Primates," in *Primate Encounters: Models of Science, Gender, and Society*, ed. Shirley C. Strum and Linda Marie Fedigan (Chicago: University of Chicago Press, 2000), 69.

87. Vinciane Despret, "Sheep Do Have Opinions," in *Making Things Public: Atmospheres of Democracy*, ed. Bruno Latour and Peter Weibel (Cambridge, Mass.: MIT Press, 2005), 363.

88. Haraway, *When Species Meet*, 17–18.

4. The Fictions and Futures of Farm Animals

1. Garry Marvin, "Perpetuating Polar Bears: The Cultural Life of Dead Animals," in *nanoq: flat out and bluesome: A Cultural Life of Polar Bears* by Snæbjörnsdóttir/Wilson (London: Black Dog Publishing, 2006), 164.

2. In her pioneering cookbook, *Diet for a Small Planet: Tenth Anniversary Edition* (New York: Ballantine Books, 1982), Frances Moore Lappé notes, "Like drinking Coca-Cola and wearing Levi's, eating beef is a symbol of the American way of life, imitated from Tegucigalpa to Tokyo" (90).

3. Ritvo, *The Animal Estate*, 188; Carol J. Adams, *The Sexual Politics of Meat: A Feminist-Vegetarian Critical Theory* (New York: Continuum, 1991), 29.

4. Paul Robbins, "Shrines and Butchers: Animals as Deities, Capital, and Meat in Contemporary North India," in *Animal Geographies: Place, Politics, and Identity in the Nature-Culture Divide*, ed. Jennifer Wolch and Jody Emel (New York: Verso Books, 1998), 219.

5. These descriptions are from the promotional Web site of New Harvest, which is the brainchild of Jason Matheny, a graduate student in utilitarian philosophy (http://www.new-harvest.org).

6. Oron Catts, "The Art of the Semi-Living," in *Live: Art and Performance*, ed. Adrian Heathfield and Hugo Glendinning (New York: Routledge, 2004), 154. Catts notes that, while J. M. J. Jolly invented a technique for sustaining tissues excised from complex organisms in 1903, it was perfected in 1910 by Alexis Carrel, who coined the term "tissue culture" (159 n. 25). Eighty years later, the collaboration of surgeon Joseph Vacanti and material scientist Robert Langar led to the degradable scaffolding technique that allows tissue to be grown in three dimensions—"emblematized by one of the most important icons of the late twentieth century: the mouse with a human ear growing on its back"—that revolutionized biomedicine with the prospect of tissue engineering (154–55).

7. "Real artificial meat" is the preferred phrasing of Marianne Heselmans, "The Dutch Cultivate Minced Meat in a Petri Dish," *NRC Handelsblad*, September 10, 2005 (http://www.new-harvest.org).

8. Oron Catts and Ionat Zurr, "Towards a New Class of Being: The Extended Body," *intelligent agent* 6 (http://www.intelligentagent.com).

9. Patrick D. Hopkins and Austin Dacey, "Vegetarian Meat: Could Technology Save Animals and Satisfy Meat Eaters?" *Journal of Agricultural and Environmental Ethics* (2008).

10. See http://www.new-harvest.org.

11. P. D. Edelman et al. observe that the greatest quantities of cells have been produced in the shortest periods of time through experiments with goldfish skeletal muscle

tissue grown with large amounts of fetal bovine serum (659). P. D. Edelman, D. C. McFarland, V. A. Mironov, and J. G. Matheny, "*In-Vitro* Cultured Meat Production," *Tissue Engineering* 11 (2005): 659.

12. Zurr and Catts, "The Ethical Claims of Bio Art: Killing the Other or Self-cannibalism?" (http://www.tca.uwa.edu.au).

13. Catts and Zurr, "Towards a New Class of Being." By redeploying biotechnology in the realm of art in order to critique scientific classification, Catts and Zurr contribute another example to "dispute biology's claim that life only emerges in cells and organisms," according to Lauren Seiler in "What Are We? The Social Construction of the Human Biological Self," *Journal for the Theory of Social Behavior* 37 (2007): 266.

14. Catts and Zurr, "Towards a New Class of Being."

15. Adele Senior, "In the Face of the Victim: Confronting the Other in the Tissue Culture and Art Project," in *Sk-interfaces: Exploring Borders—Creating Membranes in Art, Technology, and Society*, ed. Jens Hauser (Liverpool: FACT and Liverpool University Press, 2008), 82.

16. Deborah P. Dixon, "The Blade and the Claw: Science, Art, and the Creation of the Lab-borne Monster," *Social & Cultural Geography* 9 (2008): 685.

17. Jens Hauser, "Biotechnology as Mediality: Strategies of Organic Media Art," *Performance Research* 11 (2006): 133.

18. Zurr and Catts, "The Ethical Claims of Bio Art."

19. Gilles Deleuze, *Francis Bacon: The Logic of Sensation*, trans. Daniel W. Smith (Minneapolis: University of Minnesota Press, 2003), 21–22. Deleuze includes Bacon's own famous line: "If I go into a butcher shop, I always think it's surprising that I wasn't there instead of the animal" (22).

20. Burt, "The Aesthetics of Livingness," *Antennae: The Journal of Nature in Visual Culture*, 5 (2008): 8.

21. Borrowing the term "Dolly Mixtures" from "a distinctive species of confection," Franklin uses it as a trope for the ways in which the famous cloned sheep Dolly mixes up stories of animal husbandry, operating "both as a domesticated animal and as the embodiment of a technique with the potential value to colonize or domesticate human cells" (*Dolly Mixtures*, 2, 56).

22. Vivian Sobchack, "Beating the Meat/Surviving the Text, or How to Get Out of This Century Alive," in *The Visible Woman: Imaging Technologies, Gender, and Science*, ed. Paula A. Treichler, Lisa Cartwright, and Constance Penley (New York: New York University Press, 1998), 313.

23. N. Katherine Hayles, *How We Became Posthuman: Virtual Bodies in Cybernetics, Literature, and Informatics* (Chicago: University of Chicago Press, 1999), 48.

24. Ibid., 33.

25. Nicole Shukin, *Animal Capital: Rendering Life in Biopolitical Times* (Minneapolis: University of Minnesota Press, 2009), 232.

26. McKay, "BSE, Hysteria, and the Representation of Animal Death," 158.

27. Helen Tiffin, "Pigs, People, and Pigoons," in *Knowing Animals*, ed. Laurence Simons and Philip Armstrong (Boston: E. J. Brill, 2007), 250.

28. Peter Stallybrass and Allon White, *The Politics and Poetics of Transgression* (Ithaca: Cornell University Press, 1986), 49.

29. Doris Witt, "Soul Food: Where the Chitterling Hits the (Primal) Pan," in *Eating Culture*, ed. Ron Scapp and Brian Seitz (Albany: State University of New York Press, 1998), 267; Allon White, "Pigs and Pierrots: The Politics of Transgression in Modern Fiction," *Raritan* 2 (1982): 57.

30. Although, as Lappé notes, beef now is associated most clearly with American diets, Roger Horowitz clarifies that such perceptions reflect historic shifts away from rural sustainability: "A meat eaten cured rather than fresh, pork was America's preeminent meat before urban growth and home refrigeration made beef more accessible." Roger Horowitz, *Putting Meat on the American Table: Taste, Technology, Transformation* (Baltimore: Johns Hopkins University Press, 2006), 43.

31. Most concede that early nineteenth-century Cincinnati, or "porkopolis" as it quickly became known, modeled the centralization of transport exploited by the architects of Chicago's meatpacking industry, which according to Horowitz remained "hog butcher for the world" well into the twentieth century (*Putting Meat on the American Table*, 49).

32. Ann Bruce, "GM Animals—Another GM Crops?" *Genomics, Society, and Policy* 3 (2007): 4. I learned about this pig from Jonathan L. Clark, whose dissertation on Enviropig™ as a "regulatory-friendly" organism explains the significance of this creature in terms of a special kind of biotech fix, one that conceptualizes the body not as a sink but as a source of environmental toxins.

33. Adams, *The Sexual Politics of Meat*, 14.

34. Ibid., 93, 94.

35. Ford's autobiography *My Life and Work* (Garden City, N.Y.: Doubleday, 1922) records that he got "the idea" for his famous assembly-line factory design "from the overhead trolley that the Chicago packers use[d] in dressing beef," which he understood to be "the first moving line ever installed" (81).

36. Jimmy M. Skaggs, *Prime Cut: Livestock Raising and Meatpacking in the United States, 1607–1983* (College Station: Texas A&M University Press, 1986), 118. On *The Jungle*'s transformation of black people from spectacularized individuals to a more threatening body of "scab" labor, see Shukin, *Animal Capital*, 255–56.

37. Horowitz, *Putting Meat on the American Table*, 68, 99–100.

38. Burt, "Conflicts around Slaughter in Modernity," in *Killing Animals*, 268.

39. Anna Williams, "Disciplining Animals: Sentience, Production, and Critique," *International Journal of Sociology and Social Policy* 24 (2004): 54.

40. Burt, "The Illumination of the Animal Kingdom: The Role of Light and Electricity in Animal Representation," in *The Representation of Animals*, 206.

41. Discussing the extreme example of zooerasts (or perpetrators of pathological bestiality), Akira Lippit accounts for such people's fascination with the sight of dying

animals as making "animals, or rather images of animals, mediate this violent act," mutating identification into a form of avoiding the responsibilities of the subject (*Electric Animal*, 181).

42. Skaggs, *Prime Cut*, 119.

43. Sinclair, *The Autobiography of Upton Sinclair* (New York: Harcourt, Brace and World, 1962), 126.

44. Brecht, quoted in Frederic Grab, introduction to *Die heilige Johanna der Schlachthöfe [Saint Joan of the Stockyards]*, by Bertolt Brecht, trans. Frank Jones (Bloomington: Indiana University Press, 1969), 9. Brecht's elaboration of this play as "non-Aristotelian drama" intimates how individual roles, scripted by groups pitted against one another in the meatpacking industry, evoke a serious breakdown in form, in which "certain modes of representation are destroyed by the demonstration of their social function" (quoted in Grab, 13).

45. Illuminating his theory of "feral agency," Armstrong points to this moment in the narrative to argue that "the fates of the human and nonhuman elements of the system are conjoined; the desperate unpredictability of the animal matches that of the workers, and all are equally vulnerable to the butcher's knife and the boss's gun" (*What Animals Mean*, 137).

46. Charles Patterson, *Eternal Treblinka: Our Treatment of Animals and the Holocaust* (New York: Lantern Books, 2002), 63. Marian Scholtmeijer counters that Sinclair's disruption of traditional representational linkages contributes to the further victimization of animals: "The metaphoric use of animals vacillates because it is not grounded in narrative allegiance with the animal." Marian Scholtmeijer, *Animal Victims in Modern Fiction: From Sanctity to Sacrifice* (Toronto: University of Toronto Press, 1993), 151.

47. Monica Chiu, "Postnational Globalization and (En)Gendered Meat Production in Ruth L. Ozeki's *My Year of Meats*," *LIT: Literature, Interpretation, Theory* 12 (2001): 111.

48. Nina Cornyetz, "The Meat Manifesto: Ruth Ozeki's Performative Poetics," *Women & Performance: A Journal of Feminist Theory* 12 (2001): 207.

49. Michael Zyrd, "Ironic Identity Frames and Autobiographical Identity: Ruth L. Ozeki's *Halving the Bones* and *My Year of Meats*," *Literary Research* 18 (2001): 125.

50. Ruth Ozeki, "A Conversation with Ruth Ozeki," in *My Year of Meats* (New York: Penguin, 1998), 7.

51. Steve Baker, *The Postmodern Animal*, 116.

52. Baker argues that Coe's images "constantly risk being drawn close to a stylistic sentimentality in order to express the artist's moral and political outrage," and that this is a critique that Coe herself counters by noting that "the accusation of sentimentality is typically used 'to prevent an outcry against cruelty, to silence criticism against bad science'" (*The Postmodern Animal*, 178).

53. D. Stull and M. Broadway, "Killing Them Softly: Work in Meat-Packing Plants and What It Does to Workers," in *Any Way You Cut It: Meat Processing and Small-Town America*, ed. Stull, Broadway, and D. Griffith (Lawrence: University Press of Kansas, 1995), 61–83.

54. Sue Coe, *Dead Meat* (New York: Four Walls Eight Windows, 1995), 72.

55. Ibid. At such moments, Coe moves from "cross-mapping" to collapsing human-animal distinctions, and so complicates critiques like Cary Wolfe's in *What Is Posthumanism?* that her project "reinstalls a familiar figure of the human at the center of . . . representation" (166–67).

56. J. M. Coetzee, *The Lives of Animals*, ed. Amy Gutmann (Princeton: Princeton University Press, 1999), 22.

57. Ibid., 53. Pointing to Costello's articulation of this point in terms of an "exercise of the sympathetic imagination," Helen Tiffin argues that, while risking an even more tightly closed circuit of anthropocentrism, such an approach "does, however, have the potential to work in the opposite direction—reading through humans to bring the (absent) animal into presence" ("Pigs, People, and Pigoons," 254).

58. Robert McKay, "Metafiction, Vegetarianism, and the Literary Performance of Animal Ethics in J. M. Coetzee's *The Lives of Animals*," *Safundi* 11 (2010): 77. Offering a rare, carefully detailed reading of the novel on its own terms, McKay also compiles sources to document the "disproportionate amount of critical energy expended on the ethics of Elizabeth's comparison of the meat industry to the Holocaust" (69).

59. See especially Charles Patterson, who cites these and other passages in Sinclair, Coe, and Coetzee almost without comment, as if they straightforwardly or self-evidently support his thesis that "the road to Auschwitz begins at the slaughterhouse" (*Eternal Treblinka*, 53).

60. Coe, *Dead Meat*, 111.

61. Ibid., 66.

62. Ibid., 73.

63. Ibid., 74.

64. Susan McHugh, "Bringing Up *Babe*," *Camera Obscura* 49 (2002): 149–87.

65. Philip Kemp, review of *Babe*, *Sight and Sound*, n.s. 5 (1995): 40.

66. Kenyon-Jones, *Kindred Brutes*, 12.

67. George Orwell clearly supports this interpretation in the following passage: "On my return from Spain I thought of exposing the Soviet myth in a story that could be easily understood by anyone and which could be easily translated into other languages." Orwell, "Author's Preface to the Ukrainian Edition of *Animal Farm*," in *The Collected Essays, Journalism, and Letters of George Orwell*, vol. 3, *As I Please, 1943–1945*, ed. Sonia Orwell and Ian Angus (New York: Harcourt, Brace and World, 1968), 405.

68. Orwell, *Animal Farm* (New York: Harcourt, Brace and World, 1954), 128.

69. Orwell, "Author's Preface," 406.

70. Margaret Drabble, "Of Beasts and Men: Orwell on Beastliness," *On Nineteen Eighty-Four: Orwell and Our Future*, ed. Abbott Gleason, Jack Goldsmith, and Martha Nussbaum (Princeton: Princeton University Press, 2005), 43. Abbot Gleason elaborates that "publishers [were] unwilling to challenge the Russophile sentiments of the English public (and to a degree, government) by publishing *Animal Farm*" ("Puritanism and Power Politics during the Cold War: George Orwell and Historical Objectivity," in *On*

Nineteen Eighty-Four, 82). Complaining that that the novel was left "lying in type for about a year because the publisher dared not bring it out until the war was over," Orwell wrote privately that he was "surprised by [the novel's] friendly reception," noting too that "the first edition of 6000 copies sold out immediately" ("Letter to Frank Barber," in *The Collected Essays, Journalism, and Letters of George Orwell,* vol. 3, *As I Please,* 402).

71. D. B. D. Asker, *The Modern Bestiary: Animals in English Fiction, 1880–1945* (Lewiston, N.Y.: Edwin Mellen, 1996), 65. Jeffrey Moussaieff Masson claims it "astonishing" that such a "revolutionary comment about humans and animals has been effaced from the public record!" in *The Pig Who Sang to the Moon: The Emotional World of Farm Animals* (New York: Ballantine Books, 2003), 239 n. 4, whereas Tiffin reads this oversight as symptomatic, "a classic example of the disappearance of animals as characters in their own right" ("Pigs, People, and Pigoons," 252).

72. Raymond Williams, *Culture and Society, 1780–1950* (London: Chatto and Windus, 1958), 293.

73. Raymond Williams, *George Orwell* (New York: Viking Press, 1971), 74.

74. Gene Stratton-Porter, *The Strike at Shane's: A Prize Story of Indiana* (Bedford, Mass.: Applewood, 2002).

75. Orwell, *Animal Farm,* 104.

76. Daniel J. Leab, "Animators and Animals: John Halas, Joy Batchelor, and George Orwell's *Animal Farm,*" *Historical Journal of Film, Radio, and Television* 25 (2005), 238. See also the chapter entitled "The Animators: Halas and Batchelor" in Leab, *Orwell Subverted: The CIA and the Filming of "Animal Farm"* (University Park: Pennsylvania State University Press, 2007).

77. Jane Doe, *Anarchist Farm* (Gualala, Calif.: III Publishing, 1996), 9.

78. Frederic Jameson, *Postmodernism or, The Cultural Logic of Late Capitalism* (Durham: Duke University Press, 1991), xvi. Jameson explains that "necessary failures" work to "inscribe the particular postmodern project back into its context, while at the same time reopening the question of the modern itself for reexamination" (xvi).

79. Jameson posits the "logical possibility, alongside both the old closed, centered subject of inner-directed individualism and the new non-subject of the fragmented or schizophrenic self, of a third term which would be very precisely the non-centered subject that is part of an organic group or collective" (*Postmodernism,* 345).

80. Donna J. Haraway, *Modest_Witness@Second_Millennium: FemaleMan©_Meets_OncoMouse™: Feminism and Technoscience* (New York: Routledge, 1997), 119–21.

81. N. Katherine Hayles proposes the expansive notion of "intermediation," or interplay through which new media forms constantly rewrite each other's potentials, in *My Mother Was a Computer: Digital Subjects and Literary Texts* (Chicago: University of Chicago Press, 2005), 33.

82. My neologism "animalacra" flags a point of overlap in two concepts. The first is Jean Baudrillard's "simulacra," which he uses to elaborate the difference between the "real" order of representation and the "hyperreal" order of simulation, and in turn how the latter have come to subsume the former in *Simulacra and Simulation,* trans.

Sheila Faria Glaser (Ann Arbor: University of Michigan Press, 1994), 12, 13. The second is Deleuze and Guattari's "desiring-machines," the agents or "organ-machines" that "cling to" or "are pinned onto" the "Body without Organs," serving as "the element of antiproduction coupled with the process, a full body that functions as a *socius*" in a model of "man" and "nature" alike as replaced by "a process that produces the one within the other," a process articulated through this expansive concept of "machines" to mean "all of species life." Deleuze and Guattari, *Anti-Oedipus: Capitalism and Schizophrenia*, trans. Robert Hurley, Mark Seem, and Helen R. Lane (Minneapolis: University of Minnesota Press, 1983), 11, 10, 2.

83. Haraway, *Simians, Cyborgs, and Women*, 161.

84. Mitchell elaborates a similar case in which "the jerky, robotic movements . . . do not, curiously enough, detract from their realism, but fit perfectly with their role as embodiments of machine technologies" (*The Last Dinosaur Book*, 171).

85. See, for instance, Teresa de Lauretis's characterization of film subjects as "not unified but rather multiple, and not so much divided as contradicted," in *Technologies of Gender: Essays on Theory, Film, and Fiction* (Bloomington: Indiana University Press, 1987), 2.

86. Joan Scott, "The Evidence of Experience," in *The Lesbian and Gay Studies Reader*, ed. Henry Abelove, Michele Aina Barale, and David M. Halperin (New York: Routledge, 1993), 401. Noting the parallel between de Lauretis's idea of experience and Raymond Williams's definition of it in *Keywords*, Scott contrasts these structuralist models with Gayatri Spivak's deconstructive theory of the "subject-effect," which emphasizes "inquiry into the process of subject-construction" as a means of flagging "a metalepsis" or "the substitution of an effect for a cause" (403, 413).

87. Jay Bolter and Richard Grusin, *Remediation: Understanding New Media* (Cambridge, Mass.: MIT Press, 1999), 5.

88. In a discussion of what happens when we think of television through Martin Heidegger's concept of *Ge-stell* or enframing, Richard Dienst argues, "This surpassing and submerging of the proper space and time of visual objects can be thought, for us, only through television." Richard Dienst, *Still Life in Real Time: Theory After Television* (Durham: Duke University Press, 1994), 113, 122.

89. The notable exception to the mice's tendency to cite only lines spoken by other characters is the intertitle, "Pig of Destiny." In light of Deleuze and Guattari's critique of Derrida's supplementarity, I propose that this significantly singular and last intertitle shifts the terms of the mice's textual supplementarity from supplying the voices that dominate the written or graphic text to being the voices dominated or supplanted by graphism in this final instance (*Anti-Oedipus*, 202–3).

90. Haraway, *Simians, Cyborgs, and Women*, 148.

91. Haraway, *The Companion Species Manifesto*, 20.

92. In Walter Benjamin's terms, the machine- and animal-mediated human's "aura"—its uniquely self-referential condition of production—recedes under these conditions of mechanical reproduction. Benjamin, "The Work of Art in an Age of

Mechanical Reproduction," in *Illuminations*, ed. Hannah Arendt (New York: Schocken Books, 1969), 221. Incidentally, this is the argument from which Berger derives his proposition that animals are disappearing in modernity, referenced here in the introduction.

93. The film's source novel, Dick King-Smith's *Babe the Gallant Pig* (1995), a reprint of *The Sheep Pig* (1983), describes him with appropriate succinctness: "Farmer Hoggett . . . never wasted his energies or his words" (11). Creating a sort of inside joke for farm folk, King-Smith does not elaborate that, in spite of its porcine resonance, his choice of surname less one "t" is the word that designates a yearling lamb headed for slaughter.

94. De Man, *Allegories of Reading*, 296.

95. Judith Butler, *Gender Trouble: Feminism and the Subversion of Identity* (New York: Routledge, 1990), 93. In *Bodies That Matter: On the Discursive Limits of "Sex"* (New York: Routledge, 1993), Butler elaborates that, while the construction of resistance to discrete identification as "subversion," on the one hand, enables the separation of the social function from bodily form, on the other hand it limits the range of potential functions to socially intelligible forms, which explains why the erasure of the gendered terms of the individual sharpens the focus on the species critique of this agency form only to cover over the ways in which gendering sets the boundaries around (by establishing the norms of) the human form (123).

96. "A Couple of Furry Black and White Pets Sitting around Talking about *Babe*," *Cinéaste* 22 (1996): 18.

97. This aspect illuminates Butler's concept of "the matrix of gender relations" as "prior to the emergence of the 'human'" (*Bodies That Matter*, 7), in contradistinction to Baudrillard's assertion that the human serves as the "principle of exclusion" linking "the chain of discriminations." Jean Baudrillard, *Symbolic Exchange and Death*, trans. Iain Hamilton Grant (Thousand Oaks, Calif.: Sage, 1993), 125. The latter point subsequently has been supported through Derridean-deconstructive critique by Cary Wolfe, who argues that attempts to denature the foundations of prejudicial social structures remain locked within a framework of "speciesism," the systematic discrimination against others based on the generic characteristic of nonhuman status that fuels a fundamental repression of concerns about human species identity among otherwise well-intentioned critics of humanism. Cary Wolfe, *Animal Rites: American Culture, the Discourse of Species, and Posthumanist Theory* (Chicago: University of Chicago Press, 2003), 6–7.

98. See Stallybrass and White's etymological history of "pig" (*The Politics and Poetics of Transgression*, 44–45).

99. Sylvia Kolbowski writes about this aspect of *Babe* in "Questions of Feminism: Responses," *October* 71 (1995): 49.

100. Roberto Esposito elaborates this Deleuzian sense of "impersonal singularity (or singular impersonality)" that "traverses men as well as plants and animals independently of the matter of their individuation and the forms of their personality." Roberto Esposito, *Bíos: Biopolitics and Philosophy*, trans. Timothy Campbell (Minneapolis: University of Minnesota Press, 2008), 194.

101. Walter R. Brooks, *To and Again (Freddy Goes to Florida)* (Woodstock, N.Y.: Overlook Press, 1998), 11.

102. Michael Card, introduction to Walter R. Brooks, *The Freddy Anniversary Collection* (Woodstock, N.Y.: Overlook Press, 2002), 5.

103. Brooks, *To and Again,* 195.

104. Ibid., 56, 55.

105. Horowitz, *Putting Meat on the American Table,* 43.

106. Shukin, *Animal Capital,* 68–70.

107. Skaggs details these historic changes in slaughter-swine production (*Prime Cut,* 186–87), noting how they relate to problematic "total confinement" operations: "Concerned consumers and health authorities alike have questioned the quality of the resulting product and the propriety of inadvertently creating mutant viral and bacteriological strains readily communicable to people" (185).

108. Bharati Mukherjee, *Jasmine* (New York: Fawcett Crest, 1989), 209.

109. Winston Churchill, "Fifty Years Hence," in *Thoughts and Adventures* (London: Macmillan, 1943), 234.

110. Warren Belasco, *Meals to Come: A History of the Future of Food* (Berkeley: University of California Press, 2006), 132.

111. Sally Borrell, "Challenging Humanism: Human–Animal Relations in Recent Postcolonial Novels" (PhD diss., Middlesex University, 2010).

112. Margaret Atwood, *Oryx and Crake* (New York: Doubleday, 2003), 26.

113. Ibid., 56.

114. Ibid., 292.

115. Traci Warkentin, "Dis/integrating Animals: Ethical Dimensions of the Genetic Engineering of Animals for Human Consumption," in *Genetic Technologies and Animals,* ed. Carol Gigliotti, special issue of *AI & Society* 20, no. 1 (2006): 94; Tiffin, "Pigs, People, and Pigoons," 260.

116. Jovian Parry, "*Oryx and Crake* and the New Nostalgia for Meat," *Society & Animals* 17 (2009): 244.

117. Lisa Lynch, "Culturing the Pleebland: The Idea of the 'Public' in Genetic Art," in *Genomics in Literature, Visual Arts, and Culture,* ed. Priscilla Wald, Jay Clayton, and Karla F. C. Holloway, special issue of *Literature and Medicine* 26 (2007): 182.

Conclusion

1. On Goodall's mastery of storytelling techniques, see Marianne DeKoven, "Women, Animals, and Jane Goodall: *Reason for Hope,*" *Tulsa Studies in Women's Literature* 25 (2006): 141–51. On the relevance of Goodall's self-presentation via zoo politics to the institutionalization of animal studies, see my essay "Sweet Jane," in *Feral,* ed. Heather Steffen, a special issue of *the minnesota review* 73–74 (2009–10): 189–203.

2. Showing how Goodall's trope of the simian–human "touch across difference" is redeployed in a 1984 ad for Gulf Oil, Haraway argues that visual-media technologies are integral to the popular version of primatology stories as "about modes of *communication,*

not history" (*Primate Visions*, 149). Updating this argument, Shukin shows how ads for Telus Mobility similarly use primate images to put a touching face on mobile media devices driven by microcapacitors containing tantalum, derived from coltan (colombo-tantalite), a natural resource currently being cheaply (and largely illegally) extracted from mines in the Democratic Republic of the Congo (*Animal Capital*, 172–79).

3. Ralph H. Lutts, *The Nature Fakers: Wildlife, Science, and Sentiment* (Charlottesville: University Press of Virginia, 1990), 32.

4. Charles G. D. Roberts, "The Animal Story," *The Kindred of the Wild* (New York: Sitt Publishing, 1905), 24.

5. Lutts distinguishes "nature faker" from "fraud," noting that, although many of these writers' "deeply held personal beliefs [led] them to spin fanciful visions of nature," few consciously set out to deceive readers (*Nature Fakers*, 176).

6. Matt Cartmill, *A View to a Death in the Morning: Hunting and Nature through History* (Cambridge, Mass.: Harvard University Press, 1993), 148–56. See also Lutts, who details the pivotal involvement of Chicago *Evening Post* journalist Edward Long (who first popularized the variant term "nature fakir") in framing the discussion largely as a public argument between Roosevelt and Long (129–30).

7. [Barbara] Barney Nelson, *The Wild and the Domestic: Animal Representation, Ecocriticism, and Western American Literature* (Reno: University of Nevada Press, 2000), 74–91. Nelson clarifies this history by analyzing the present rangeland conflicts over national parklands through a comparison of how early ecological writers John Muir (the other prominent turn-of-the-century naturalist and Burroughs's more romantic counterpart) and Mary Austin, respectively, characterize the destruction or endangerment of shepherds in Yosemite.

8. Like Martin Heidegger, Paul de Man, and other academics who lived and worked within the Third Reich, Lorenz's political compromises became the subject of posthumous speculation. See Boria Sax, who notes that Lorenz joined the Nazi party and pursued government-sponsored scientific research informed by anti-Semitic ideas later sanitized in his writing for popular audiences, a strategic development that enabled him to share a Nobel Prize with Niko Tinbergen and Karl von Frisch in 1973 ("What Is a 'Jewish Dog?': Konrad Lorenz and the Cult of Wildness," *Society & Animals* 5 [1997]: 3–21).

9. Konrad Lorenz, *King Solomon's Ring: New Light on Animal Ways*, trans. Marjorie Kerr Wilson (New York: Thomas Y. Crowell, 1952), 148, 116.

10. Lutts, *The Nature Fakers*, 133–34.

11. Ibid., 50.

12. Michael Lundblad, "From Animal to Animality Studies," *PMLA* 124 (2009): 496.

13. Moore, *Avowals*, 84.

14. Terry Eagleton, *Literary Theory: An Introduction* (Minneapolis: University of Minnesota Press, 1996), 6, 67–68.

15. Roughgarden, *Evolution's Rainbow*, 163.

16. Haraway, *When Species Meet*, 32–33.

17. Rosi Braidotti, "Animals, Anomalies, and Inorganic Others," *PMLA* 124 (2009): 530. The patterns of representing cross-species intersubjectivity and intercorporeality in narrative likewise might be seen as inscribing a perspective that Isabelle Stengers terms the "etho-ecological," one that adds to "a form self-regulation" the requirement and "advantage of presenting the 'self' as an issue," in "The Cosmopolitical Proposal," 997.

18. Deleuze and Guattari elaborate: "In the same way that we avoided defining a body by its organs and functions, we will avoid defining it by Species or Genus characteristics; instead we will seek to count its affects. This kind of study is called ethology, and this is the sense in which Spinoza wrote a true Ethics" (*A Thousand Plateaus*, 257).

19. Éric Alliez, "On Deleuze's Bergsonism," *Gilles Deleuze: A Reason to Believe in This World*, ed. Réda Bensmaïa and Jalal Toufic, special issue of *Discourse* 20 (1998): 240.

20. Sabloff, *Reordering the Natural World*, 43.

21. Erica Fudge, *Animal* (London: Reaktion Books, 2002), 12, 16.

Index

Susan McHugh is associate professor of English at the University of New England. She is the author of *Dog.*